DEATH & SURVIVAL
in Glacier National Park

True Tales of Tragedy, Courage, & Misadventure

BY C. W. GUTHRIE & DAN AND ANN FAGRE

FARCOUNTRY
PRESS

ISBN: 978-1-56037-658-3

Cover photograph: Sunrise, ponds near St. Mary Lake, Tim Rains, National Park Service.
Back cover photograph: Going-to-the-Sun Road, Tim Rains, National Park Service.

For more information about our books, write Farcountry Press, P.O. Box 5630, Helena, MT 59604; call (800) 821-3874; or visit www.farcountrypress.com.

Cataloging-in-Publication data on file at the Library of Congress.

 Produced and printed in the United States of America.

21 20 19 18 17   1 2 3 4 5 6

ACKNOWLEDGMENTS

We dedicate this book about death, courage, and survival to the ground and aerial rescue crews who willingly risk their own lives to rescue those in danger and recover those who have died. Throughout this book we chronicle many noble acts of rescue and recovery. We can never properly thank these people for their courage, skill, and dedication, but we speak from the heart to say—thank you for being there when someone needs you. You are the stuff of heroes.

This book required extensive research, poring through incident reports and newspaper articles, and listening to the voices of those who were on the scene. While gathering material and sorting fact from fiction, it's been our privilege to work with park employees, area residents, park visitors, rescue crews, and many others who have been a part of the Glacier National Park experience.

Our sincere appreciation to Deidre Shaw, GNP museum curator, and her staff. Deirdre's keen memory of historical incidents led us to many interesting discoveries. Thanks and appreciation are also due Lon Johnson, retired GNP cultural resource specialist, for providing information on pre-park deaths and burials inside the park boundaries, and to Mark Wagner, GNP naturalist, and Dave Shea, retired backcountry ranger and author of *Chief Mountain, Home of the Thunderbird*, for providing insight and historical information about Native Americans and pre-park history.

Anya Helsel, GNP librarian, was exceptionally helpful in finding information on various subjects, particularly about the Glacier Mountaineering Society. Tessie Bundick of the Minnesota Historical Society also provided extensive research, including the 1913 avalanche death of Dr. Fletcher (Chapter 10). Beth Hodder, retired USDA Forest Service employee and author of several children's books, gave us ideas and inspiration, including leading us to retired Belton Chalet, Inc. manager Lanny Luding's story of the Paisley Umbrella. We also thank Chris Peterson of the *Hungry Horse News* and former GNP public affairs officers Denise Germann and Margie Steigerwald for their help in providing information and locating photographs.

Many thanks to Dr. John Waller, GNP supervisory wildlife biologist, who kept us on track about Glacier's wildlife with his humor and insightful review of our work.

We are particularly indebted to Jack Potter, former assistant chief ranger and chief of GNP's Science and Resources Management Division. Jack is known as "the conscience of Glacier." He served the park for forty-two years, helping park supervisors steward the difficult and sometimes conflicting philosophies of park management—protecting the wilderness while providing recreational use for visitors. Thank you, Jack, for your service and your gracious and candid review of our manuscript.

In writing this book we are privileged to tell the stories of the personal experiences in the park of noted author (*Politics and Parks*) and national parks crusader George Bristol, retired GNP public information officer Amy Vanderbilt, retired park rangers Gary Moses and Charlie Logan, Belton Chalet manager Lanny Luding, Kathleen Marshall, ALERT pilot Ken Justus, and Two Bear Air pilot Jim Bob Pierce. We also tell, with their permission, the riveting grizzly encounters of Johan and Jenna Otter and Smitty Parratt and wildlife photographer Buck Wilde's experience in the John Petranyi grizzly attack as reported in Scott McMillion's book *Mark of the Grizzly*. We are extremely grateful to all who have allowed us to share their stories.

We also want to thank those who graciously contributed photographs from their personal collections. They are indeed worth a thousand words. Our thanks to Mark Wagner, Luci Yeats, Montana House's Monica Jungster, award-winning wildlife photographer Sumio Harada, Somer Treat, Ed DesRosier of Sun Tours, Two Bear Air, ALERT, and Glacier and Great Northern Railway historian and collector John Chase.

Special thanks to our editor Will Harmon, who was well suited for this project. It's been our pleasure to work with Will and the talented staff at Farcountry Press. We are grateful for their confidence in us, their patience and good advice, and for producing this book. It's been our pleasure.

Glacier National Park encompasses more than 1 million acres in northwest Montana.

LIFE *and* DEATH
in GLACIER
NATIONAL PARK

There have been several books written on deaths in national parks. They provide cautionary tales about incidents relating to the specific natural features of the individual park. This book about Glacier National Park also showcases cautionary tales of park deaths, but we have also included stories about courage and survival. We have chronicled the most compelling incidents from the distant past as well as recent times; these stories convey intriguing park history and an awareness of the inherent natural hazards of a mountainous national park and people's decisions that often made the difference between life or death.

The introductory story that follows is about courage and survival. In this story, death takes a holiday.

SOUTHERN FLANK OF MOUNT GRINNELL, GLACIER NATIONAL PARK, 2005

Johan Otter looked up.* His daughter Jenna was coming toward him, shouting. Then he saw it. The open mouth, the tongue, the teeth, the flattened ears. A grizzly bear charging right at him. It caught him by his

---

* The following account is adapted and condensed, with permission, from the article "A hike into horror and an act of courage" by Thomas Curwen that originally appeared in the April 29, 2007, edition of the *Los Angeles Times*. Some details were extracted from park incident records and other newspaper and magazine articles about the attack.

Grizzly bears are powerful and unpredictable. JIM PEACO, COURTESY OF NATIONAL PARK SERVICE.

left thigh. The bear bit and pulled away, then bit again and pulled away. Teeth hitting bone and pulling flesh with each bite. Johan later said that he saw oozing blood but felt no pain, just disbelief.

Johan and Jenna were on a father-daughter get away, celebrating her graduation from high school. Johan, his wife Marilyn, and their two daughters lived in Escondido, California. He worked as an administrator at Scripps Memorial Hospital in La Jolla.

Father and daughter had been hiking about an hour. As they walked they talked loudly, which they knew is what you are supposed to do in bear country. Jenna was trying to figure out how she could be both a dancer and a doctor, and Johan was wondering if he would be able to qualify for the Boston Marathon. They had skirted Lake Josephine and were above the tree line, making their way along the southern flank of Mount Grinnell. Ahead were the Gem and Salamander Glaciers. Below, a stream flowed into the turquoise stillness of Grinnell Lake. Johan watched a golden eagle swaying back and forth trying to catch a thermal. Johan and Jenna fell silent, lost in the sounds of the wind and the water and the beauty. They had hiked a series of switchbacks above Grinnell Lake and were on a narrow ledge cut into the cliff. Jenna had just been about to walk around a twenty-foot-tall boulder on the trail when a bear came around from the other direction followed by two cubs.

The bear kept biting at Johan. He had to get away, but how? The wall of the mountain was on his right and on his left was a sheer drop off the cliff. In an emergency, the mind is often amazingly keen; flashes of life-saving details emerge. Johan recalled that slightly behind him and twenty feet below the trail grew a thimbleberry and alder patch on a small slope jutting from the cliff. He dived for the thimbleberry patch. The landing hurt, but he was alive and conscious. His right eye was bleeding. His concern now was for his daughter Jenna. She was on the trail above, alone with the bear.

A canister of bear spray had fallen out of the side pocket of Johan's daypack and was lying on the ground. Jenna grabbed it but couldn't remove the safety clip. The bear was coming at her. She screamed. Johan heard her and yelled back, "Jenna, come down here!" But she never heard him. She had backed off the cliff and was falling.

The bear, however, did hear Johan and charged down the slope. Johan tucked into a fetal position. The bear clawed and bit at his back, but the daypack protected him. Johan's mind raced with thoughts. Jenna did not have a pack. If the bear got to her, it would easily tear her apart. Johan turned, swung to his right and fell off the slope. It was a straight drop to where Jenna had landed. He had hoped that the bear would be discouraged and go away. But it didn't. The bear came after them. Jenna scrambled away and the grizzly, in a flash of movement, was on top of Johan.

It was fight or die. Johan grabbed the bear by the fur on its throat. For a moment the bear just stared at him, its snout straight in his face. No fear, no anger, just amber-brown eyes looking down at him. Johan reached for a rock, but it was shale and crumbled in his hand. Then he tucked his knees to his chest and tried to cover his head.

The bear bit again and again on his right arm. Johan tossed about trying to avoid the bites. Then the bear tugged on his back and began jumping up and down on him. Johan knew the bear would pound him to death if he didn't do something. He rolled and fell, sliding twenty feet down the slope to a small ledge and then over that and onto a narrow shelf. By luck he landed on his feet, stopping his fall. He would not have survived the next long, straight drop. The bear stood above watching, then, unable to reach Johan, headed uphill toward Jenna.

Jenna heard the bear panting as it came closer to where she was lying beneath the branches of a low alder. She had a knot on her head and was woozy from her fall. Her back ached and her ankle was bleeding. She tried to stay tucked within the branches, but when the bear got close to her face she pushed it away. It nipped at the right corner of her mouth, at her hair and her right shoulder. She screamed.

Johan heard Jenna's scream and then there was nothing—just an eerie silence. And he was helpless. He could not do anything to save his daughter. He was pressed against the mountain. There wasn't room enough to lie down or even sit. He stood as best he could, shifting his weight away from the painful left thigh. Johan was wet, dirty, soaked with blood, and shivering. He looked at his right arm and saw exposed tendons, but no major nerves or arteries had been cut. Nothing seemed broken. He touched the top of his head and felt only bone. His scalp had been torn off. He couldn't see out of his right eye. It was full of blood and caked over. He parted his eyelids and was relieved that he could see.

Johan called out to Jenna. She replied with "Dad." Hope and happiness flooded over them both. She had played dead and the bear moved on. She had a bite on her shoulder and her lower lip was torn down to her chin. Her hair was caked with blood.

They yelled back and forth reassuring each other they were okay. Johan could tell by the sound of Jenna's voice that she really was all right. "Thank you, God," he said to himself. He looked up at the sky and thought of his mom and dad who were both dead. "Thank you, Mom, and thank you, Dad," he mouthed, for being an energy to draw on. Somehow he was less afraid.

Both Johan and Jenna began to yell for help.

Johan knew he couldn't stand much longer. He needed to climb to the ledge above where he could at least sit. He didn't know how he would manage to carry his pack and camcorder with his badly damaged right arm. Then he remembered what they say on airplanes: leave your luggage and take care of yourself. Johan took off his daypack and camcorder. He pulled a jacket out of the pack and put the hood over his head. The night before, he'd read a book about bear attacks and how a woman in Alaska had stopped the bleeding of her scalp by covering her head. Then he crawled off the narrow shelf and up to the ledge. He felt dizzy and sat down.

Jenna, too dizzy to move and uncertain of her injuries, had decided to stay where she was. The two survivors, about seventy-five feet apart, were precariously sitting on the side of the mountain looking down into the valley below. It was windy and cold and quiet.

They alternated their calls for help. Then Jenna spotted the tour boat that ran a regular service across Lake Josephine. The arrival of the boat gave them hope. Hikers would soon be coming along the trail and would hear their calls. About forty-five minutes later, Jenna called out to Johan, telling him, "Dad, there are people here now. They're getting help."

Soon, although it seemed like forever to Johan, he saw a man cutting through the bushes and sliding down toward him. Jim Knapp and his wife had started hiking that morning about 8:30 A.M., well ahead of the tour boat. They were an hour on the trail when they heard what sounded like a coyote or a hawk or some animal being attacked. Then there was more, and it sounded human. They started running toward the sounds, thinking someone must have fallen or sprained an ankle and needed help.

They first came to Jenna and she sent them on to Johan. When Jim reached Johan he thought it was "the most gruesome sight he had ever seen." Blood covered Johan's face. His arms and legs oozed blood. His voice was jerky, his sentences repetitive, and his sweatshirt was pulled up over his head.

"Jenna's okay," Jim said, as he began to get a sense of Johan's injuries. He noticed the daypack on the shelf beneath them and climbed down to get it. Inside were a sweatshirt and four bottles of water. He covered Johan and tried to make him drink. Jim took off his T-shirt and wrapped it around the deep gash on Johan's leg. He laid out some nuts and a granola bar and took some water to Jenna.

Then Johan saw a girl sliding down to him. It was Kari Schweigert. She and Heidi Reindl had been car camping in Glacier. They were just starting on an eleven-mile hike when they ran into Jim Knapp's wife running down the trail to get help. Shortly, two teenage boys also came along to help. "What can we do? How can we help?" they asked.

All Johan wanted at the moment was to sit up, have a drink of water, and lie down again. He was fading. Voices told him help was on the way. Kari Schweigert was sitting beside him, talking. Kari had put her jacket over him, but he was still shaking and numb with cold.

"How are you doing?" she asked.

"The pain is okay," he said. "I'd just like to take a nap."

Kari moved closer. She knew he was cold and needed to be warmed up. She angled around him and covered his abdomen and chest with her body. Her legs were off to one side. She couldn't cover him completely because of his torn left thigh, but she did shield him from the wind. How strange, he thought, to be hiking along on this trail one moment, thinking about running in a marathon, and then suddenly not being able to walk, being dependent upon strangers, and now this girl so close to him, so tender and different from the savagery of the attack.

Kari kept talking to him. She told him not to fall asleep. He knew she was right. He had lost a lot of blood and probably was in shock. Then the wash of voices and movement of people around him began to blur.

A park ranger and a dozen hikers were on the trail above them. The ranger radioed a report on Johan and Jenna's status to the ranger station at Many Glacier, where the incident commander was assembling a rescue team.

A few hikers peered over the edge. "Do you need anything?" they yelled.

"More jackets," came the reply, then someone tucked one under Johan's head. His neck felt broken.

Ranger Katie Fullerton had pulled into the Many Glacier parking lot expecting just another summer day. Then she heard about the attack. She and another ranger were ordered to get to Johan and Jenna as soon as possible. Since 1910, when Glacier became a national park, there had only been ten bear fatalities. That was enough!

Katie, balancing a medical kit and shotgun in her hands, slid down the slope toward Johan.

"What's your name?" she asked.

"Johan Otter," he replied.

"Where are you?"

"Glacier National Park."

"What time of day is it?"

"Late morning."

"What happened?"

"Bear attack."

Once she determined he was alert and oriented, she started dressing his wounds. Meanwhile, the incident commander at Many Glacier had put a call out for additional rangers. Some were stationed on the west side of the park, a two-hour drive away. He called in a helicopter, chartered from Minuteman Aviation, to ferry the west-side rangers to the site of the attack. The chopper would also be used to shuttle equipment and personnel up the mountain.

Katie looked up as the whop, whop, whop of the helicopter drew close. The chopper had flown through a U-shaped notch in the Garden Wall and was circling above, looking for a place to land. Johan and Jenna could not have fallen in a less accessible place.

It was now three hours since the attack. Johan's metabolism was slowing down. The blast of adrenaline triggered by the attack was gone. He was crashing mentally and emotionally. He needed to stay warm and awake. Nature didn't help. Gusts of wind blew along the cliff; temperatures went from warm to freezing as clouds drifted beneath the sun. Thankfully, hikers on the trail tossed down energy bars, water bottles, and more jackets.

Ranger Gary Moses jumped out of the chopper and crouched down beside Johan. He had arrived with fifty pounds of gear, including a life-support pack with intravenous fluids, medications, and an oxygen tank. He cut away Johan's jackets and clothing. While he worked, he introduced himself to Johan and explained that they were going to place him and Jenna on litters, have them lifted up to the trail and then carried down to a landing zone where the chopper would take them to the Kalispell Regional Medical Center west of the park. While he was explaining the plan, Gary took Johan's vitals. His blood pressure was eighty over thirty, pulse forty-four, and his temperature was dropping. Gary prepared an I.V. line.

The rangers setting up the belaying system knew they had to work fast if they were to save Johan Otter.

Johan tried to lie still while Gary was preparing the I.V. line, but he was shivering uncontrollably. Then he heard Katie Fullerton crying. The sound startled him.

"Do you want to stand down?" Gary Moses asked Katie.

She shook her head no. This was her first season as a patrol ranger, and her first major trauma. Last year she had been collecting user fees. Katie had grown up near the park, and she and her family had hiked these trails. This could just as easily have been her father. It was an emotional moment, then she collected herself.

The helicopter made a second drop, and a second medic joined Gary Moses and Katie Fullerton.

"How's Jenna?" Johan asked. "There're people with her," came the reply.

Gary Moses and the other medic put a cervical collar around Johan's neck and got ready to insert a urinary catheter. Johan reminded them about a scene in *Seinfeld* in which George Costanza is caught naked and complains about "shrinkage." They burst out laughing and Johan relaxed a little. This is who he was: not just a bloodied man, but someone always there with an easy line, ready to lighten the mood.

Gary Moses reassessed the rescue plan. Carrying Johan out, lifting him to the trail and then down to the helicopter landing zone was going to be too traumatic and take too long, and the afternoon was getting on.

He thought a helicopter could lift Johan directly off the ledge. It would be quicker but riskier. Still, he didn't see any way around it. He radioed

With Johan Otter in the Bauman bag, Ranger Gary Moses and rescuers ready him for a short-haul flight. COURTESY OF HEIDI REINDL-HARPER.

in his recommendation. The incident commander agreed. They called in the ALERT rescue helicopter.

While they waited, Johan remembered an Air Force chopper that had crashed during a rescue on Mount Hood about three years earlier. The plummeting helicopter rolling down the slope in a cascade of snow had been televised on the evening news. It made him nervous. "Am I going to die?" Johan asked.

"You're not going to die up here," the second medic said.

First they heard the whop, whop, whop of the rotor blades and then the red short-haul helicopter came into sight. "Hear that?" Gary Moses said. "That's the sound of your rescue."

Pilot Ken Justus maneuvered the foot pedals and hand controls to bring the Bell 407 closer to the cliff. Travis Willcut, the flight nurse, sat next to him, calling out

Rescuer Jerry Anderson signals the helicopter pilot to begin lifting. COURTESY OF HEIDI REINDL-HARPER.

Rescuer Jerry Anderson steadies
the basket carrying Johan Otter as
the ALERT helicopter lifts them from
the ledge far above Grinnell Lake.
COURTESY OF HEIDI REINDL-HARPER.

positions, monitoring radio traffic. Jerry Anderson, a medic, dangled 150 feet beneath them on a rope with a red Bauman bag and body board at his waist.

Johan was still stiff and cold, but the I.V. had kicked in and he was wide awake and not in pain. He still felt a little afraid at the thought of the helicopter ride.

"You'll have the best view of your life," Gary Moses said, hiding his own worry. He knew just getting Jerry Anderson in would be tricky. Helicopters don't cast sharply defined shadows on steep terrain, and pilots flying short-haul missions in this terrain have trouble judging closing speeds and distances.

Anderson, dangling at the end of the rope, had a radio in his helmet to call out his position to direct Ken Justus lower and closer to Johan. Suddenly the radio died. Gary Moses, on the ground, instantly realized what happened and broke in with his radio. "I'm at your eleven o'clock position, a mile out."

Then it was a "half mile, twelve o'clock."

"Do I need to come up or down?"

"Up about ten feet."

As Ken Justus got closer, he caught Anderson's shadow on the ledge and set him down about twenty feet to the right of Johan. Anderson unhooked himself, and he and the other rangers slid the body board under Johan and strapped the Bauman bag around him. Then Anderson signaled Ken, "We're ready to lift."

"Roger, ready to lift."

Johan couldn't tell when he was off the ground. With Anderson beside him beneath the helicopter, all Johan could see was Anderson's face, the blue sky, and the belly of the chopper. He could hear the wind whistling around him.

"Woo hoo!" The hikers and rangers on the mountain cheered and clapped.

The chopper, with Johan and Jerry Anderson dangling beneath, flew down the valley to the helipad at Many Glacier. Johan was transferred into an ambulance and Ken Justus went back to pick up Jenna.

A short while later, Johan heard someone say, "Jenna is here." His head wrapped in bandages, Johan couldn't see her. He had mummy slits for his eyes and a C-collar on his neck. "Hi sweetie," he called out as they prepared to fly him to the medical center in Kalispell. "Make sure when they call Mom that you talk to her. Otherwise she'll totally freak out."

EPILOGUE

Johan had three broken vertebrae in his neck, broken ribs, numerous lacerations, a badly torn scalp, and eye damage. He recovered after several surgeries and a long rehabilitation, all met with Johan's humor, determination, and courage. Eleven months after the attack, Johan and Marilyn returned to the park to retrace Johan and Jenna's fateful journey of the year before. Ranger Gary Moses joined them on the hike. Just as her father did the year before, Jenna returned to the park in 2007

Jerry Anderson and Johan Otter head to the helipad at Many Glacier. COURTESY OF HEIDI REINDL-HARPER.

to face the memory of their chance encounter with a grizzly, to remember the beauty of the mountains, and to heal.

For Johan and Jenna's complete story, including their amazing recovery, we recommend Johan Otter's 2016 book, *A Grizzly Tale, A Father and Daughter Survival Story.*

Park officials convened a board of inquiry and determined that the bear was protecting her cubs. She was not destroyed.

According to Dr. John Waller, Glacier National Park wildlife biologist, the Otters survived because they kept their wits about them, made non-threatening movements, and had a little good luck. Their only mistakes were not making enough noise as they hiked and leaving their bear spray in their backpacks and not instantly accessible (see Chapter 13).

AMERICA'S BEST IDEA

National parks serve many purposes. Congress established our first national park, Yellowstone, as a "pleasuring-ground for the benefit and enjoyment of the people." The Organic Act of 1916, creating the National Park Service, clarifies that the purpose of national parks is "to conserve the scenery and the natural and historic objects and the wild life therein and to provide for the enjoyment of the same in such manner and by such means as will leave them unimpaired for the enjoyment of future generations." This founding legislation reflected Congress's intent that Americans would visit their parks to relax, explore, and be inspired. It is likely the founders did not envision the degree to which this visitation would occur. Americans have responded by loving their parks, visiting often, and consistently ranking the National Park Service as one of the most admired parts of government. Indeed, Wallace Stegner called the national parks "America's Best Idea." People choose national parks as vacation destinations now more than ever before; the rate of visitation by both American citizens and international tourists has increased, proving they are wonderful places to visit.

So how is it that people die in America's Best Idea? Actually not many do. The vast majority come and enjoy a unique and amazing nature experience. During the 100-plus years that people have enjoyed adventures in Glacier, an average of two to three people a year have died in the park for one reason or another. Often, people who are in vacation mode are less cautious than in their everyday lives. In some cases, visitors may have the sense that they are being looked after by national park staff, that hazards have been identified and mitigated, that aid and rescue are minutes away, that Glacier is, by the mere nature of it being a "park," a safe environment.

In truth, most visitors are out of their normal environment, and many lack experience being in mountains, near cold and turbulent waters, or around wild animals. They may fail to recognize risk and then struggle to make appropriate judgments in suddenly dangerous situations. Even very experienced outdoor enthusiasts face death or near-death incidents while confronting nature's unpredictability. A few visitors have simply been in the wrong place at the wrong time. Unfortunately, national parks also attract people with motivations other than recreation and renewal, including darker urges like suicide or murder. For these and other reasons, people have died in Glacier Park since its beginning.

As we noted earlier, this book chronicles those deaths and looks at near-death incidents and how and why some survive and some don't. Our goal is to extract key lessons from the incidents so that we are all better informed when venturing into Glacier Park and similar wild, mountainous terrain.

PART ONE

LAWS OF THE LAND

Nature is in charge and oh, how she makes it plain!
—ROBERT SERVICE

In the northwest corner of Montana lies the more than 1-million-acre expanse of glacier-carved mountains, swift streams and rivers, bone-chillingly cold lakes, glaciers, deep valleys, and expanses of dense forests that since 1910 have been known as Glacier National Park. People give it well-deserved status, ranking it as one of the ten most favorite national parks and one of the most visited parks despite its isolation from major urban centers.

Glacier National Park adjoins Waterton Lakes National Park in Alberta, Canada, and together they form the world's first international peace park. Established in 1932, Waterton-Glacier International Peace Park sits at the heart of the Crown of the Continent Ecosystem, a 9-million-acre expanse of national forests, Native American and First Nations reservations, wildlife refuges, state forests and parks, and a largely rural landscape of towns, farms, and ranches.

This relatively wild and natural landscape is one of the largest, most intact mountain ecosystems in the United States and is valued worldwide for its natural assets and as a haven for threatened wildlife populations.

The park is also increasingly valued as a top outdoor recreational destination. Glacier National Park finished 2015 with its highest visitation ever, 2.37 million, which bested the next highest number of visitors set the previous year. In 2016, nearly 3 million visited, a new annual record. These rising visitor numbers are due, in part, to milestones such as Glacier's centennial celebration in 2010 and the National Park Service centennial in 2016. Other social trends such as campaigns to change the sedentary lifestyle of the digital age are leading to increased visitation rates for the entire national park system. More than 320 million people visited national parks in 2015—that's more than the entire population of the United States. This recent influx of visitors likely includes a larger component of people from urban areas than in the past, reflecting the increasing urbanization of our country. In addition, there is likely a lower percentage of visitors with experience in outdoor activities like climbing, hiking, or whitewater boating, given that the growth of such nonmotorized outdoor sports has not kept pace with U.S. population growth.

The terrain around Redgap Pass exemplifies the wildness and beauty that draw people to Glacier National Park. GEORGE GRANT, COURTESY OF GLACIER NATIONAL PARK ARCHIVES.

Although such renewed interest is welcomed by advocates of national parks, it also brings more people into environments with inherent dangers that they may not recognize. When they get into trouble, there is a tendency to assume help is a cell phone call away. What they may not realize is coverage is still spotty in many parks, and park search and rescue staff may be many hours away.

No matter how civilized this wilderness park may appear to some, the forces of nature are still in charge, as the deaths and near deaths in this book will attest.

CHAPTER ONE

NATURE—
WILD, WONDERFUL,
UNPREDICTABLE

MOUNTAINS

Glacier National Park's wild and wonderful characteristics also con-
tribute to its inherent dangers. As a mountainous park, the first char-
acteristic that comes to mind is its verticality and therefore the force
of gravity. Consider the potential for rockfall. The mostly sedimentary
rock layers that make up Glacier's mountains are highly erodible and
lead to much loose rock. Water trickles down into cracks, freezing
and thawing, loosening rock pieces on steep slopes or cliffs. People,
animals, strong winds, flowing water, or slumping snow can dislodge this
loose rock.

The Going-to-the-Sun Road climbs from valleys on the eastern and
western sides of the park to reach Logan Pass at 6,646 feet. An enormously
popular attraction of Glacier, the road is traversed by nearly seventy percent of park visitors each year, either by personal vehicles or shuttle buses.
Most are blissfully unaware of the low-probability but high-consequence
risks to which they are exposed. Boulders that dislodge from above
the road gather so much momentum, especially if free falling, that even
medium-sized rocks are capable of flattening cars. Large boulders have

the momentum to flatten an army tank or knock it over the edge of the road. On September 10, 1986, Brian Kennedy, the editor of a local newspaper, the *Hungry Horse News*, was driving his car up the western side of the road toward Logan Pass with his wife when they were shocked by a loud bang and violent jolt to his car. He stopped and got out to investigate. A rock two feet in diameter was embedded in the trunk of his car. This missile had missed the passenger compartment by tiny fractions of a second as the car moved up the road. The car was totaled, and he and his wife were injured by flying glass. Both of them briefly went to the hospital for treatment. This close call underscores the risks that are posed from above and normally not considered by people traveling in the mountains. Most people are more focused on staying on the winding road or not falling themselves while standing at an overlook or hiking on trails along the edge. Even small rocks, dislodged by mountain goats above or by strong winds blowing off ridges, have injured climbers. Such falling rocks are natural hazards because they are not triggered or caused by human actions.

The Garden Wall viewed from Granite Park. COURTESY OF DAN FAGRE.

Situated at the base of Mount Jackson—and in a major slide path—Gunsight Chalets, shown here circa 1915, were destroyed by an avalanche in March 1916. R. E. MARBLE, COURTESY OF GLACIER NATIONAL PARK ARCHIVES.

Human-triggered hazards are due to decisions and actions that people make. When climbers dislodge rocks that then fall onto climbers below, that's a combination of geology and human decisions. Some of the deaths and near misses in the park have been caused by natural hazards—the person just happened to be in the wrong place at the wrong time. But most deaths and near misses are human-triggered. Some degree of human judgment and error was involved, whether climbing a risky route, skiing an avalanche-prone slope, fishing in bear habitat, or hiking an exposed ridge during a storm.

What other gravity-related natural hazards should park visitors be aware of? Snow avalanches that released naturally (meaning there was no human trigger such as skiing onto the unstable snow) have swept down from slopes near the Garden Wall ridgelines and pushed massive, multi-ton bulldozers off the Going-to-the-Sun Road. In a few cases, these heavy-equipment vehicles (front-end loaders, giant snow throwers, and bulldozers that clear the road of big snowdrifts during the annual spring opening) tumbled hundreds of feet to the valley below. Amazingly, they were winched back up to the road and put back to work. In the early 1900s, several backcountry cabins and chalets, including buildings at Gunsight Lake and on the slopes of Mount Altyn near Swiftcurrent Lake, were wiped out by snow avalanches before the builders realized where not to site a building. In 2011, a large avalanche did significant damage to Sperry Chalet, requiring major repairs. In all these cases, the avalanches occurred during winter when no one was in the buildings, but in other circumstances snow avalanches have been lethal to people.

Debris flows are another natural hazard caused by heavy rain on slopes covered with loose rock. With enough water volume provided by a downpour, a slurry of soil, water, and rock drains off steep slopes and courses down streambeds with enough force to move large boulders and uproot sturdy trees. Although no one has died in Glacier from one of these events, people have been trapped on the Going-to-the-Sun Road when debris flows piled material onto the road above and below their vehicles (see Chapter 10).

Landslides are massive failures of entire slopes, sometimes triggered by heavy rain. In contrast to debris flows, landslides are structural collapses, and they tend to occur suddenly, without warning. In Glacier, there have been no known deaths due to landslides, but their handiwork is seen throughout the park and has created distinctive features like Slide Lake.

WEAK ROCK

Another factor inherent to Glacier's natural hazards stems from the titanic processes that formed the mountains we see today. Most of the rock is layered because it was formed at the bottom of vast, shallow seas

Much of Glacier's rock is sedimentary and easily fractured. TIM RAINS, COURTESY OF NATIONAL PARK SERVICE.

that came and went over millions of years. Fine sediments settled out of the seas, eventually forming layers of sedimentary rock as the seas receded. This rock is more easily fractured than harder rock such as igneous rock (granite, for example).

As Earth's crustal plates collided, thousands of feet of sedimentary rock were uplifted. The process wasn't gentle. As if that wasn't enough, Glacier's mountains have their origins from a giant slab of rock layers (many thousands of feet thick) that was shoved here from fifty miles to the west. All that heaving and shoving of rock was then followed by 3,000-foot-thick glaciers that covered all but the highest peaks. The end result, while beautiful, is a mountain landscape that adds to the risks people take while scrambling up fractured and relatively weak rock that is still being worked over by rain, wind, and snow. Indeed, this instability led one of the road foremen, responsible for keeping the Going-to-the-Sun Road free of rock debris, to remark, "These mountains are always trying to fall down!" Despite the fact that the relative softness of the rock leads to more hazard than, say, the granite of the Sierras where the rock is harder and more reliable for climbing, people are willing to take the risk. Perhaps this is because modern mountain climbing originated in Europe where some of the peaks are made up of similar sedimentary rock. Indeed, one climber from Germany, Helmuth Matdies, established a direct rock-climbing route on the face of Mount Clements overlooking Logan Pass. He pronounced the rock to be perfectly fine. Clearly a person's view of the hazard posed by Glacier's rock depends somewhat on what he or she is accustomed to climbing.

Falling is one of the most common causes of death in Glacier, and fatalities can occur over very short distances, although most lethal falls are long ones. Many of these deaths are due to the underlying geology and weathering process- es that make for untrust- worthy hand- and foot-

Scree-covered slopes (here on Ninaki and Papoose Mountains on the ridge leading to Chief Mountain) make for treacherous footing. COURTESY OF DAN FAGRE.

holds. The erodible rock also leads to scree—a lot of small, loose rocks—underfoot that acts like ball bearings, making for treacherous footing on slopes. The scree accumulates on ledges, sloping outward from the vertical wall to the edge of the ledge, often forcing climbers to traverse or step up at the edges. Because of the layered structure of sedimentary rock, with some layers more resistant to erosion and other layers more easily eroded, many steep mountain slopes in Glacier have an alternating pattern of low cliffs and ledges with steep slopes of rock debris. People who fall even a short distance over a low cliff will, in most cases, land on a steep, slippery scree slope and be unable to stop their fall. They are likely to bounce over yet another small cliff and maybe another.

EARTHQUAKES

Glacier National Park is in an area of high earthquake activity. West Glacier has had fifty-three detectable earthquakes since 1931, but none of these were major (over 5.0). The largest earthquake within thirty miles of West Glacier was a 4.6 magnitude in 1975. The U.S. Geological Survey database shows that there is a 57.15 percent chance of a major earthquake (over 5.0) occurring within thirty-two miles of West Glacier over the next fifty years. Although a July 1992 earthquake fractured a large pane of glass at the St. Mary Visitor Center and caused a landslide on Chief Mountain, the earthquake history since the park was founded in 1910 has been fairly quiet. No one has died from earthquake activity . . . so far. Given the potential for a significant earthquake, that could change. As natural hazards go, earthquakes are unique because they are typically very low probability (unlikely to happen in any given human lifetime), but even a moderate earthquake can have very high consequences for people. In Glacier's case, the relatively weak sedimentary rock and the considerable amount of loose rock that covers much of the higher elevations poses the potential for massive damage and, depending upon the time of year, could lead to large numbers of deaths. Scenarios like these have been taken very seriously at Mount Rainier National Park where volcanic activity can unleash a combination of snow, water, and volcanic gravel downslope at high speeds. These "lahars" have the destructive force of a slurry of cement. Past lahars have overrun campgrounds (empty at the time), destroyed roads, and covered forests to depths of twenty feet so that only the largest trees remained. At Glacier National Park, in the Superintendent's Annual Report for 1936, Eivind Scoyen reported that earthquakes were felt at park headquarters (West Glacier) on October 12, 18, and 31, 1935, of sufficient force to sway floor lamps and move the office safe a few inches.

WEATHER

Glacier's weather is notoriously unpredictable and thus presents natural hazards too. Weather forecasters have vastly improved their ability to provide accurate descriptions of weather conditions for several days into the future, sometimes up to a week. But forecasting weather in the mountains is particularly challenging because the peaks' sheer height and mass reshape weather patterns.

The first feature to alter weather systems is the Continental Divide, the highest continuous ridge running through the mountains, which meanders north to south and effectively divides Glacier into two distinct climate types. On the west side, storm systems approaching from the Pacific Northwest are forced up when they encounter the mountains. This cools the air and, because cooler air cannot hold as much moisture, that moisture falls as rain or snow. Once over the divide, the drier storm system descends again as it heads east, warming in the process and again able to hold higher amounts of moisture. Because of this, precipitation tends to be less on the eastern side of the park. This "rain shadow" is a typical feature of western North American mountain ranges.

The Continental Divide also acts as a wall to keep arctic air coming from the northeast from crossing to the western side. Particularly in winter, air masses will occasionally come across the plains of Canada down to north-central Montana, lowering temperatures dramatically. The dense, cold air piles up against the eastern front of Glacier's mountains and

Storm clouds threaten to spill over the Continental Divide. COURTESY OF DAN FAGRE.

only occasionally builds up enough to spill over passes. Then, like an invisible wall of approaching water, it pushes down the valleys on the west side of the park, bringing abrupt cold temperatures.

The warmer, wetter systems from the west and the colder systems pushing from the east along the Continental Divide create the potential for rapid and extreme changes in temperature and precipitation. One avalanche forecaster from the Glacier region called it a "sumo wrestling" contest between such different air masses. This clash also helps create snow conditions conducive to avalanches. Very cold temperatures that occur for several nights can lead to beautiful and expansive ice crystals on the snow surface, called surface hoar. If "sumo wrestling" by air masses causes a storm to quickly bury that surface hoar of delicate crystals, it creates a weak layer in the snowpack. The weak layer cannot support the accumulating weight of snow as winter progresses or the sudden weight of a skier or snowshoer, presenting a danger for both natural and human-triggered releases of avalanches.

In addition to the grand weather wall that is the Continental Divide, numerous other tall peaks and connecting ridges trap and channel air flows to create a mosaic of different mini weather systems. Thus, a mountaineer standing on a high ridge might look down to one valley that is enshrouded by dense fog, while the valley next to it, perhaps a mile or two away but separated by a ridge, will be basking in sunlight. Summer snowstorms (yes, it sometimes snows here in summer) have dumped six inches of snow in one valley while an adjoining valley saw only rain. On average, of course, the higher elevations have the stormiest weather. A mountaineer can be on a summit in a bitterly cold wind with hail slapping their parka and look down to a sunny valley where hikers are wearing T-shirts and shorts.

Due to a strong chinook wind (which means "snow eater" in some Native American dialects) coming down off Glacier's east-side mountains, a record-breaking temperature change was recorded east of the Rockies over twenty-four hours at Loma on January 15, 1972. The temperature rose exactly 103 degrees, from 54 below zero to 49 above zero. This is the world record for a twenty-four-hour temperature change. Nearby Fairfield, Montana, holds the U.S. record for the greatest temperature change over twelve hours. On December 14, 1924, the temperature dropped from a balmy 63 above zero to 21 below zero at midnight, a drop of 84 degrees. Although these are rare events, they clearly underscore the uncertainty of what the weather will do in these mountains and plains environments.

Finally, as the mountain topography channels and uplifts air masses, often with radically different temperatures and moisture content, it creates winds. Extraordinary winds. Stories of Glacier's winds are legendary. One account tells of an outhouse next to the Swiftcurrent fire lookout that vanished in a ferocious wind. And there was a weather station that was stripped of its wind monitor propeller with a 166 mile-per-hour wind gust; the propeller may well be in North Dakota! On east Flattop Mountain, persistent and strong winds have piled scree into drifts, some of which have engulfed the low-growing fir trees with mounds of fine rock.

When you have such a tumultuous mix of temperatures, moisture, competing air masses, and windy conditions that change rapidly, it is easy to see why a prudent park visitor is always prepared for poor weather conditions even on a warm, sunny day. It's been said by many people about many places, but truly, in Glacier Park, if you don't like the weather, wait five minutes. It will change.

HYPOTHERMIA

Park visitors have the potential for exposure and loss of body heat with this changeable and sometimes dire weather. Hypothermia occurs when a person's core body temperature drops below a threshold, usually defined as 95 degrees F. Symptoms of early hypothermia include violent shivering of the teeth-chattering kind, some reduction in motor coordination, and some mental confusion. As hypothermia progresses, shivering actually stops and people show profound confusion and may be unable to talk. Without reversal, hypothermia leads to death. This loss of body heat is a leading cause of deaths in mountains worldwide and is usually due to lack of being prepared with appropriate clothing and shelter when the conditions change. A person might be hiking on a clear, warm summer day when a squall abruptly comes over a ridge and the sun disappears. The wind rises and the temperature drops ten to twenty degrees. A pleasant day can quickly become chilly and miserable just with the drop in temperature. Winds, however, can exponentially increase loss of body heat, so the presence or absence of wind and its force is often more important than the drop in air temperature.

However, the greatest vulnerability that people have when caught by a sudden change in mountain weather is getting wet. Wet clothing and wind allow body heat to be wicked away with stunning speed, and so efficiently that people have died of hypothermia in a summer squall at temperatures well above freezing. Boaters getting doused while navigating whitewater or an angler who slips into a stream are at greater risk of hypothermia because they have already lost some body heat.

Another scenario for hypothermia is being caught out at night. This might be due to route-finding errors, a sprained ankle, or misjudging the amount of time needed to complete a hike. Glacier's changeable weather, however, is also a big factor when storms or dense fog slow or stop a hiking party and require an unplanned overnight stay. This is a fairly common occurrence during the peak of summer visitation and is not confined to naïve hikers and climbers. At least one experienced park service employee who was solo hiking the Floral Park traverse from Logan Pass to Sperry Glacier was engulfed in clouds and fog so thick and disorienting that she (wisely) had to stop and hunker down, even though she was intimately familiar with the route. The fog lasted into the night, then cleared; it made for a long, cold bivouac. Mountains can radiate their daytime accumulated heat into a clear, dark sky very efficiently. This nighttime radiation can drop temperatures close to freezing high on a mountain slope by dawn, even if the daytime temperatures had been a toasty 80 degrees F. One of this book's authors has experienced several overnight bivouacs while climbing and can attest to the misery and uncontrollable shivering that accompanies mild hypothermia. Such incidents quickly teach a person to carry extra clothing and a rudimentary shelter on every hike or climb even if Glacier is basking in summer sunshine when beginning a trip.

Other less common weather-related hazards are high winds and sudden gusts that can cause hikers and climbers to lose their balance and fall. Even large, sturdy hikers weighing over 200 pounds and carrying a fifty-pound pack have been blown so hard by a gust that they abruptly staggered twenty feet off trail onto a talus slope of boulders. Skiers have been sent tumbling down slopes and injured. Although official accounts of deaths often don't detail wind as the cause for a fatal fall, numerous accounts and stories speak to wind as a contributing cause.

Extreme weather events that last more than a few hours are another hazard due to Glacier's mountain climate. The mountaineering literature includes plenty of examples of climbers partway up a climbing route forced by nightfall or worsening weather to bivouac in mid-climb. In the morning, they wake to find snow or freezing rain coating the rock with ice, making their route up or retreat down a suddenly more daunting and technical challenge.

Snowstorms that leave a foot or more of snow are expected during the winter and, to a lesser degree, in the shoulder seasons of spring and autumn. However, even experienced hikers and longtime park visitors aren't usually prepared for such an event at the height of summer. In August 1992, a significant storm system brought heavy snow to Glacier Park, leaving the summer flowers at Logan Pass under at least twelve

Fresh snow—in July—blankets a backcountry campsite in the park. COURTESY OF U.S. GEOLOGICAL SURVEY.

inches of snow. In addition to the problems this created for drivers on the Going-to-the-Sun Road and other disruptions, the snowstorm stranded hundreds of backcountry hikers at higher-elevation backcountry camps. Some campers were faced with three feet of snow, and snowdrifts had piled snow even higher in places. Many people had only summer foot-wear and clothing—not suitable for the sudden onset of winter! Rangers spent days heading into the backcountry and helping to evacuate various parties. Although no deaths were recorded from this extreme and wide-spread weather event, it illustrates the fickle nature of mountain weather and underscores the hazards that park users should be prepared for when venturing into the backcountry.

LIGHTNING

And then there is lightning. The uplift provided by mountains to colliding air masses with different temperatures and moisture can give rise to rapid thunderstorm formation, sometimes so local that the thunderhead builds over only one mountain. Although these convective and powerful storms occur mostly in the summer, "thundersnow" has been documented in Glacier during the winter and early spring when an unstable storm produces snow, lightning, and thunder all at once. Hikers, climbers, and boaters are likely to be miserable when caught in a gusty, wet downpour, but it is the lightning that is of greatest concern.

Using data from 1985 to 2014, an average of 49 people are killed each year by lightning nationwide; about 260 people are injured. The Rocky Mountain states have the most lightning-related fatalities per capita, but populous states like Florida that also have high lightning potential see the greatest number of total fatalities. According to the National Lightning Detection Network of the National Oceanic and Atmospheric Administration (NOAA), Montana had only three lightning fatalities from 2005 to 2014, but Colorado had seventeen during the same period. However, when weighted by population, Montana is right behind Colorado in lightning deaths. According to NOAA, the odds of a person being struck by lightning in their lifetime is one in 12,000, but only ten percent of those struck by lightning are killed. Although rare, some people were struck on clear days when no obvious storm system was producing lightning. These seem to be cases of massive static buildup between the atmosphere and the mountains. The rarity of this phenomenon likely is the origin for the saying "a bolt out of the blue."

To date, Glacier Park has no recorded deaths due to lightning strikes, but people have been struck and knocked unconscious. In July 2013, three people were struck while on a hike to St. Mary Falls on the east side of the park. Travis Heitmann and Kinsey Leishman were dropped to the ground by the bolt, and the eleven-year-old boy hiking with them was thrown from the trail. Hikers who came upon them shortly afterward thought that all were dead; two of the victims' boots were partially melted by the high-voltage bolt. Leishman was not breathing but her eyes were open. CPR was started immediately and the rescuer, Steven Keith, later said he could taste electricity as he breathed air into her. The hikers were able to revive all three and the boy was airlifted to the regional hospital, while Heitmann and Leishman were transported by ambulance. CPR is particularly effective on lightning strike victims because it restarts the heart muscle contraction rhythm that is electrically halted by lightning. Lightning is a particular concern of mountaineers and high country hikers, but this strike occurred in a valley bottom surrounded by forest, a seemingly unlikely place. The *Flathead Beacon* interviewed Heitmann in April 2016, and he recalled waking up in the hospital surrounded by family but having only fuzzy memories of the whole experience. He received multiple burns to his feet and suffers chronic neck pain that requires specialized care. Heitmann now works as a youth counselor and still hikes in Glacier Park, albeit with a careful regard for the weather. "After that day in Glacier I decided I needed to do something cool with my life," he said. "Your life can end in an instant and it's too precious to waste."

Although Glacier averages between 2 and 3 million visitors each year, it is a bit curious that there have not been any lightning-caused deaths in all the years records have been kept. Lightning certainly occurs here (150-plus strikes when an average thunderstorm passes across the park), and lightning-caused fires aren't uncommon. How can the lack of lightning-caused fatalities be explained? Overall climate differences might explain more frequent lightning in places like Colorado and New Mexico (more static buildup), but a big factor is that more people may be out playing and working in the mountains in those other states. Thus, it is partly a matter of more opportunities for people to be struck.

WATER

Glacier's streams, rivers, and lakes are all cold, fed by copious snowmelt and, in some cases, by glaciers. Some lakes are so cold that sheets of winter ice and icebergs calved from glaciers will persist all summer. In fact, an alpine insect known as the meltwater stonefly (*Lednia tumana*) requires stream environments below snow or glaciers with very cold water (just above freezing). Originally discovered in Glacier National Park and thought to live there exclusively, *L. tumana* has now been found in similar environments in other western mountains. Although cold-water fish, such as bull trout, and the alpine stream insects such as the meltwater stonefly are highly adapted to thrive in these breath-takingly chilly waters, people are not. Even strong swimmers in an alpine lake can find themselves barely able to swim within minutes as the water sucks body heat from major muscle groups. Hypothermia sets in quickly with total cold-water immersion because water is such an effective conductor of heat energy. This makes accidental immersion in a cold lake, even on a hot day, a potentially dangerous situation if the person is unable to get out. So, while drowning in rivers and lakes can occur anywhere, the cold waters of Glacier Park present an additional, and often unrecognized, threat.

WILDLIFE

Lastly, there are hazards posed by wildlife. Although grizzly bears are the first things that most people associate with Glacier National Park as a danger, bears have not caused many deaths compared to drowning or falling (see table on page 299). Despite this fact, people are highly sensitive to this large and toothsome carnivore and attribute to it much ferocity. Nearly all bears try to avoid people nowadays, but the deaths of two women in 1967 that led to the book *Night of the Grizzlies* by Jack Olsen helped to create a visceral fear of grizzlies that is strong enough to make some people avoid visiting Glacier altogether. The "bearanoia" of some people toward bears is in contrast to other park visitors who deliberately seek out grizzly bears for photo opportunities or the thrill of seeing a powerful animal in its habitat. Deaths due to bears are addressed thoroughly later in this book, but park visitors should be aware that other wildlife can be dangerous too, though there are no records of people being killed by other animals.

This mountain goat seems curious about what mischief he might have caused below.
COURTESY OF SUMIO HARADA.

For instance, moose can weigh up to 1,500 pounds, can move quickly when agitated, can kill wolves with powerful kicks, and can act unpredictably (especially bull moose during the mating season). In other national parks, bull moose have attacked and nearly killed people while they were cross-country skiing. In Glacier, a hiking party of three reported that an aggressive moose blocked them from hiking down a path from Cobalt Lake in the Two Medicine Valley. It is wise to give all moose a wide berth even if they appear to be calmly feeding.

Similarly, other ungulates like bighorn sheep and mountain goats don't behave or look as if they are dangerous, but they are powerful creatures with horns and sharp hooves. In Olympic National Park in 2010, for instance, a mountain goat fatally gored a man who got too close trying to shoo the goat off a trail. Mountain climbers in Glacier have reported goats above that knocked large enough rocks down in their direction that they took an alternative route. In an account in the Glacier Mountaineering Society's annual publication, climbers suggested that a goat stayed above them and deliberately kicked rocks down on them. If true, it is hard to know what motivated that goat, but it underscores the fact that all wildlife can be unpredictable.

WHEN LIFE HUNG
by a HAIR

HUMAN HISTORY OF THE PARK

Paleo-Indians used this landscape for at least the past 10,000 years, likely much longer. As they sought to survive and thrive, they improved their hunting and fishing methods—better spearheads and then bows, weirs, and nets for fishing—and developed expertise in the use of local plants for food, medicine, spiritual purposes, clothing, implements, containers, and canoes. Life remained challenging,

Two Guns White Calf (center) and two other Blackfeet men ride below Atlantic Falls near Medicine Grizzly Peak in the upper Cut Bank Valley. R. E. MARBLE, COURTESY OF GLACIER NATIONAL PARK ARCHIVES.

however, a struggle against cold, hunger, and the inherent dangers in hunting and gathering, as well as conflict with other Paleo-Indians. These all took their toll in fatal accidents and near-death incidents.

The Piegan (also known as Piikani) Blackfeet have a historical and religious association with what are now Glacier Park lands. In the early 1800s, maps such as Lewis and Clark's post-expeditionary map of 1806 and Arrowsmith's 1819 map showed Piegan territory located "in the country bordering the Rocky Mountains from the Red Deer River [in Alberta, Canada] to the Missouri."

The 1855 Lame Bull Treaty established the Blackfeet Reservation and included the mountains along the Continental Divide within its western boundary. These mountains are sacred to the Blackfeet, who know them as

Chief Mountain (Ninastakis) leads neighboring peaks ("the Warriors") toward the plains. BOB FRAUSEN, COURTESY OF GLACIER NATIONAL PARK.

The mountain is called Chief Mountain because it appears to be the leader of a procession of mountain peaks marching outward onto the plains. As James Willard Shultz wrote in Blackfeet Tales of Glacier National Park, *Blackfeet elders explained to him that "a chief should always be taller and more conspicuous than his followers." The elders "consider the Up Above Person of this place to be the most powerful of all the Up Above Persons that reside in the Backbone."*

There is also a legend that has been passed down through the
ages about a Piegan warrior who was known for his bravery and
became a war chief. He and his wife and baby lived in the village
near the base of the big mountain. A war party went out from his
village and all but four men were killed by the enemy tribe. The
war chief then led a party of brave warriors to avenge the deaths of
their friends and relatives, saying, "I will lead a party on the warpath
to avenge their deaths. If we do not, the enemy will think we are
women and will attack us again. Let us not permit them to attack us
here in the camp." The war chief led the war party to the camp of
the enemy and defeated them, but he was killed in the battle. His
wife was crazed with grief. For many days she wandered about the
camp calling his name. One day the villagers saw her far up on the
side of the tall mountain. She was carrying her baby, the war chief's
son, in her arms. The head man of the village sent runners after her.
From the top of the mountain she signaled that they should not
try to reach her. She threw her baby out over the cliff and then she
jumped from the mountain to the rocks below. Her people buried
her and the baby among the rocks where they fell and they brought
the body of the war chief and buried him with them. From that time
on, the mountain that towers above the graves was known as "the
mountain of the chief."

Mistakis (the Backbone). It is a place of great power where most sacred
things—materials to make paints for religious ceremonies, edible and med-
icinal plants, and spirit animals (bison, otter, bear, wolf, eagle, and raven)—
began and continue to live. For the Blackfeet, it is a place for vision quests.
Favored peaks for vision quests are Chief Mountain, Rising Wolf (Red
Mountain), and Mount Henry (Wolf Calf) in the Two Medicine area.

In 1895, after considerable pressure from the U.S. government, the
Great Northern Railway, and naturalist George Bird Grinnell (for whom
Mount Grinnell is named), the Blackfeet ceded 800,000 acres of mountain

White Calf was a respected elder of the Blackfeet. CHARLES S. FRANCIS, 956-020, COURTESY OF MONTANA HISTORICAL SOCIETY, HELENA MT.

lands along the western edge of the Blackfeet Reservation. The U.S. government opened the land to mining claims and oil and gas drilling, but prospecting was poor. In the meantime, conservationists were lobbying to set the majestic landscape aside as a national park, and in 1910, much of these ceded lands became part of Glacier National Park. Partially included in the ceded lands was Chief Mountain. This most sacred mountain to the Blackfeet and other tribes now lies partly in the Blackfeet Reservation and partly in Glacier National Park.

White Calf, the last chief of all the Piegan, was one of the reluctant signers of the agreement to cede the mountain lands. "Chief Mountain is my head," he said. "Now my head is cut off. The mountains have been my last refuge." But White Calf continued to fight for the rights of his people.

In January 1903, the U.S. Indian Office proposed to lease Blackfeet lands to cattlemen. The Blackfeet, who were themselves raising cattle, objected. Grinnell was commissioned to lead a delegation of Blackfeet headmen to plead their case; White Calf was among those who went east. While in Washington, D.C., White Calf was the guest of President Theodore Roosevelt. Sadly, the chief fell ill and died at Providence Hospital of pneumonia. The other headmen had already gone back to Montana, and there were no Indians at his deathbed. The old warrior died, but he had won his last battle—the tribe kept possession of the million acres where they ran their cattle.

President Roosevelt held the old chief in such high regard that he ordered White Calf's body be returned to Montana in a private railway car with full military escort. White Calf was buried in the Cut Bank area.

The Kootenai (aka Ktunaxa, Kutenai) also have historical and religious ties to the park. Their traditional territory encompassed most of the Flathead Valley west of the mountains. They seasonally camped at the foot of Lake McDonald and had religious ceremonies at the "Place of Dancing." According to a Glacier National Park ethnographic report titled *Our Mountains Are Our Pillows*, the Place of Dancing is at the foot of Lake McDonald or more probably near West Glacier on the Middle Fork of the Flathead River.

Other tribes, notably the Cree, Assiniboine, and Nakota (Stoney), traveled through and briefly camped in the area, but of these it was the Salish and Pend d'Oreille (aka Upper Kalispel) who most frequently camped in the area that is now the park. The 1700s and early 1800s were times of increased conflict between the tribes. The Blackfeet raided the western tribes for horses, and when the western tribes tried to cross the mountains to the plains to hunt buffalo, they often encountered battle-ready Blackfeet guarding the passes and access routes. An unknown number of deaths and nearly fatal injuries resulted.

There are also numerous accounts of killings in the early 1800s over

A Kootenai man paddles his sturgeon-nosed, reverse-prow canoe, well designed for turbulent waters. COURTESY OF ARCHIVES AND SPECIAL COLLECTIONS, UNIVERSITY OF MONTANA-MISSOULA.

the beaver trade. The Blackfeet hated the mixed-blood Canadian free-men who came to the foothills of the Rockies to trap beaver, which then deprived the Blackfeet of pelts to trade with the English on the Saskatchewan River and the American traders to the south. However, all of these battles together do not compare in death count to the 1837 smallpox epidemic when more than fifty percent of the Blackfeet died, or the Starvation Winters of 1883-1885 when 400 to 600 Piegan Blackfeet died due to the near extinction of buffalo and the failure of promised government annuities to arrive.

Aside from deaths that occurred in tribal battles and trapper feuds, the people's mortality and the struggle to survive were a natural part of the circumstances of living in a rugged landscape.

Few deaths were officially recorded during the period of exploration by fur trappers, miners, and early settlers because there was little official local presence. Fort Benton in central Montana was the military-run government hub, and people tended to disregard procedures for investigating or reporting deaths. Montana was designated a territory in 1864 and reached statehood in 1889. With completion in 1893 of the transcontinental Great Northern Railway from St. Paul, Minnesota, to Seattle, Washington, the number of people who settled in northwest Montana increased dramatically. Newspapers were established, county governments formed, and laws passed; deaths, if they were reported, were recorded somewhat more systematically.

Beginning in 1897, the area now Glacier Park was administered as the Flathead Forest Reserve. The purpose of the reserve was to prevent poaching and illegal logging and, as an aside, to address other crimes. For the most part, the denizens of the area were left to themselves. People actively developed businesses, mined, and made some attempts at ranching or farming within the current boundaries of the park. There were 400 private properties or claims ringing Lake McDonald alone.

At that point in Montana's history, there were no such things as safety regulations, written procedures, training by experts, or anything else to guide people's decisions about how to live in a wilderness. Many

Filling a trough carved by glaciers, Lake McDonald is ten miles long and 464 feet deep. GEORGE GRANT, COURTESY OF GLACIER NATIONAL PARK ARCHIVES.

activities were inherently more dangerous than they are now. The focus was to get things done. Safety was secondary if thought about at all, and people usually learned how to survive in mountainous country through harsh—sometimes deadly—experience. Such lessons were passed on from father to son, mother to daughter, and neighbor to neighbor, or not at all.

DEATH AND SURVIVAL BEFORE IT WAS A PARK

The few deaths and near misses told here help to illustrate what life was like for the early settlers before the area was under the official purview of federal park administrators.

In November 1890, Frank C. Geduhn, a young German from North Dakota, was lured to Demersville, Montana (near today's town of Kalispell), by a letter from a friend and some Great Northern Railway advertising literature. Almost immediately, Frank Miles, the superintendent of the Butte and Montana Commercial Company, hired him. The following February, Miles sent Geduhn to McDonald's Lake (as it was called then) to secure water rights at the outlet of the lake for his company. A local trapper named Palmer held the water rights at that time.

On his first trip to McDonald's Lake, Geduhn followed the tote road (built to haul supplies and building materials) from the western entrance of Bad Rock Canyon to near the beginning of Seven Mile Canyon. At Belton (now West Glacier), he picked up a guide named Dan Doody, a trapper and hunter who in 1910 would become one of the park's first six rangers. Geduhn and Doody went down the Middle Fork of the Flathead River to just above the confluence with McDonald Creek. Describing the journey up the creek, Geduhn wrote, "The jungle in the timber [thick stands of old-growth cedar and spruce] was too difficult to overcome. There was no trail to follow. We just travelled."

In 1891, there were two trapper cabins at McDonald's Lake, one at the head of the lake and one at the foot, both small. According to historian L. O. Vaught's papers, one was built by trapper John McDonald in the early 1880s. McDonald ran his trap lines from his cabin near the lake. He traded at the Ramsdell Brothers' store at Egan's Landing and was well known in the upper Flathead Valley. Despite claims to the contrary, the lake first became known to the early settlers of the Flathead Valley as McDonald's Lake because they first knew about the lake from trapper John McDonald. After a winter or maybe longer, McDonald moved to the east side of the mountains. In 1885, he and a man named Felix Constant were hanged by a mob on Birch Creek, presumably for horse stealing. There was no hearing or judicial procedure. The citizens of the Flathead Valley liked McDonald and did not believe he and Constant were guilty. They believed that it was a frame-up by two or three men who suddenly came into possession of several hundred dollars that McDonald was known to have and which mysteriously disappeared after the hanging. Whether the hangmen were ever prosecuted is unknown.

The cabin at the head of the lake on the inlet, between the falls and the lake, was built by trapper Frank McKisson in the 1880s. The walls were not over four feet high and it had a "scoop" or pitched roof. McKisson was probably the first full-time resident on McDonald's Lake. He trapped marten and lynx in the upper reaches of McDonald Creek. McKisson's nearest neighbor was "Dutch" John Elsner, another early settler who built a cabin at the small lake a half mile east of McDonald's Lake inlet now known as John's Lake.

McKisson was known as a good-hearted, rough-and-tumble pioneer who liked whiskey and never refused a drink. He eventually gave up trapping and either gave up his claim or sold it and bought a farm in Helena Flats on the Whitefish Road. He then married the widow Bennett, whose farm joined his, and the couple apparently lived happily ever after, finally moving to California.

Other trappers occupied the cabins after McDonald and McKisson. Ernest Christensen trapped a little while living at the foot of the lake. Fred McCrimon had a timber claim on lower McDonald Creek and water and placer rights at Upper McDonald Creek Falls and at six different sites around the head of McDonald's Lake.

Sometime after Geduhn's first visit to the lake, McCrimon moved into the cabin at the head of the lake, made the walls higher, and did some other assessment work to hold his claims. He left in 1896 to join in the Klondike Gold Rush and did not return, forfeiting his McDonald's Lake claims.

When Frank Geduhn and Dan Doody arrived at McDonald's Lake, Palmer was the only person there. Geduhn and Palmer parleyed for a bit, and then Geduhn bought the water rights on behalf of the Butte and Montana Commercial Company for $100.

Geduhn would later write, "I have never forgotten the moment when my gaze first encountered that lake and its surrounding mountains." He had "found his heart's desire, had reached trail's end." In March 1891, he returned to McDonald's Lake. He brought his friend John Frost with him and a sleigh load of food and tools. The two men packed the goods down the river and up the creek, which were still partially frozen over.

Geduhn located his homestead at the foot of the lake and built his claim

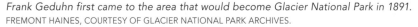
Frank Geduhn first came to the area that would become Glacier National Park in 1891.
FREMONT HAINES, COURTESY OF GLACIER NATIONAL PARK ARCHIVES.

cabin west of the outlet. "Every morning," he wrote, "noon and night I had to go to the beach and look, and admire and worship that wondrously beautiful creation of the Sublime Architect. While my friend John would be cutting holes in the ice, baiting hooks and pulling out trout, I would stand and gaze enraptured at lake and mountains, and tried to solve the lofty messages of poise, serenity, patience, peace and love to all God's creation, which they were conveying to me." (L. O. Vaught once described Geduhn as a mixture of poet and Teutonic realist.)

Soon after Geduhn was settled in at the lake, he welcomed a new neighbor—James "Scotty" Findlay, one of the Great Northern Railway surveyors who took up a claim at the Big Cedars, a half mile below the lake. Geduhn described him as a sunny-tempered young Scotsman. There were very few people in the area then; it was a lonesome life. The two young men immediately became close friends.

In June that same year, Geduhn had more new neighbors when Milo Apgar and Charles Howes and their families came from Great Falls to homestead at the foot of the lake.

On a Sunday morning in May, Findlay went to visit Geduhn. The two men talked to each other for a few minutes across the creek. Then, against Geduhn's fervent protest, Findlay went to the outlet of the lake to cross over. He started to wade across, but the water was deeper and the current swifter than he anticipated. He was swept downstream. Geduhn ran to the cabin for a rope, but by the time he returned Findlay had disappeared. Geduhn walked along the bank of the creek for "I don't know how long" hoping to find Findlay. He wrote, "I loved him as my brother and we surely were bosom friends. I pulled him out of a deep hole . . . dead."

Friends feared Geduhn would become a mental wreck. But as Geduhn wrote forty-two years later, "Time heals. Though this also be true I still often, too often, think of Scotty."

The grieving Geduhn relinquished his claim at the foot of the lake to Milo Apgar and took up the claim McKisson abandoned at the head of the lake. Here he added cabins to his site, and along with Denis Comeau,

Frank Kelly, and George Snyder, ran a thriving business renting to tourists. Geduhn also served as a forest ranger for a while when the area was established as part of the Flathead Forest Reserve in 1897.

THE TREAT PARTY—GLACIER'S FIRST TOURISTS

Up until the 1890s, the footpaths of people roaming the country we now call Glacier National Park were those of the Kootenai, Blackfeet, Stoneys, Cree, trappers, prospectors, explorers, a few lost souls, and those who came to homestead. In the Northwest, the idea of an "outing" just for the fun of it had not yet caught on. The Treat Party made one of the first—or at least one of the first recorded—tourist trips. Their haps and mishaps on their first trip to Glacier country were a harbinger of tourists to come.

At that same time, the Great Northern Railway was laying track from St. Paul, Minnesota, to the West Coast, and was about to feature Glacier as its premier tourist destination.

In September 1892 George Treat, the city marshal of Great Falls, wanted to give his father, S. C. Treat, an outing with some old friends from Decorah, Iowa. In addition to the Treats, the party consisted of Iowans Dr. Curtis L. Beard, J. J. Marsh, S. W. Matteson, H. H. Matteson, C. E. Dickerman, and Frank Day, and Great Falls friends and residents Robert (Bob) Phillips, C. E. LeMunyon, and Billy Ackerman. Frank Geduhn agreed to be their guide.

While the party waited at the head of McDonald's Lake for one of the group members who was arriving late, Geduhn told them about a little lake hemmed in by a great wall that he had recently seen, and which as far as he knew had not been visited by other white men. Captivated by the tale, the men decided to do "a little pioneer exploring and pay that lake a visit." (It would later be known as Avalanche Lake.) For this venture, Chris Keenan was their guide. Base camp was at the Box Canyon (Avalanche Gorge), where Geduhn would join them the next day after he returned from the foot of McDonald's Lake to meet the late arrival.

When Geduhn arrived at the camp late the next afternoon, he found a weary but contented bunch of tenderfoot tourists. After fighting their way through buck brush, devil's walking stick (aka devil's club), and downed timber for several hours, they despaired, gave up, and went back to camp. One of them killed a deer, and with meat in camp, everybody cheered up.

The next day they headed back to McDonald's Lake. On the way, they stopped at the Big Cedars. One of the men cut a big chip out of one of the largest cedars. On the smooth surface of the inner wood of the tree he penciled the date, their names, and a short history of their recent venture, which they jokingly referred to as "the Lost Lake Expedition." (In writing of this incident, L. O. Vaught said that six years later when he first saw the writing it was still legible.)

A few days after the party returned to McDonald's Lake, Marshall Treat, Bob Phillips, and Billy Ackerman brought in a string of riding and pack horses to take the party to Langerman Lake. (A man named Langerman, whom we don't know much about, drowned in what today is known as Trout Lake; for a brief period the locals referred to it as Langerman Lake.) According to Vaught's manuscript, Iowan H. H. Matteson told the following story about this trip in letters to Vaught.

> When we went over the divide from McDonald's Lake to Langerman Lake, we did not get started until much later than we anticipated. The only ones who had experience in packing were George Treat and Frank Geduhn. Treat had been familiar with the diamond hitch but in applying it to his packs he had some difficulty, and we spent the morning developing the right hitch. The trail over the ridge was a blind one which scarcely disclosed itself. We were off it as much of the time as on it. Much of the way, especially on the western side of the ridge where the mountain side was the steepest, our horses had a great deal of trouble maintaining a foothold. Among our party was Dr. Curtis L. Beard, a man then about sixty years of age. He was learned in medicine but had in his head more useless knowledge than any man I ever met. He knew the pedigree and record of almost every race horse, but was not a horseman.

He knew the date of every cockfight, but had never seen one. His fishing equipment was the most complete and the finest I have ever seen, but he had never fished. His hunting outfit was the most expensive produced, but he had never discharged a gun. Examining his equipment, I noted he had a ball of strong twine which I thought possibly was for fish stringers. I said to him: "Doc, you must be expecting to catch a lot of fish." "No," he replied, "that is an idea of my own. I am going to hunt bear. One end of that ball of twine will be fastened to my gun; the ball will be in my pocket. When a bear takes after me I will climb a tree, the ball unwinding, and when I get up (the tree) I can pull up the gun."

(There was little anyone in hearing distance could say. They just shook their heads.)

On the way over the divide the Doctor kept reining in his horse. We advised him to let the horse have his head but he seemed possessed to pull the horse off its feet. Suddenly the Doctor sung out: "Boys, I am going." We saw the doctor's horse sliding down the mountain side with the doctor on its back. Four or five hundred feet down the mountain side was a clump of bushes, which luckily was in the horse's course and against it they came to a stop. Finally after much effort we got the doctor and his horse back on the trail.

We reached the lake after dark. It was raining and we could find no place to pitch the tent. The next morning we pitched our tent right at the edge of the log jam which reached across the lake. From the jam we fished and such trout fishing. There was no sport in it. As fast as the line was dropped in, a strike was had.

In two or three days, four of us tramped to the head of the lake, and camped there overnight. We remained in camp there until the following day. Shortly after noon Billy Ackerman came up the lake in a folding canvas boat with very short oars and landed where we were fishing. He was in a hurry to return because the water was beginning to get rough. We endeavored to get him to remain with us but he decided not to do so. He had proceeded about a quarter

*of a mile when we heard a cry from him and saw that his
boat had capsized. In less than a minute he sank. The water
where he sank was 75 feet deep. Rafts were made and the
lake was dragged but the attempts to recover the body
were finally given up.*

Three weeks later Frank Geduhn found the body and, at the request
of the Ackerman family, buried Ackerman at the head of the lake just east
of the inlet.

THE CATTLE QUEEN
AND THE MAN WITH A PAST

One example of the precariousness of life back in the old days
involved boating. In those days, many people never learned to swim and
they did not have any form of lifejackets or personal flotation devices.
They also tended to wear heavy woolen clothing. These combined factors
made capsizing a boat likely to lead to drowning. Drinking alcoholic
beverages was common in those days and often contributed to drownings and other deaths. This latter situation is colorfully illustrated by a
signature death prior to the park's establishment.

Elizabeth "Libby" (Smith) Collins, later immortalized as the Cattle
Queen of Montana, gave an account of the drowning of her mining
partner, Frank McPartland, in her book *Cattle Queen of Montana*. L. O.
Vaught, an Illinois attorney and Glacier Park historian (Mount Vaught is
named for L. O. and his wife Helen), considered Libby's account somewhat fanciful, so he
decided to interview

*McPartland Mountain
is named for prospector
Frank McPartland. The
Kootenai name for the
mountain means
"Crossing over Victory."*
COURTESY OF GLACIER
NATIONAL PARK.

local residents. In his lawyerly way, Vaught required the interviewees to sign affidavits swearing to the truth of their stories. According to Vaught's interviews—including one with Libby's brother Chandler "Chan" Smith—and stories from the 1895 *Inter Lake* newspaper and the 1913 *Columbian*, prospector Frank McPartland was definitely a man with a past.

McPartland, along with "Skookum Joe" Anderson, David Jones, J. R. Kempet, and C. Snow, discovered the richest mining ground in central Montana, an area in the Judith Basin known

Elizabeth "Libby" Collins was a mining partner of Frank McPartland.
E. R. SHEPARD, COURTESY OF MONTANA HISTORICAL SOCIETY, HELENA.

as the Maiden District. Sometime later, as men with gold fever often do, McPartland left the Maiden and went to the Sweet Grass Hills when gold was discovered there. While in the Sweet Grass, he had an unexplainable dispute with his partner John Moy over the boundaries and size of Rhode Island. During their fight, McPartland cut Moy nearly to pieces and the man bled to death. Since the killing was on the Blackfeet Indian Reservation, some time passed before McPartland's trial came up in the U.S. court at Miles City. No prosecuting witnesses appeared and he was discharged.

McPartland returned to northern Montana in 1886 and later joined Chan Smith and Libby Collins in copper mining ventures at Mineral Creek along the east fork of McDonald Creek. This area later became part of Glacier National Park. He took up a claim west of Frank Geduhn's cabin at the head of McDonald's Lake and built a two-room cabin at the start of the trail to the copper mines.

By 1895, the vein of copper-bearing quartz pinched out, and a mining expert from St. Paul declared the vein lost. Funds were exhausted. Libby's opinion was that the best thing to do was abandon the mine.

In August the three partners—Collins, Smith, and McPartland (who was wearing a six shooter and a prospector's pick on the ammunition belt around his waist)—were at Snyder's Hotel drinking and quarreling all day. Toward evening they left Snyder's Hotel to go to McPartland's cabin at the head of the lake. All three climbed into a rowboat. Chan was rowing, McPartland was in the prow, and Libby, who weighed around 300 pounds, and a jug of whiskey were in the stern.

About halfway up to the head of the lake, McPartland asked for the whiskey jug. Chan said, "No, wait until we get to the head of the lake." A quarrel started and McPartland got up to get the jug.

The boat capsized and they all went into the water. Chan was on one side holding hands across the boat with Libby who was on the other side. Libby was wearing a Dolman cloak fastened around her neck with a chain. McPartland had grabbed the cloak to keep from sinking, and the weight on the chain was choking her. Chan called out to Libby to unfasten the chain. She did. Down went McPartland and the cloak.

Chan and Libby's cries for help alerted the people in the hotel. According to George Snyder, Billy Elsworth, and the other people

Snyder's Hotel at the head of McDonald's Lake, shown here (left) in 1905, was sold to John and Olive Lewis in 1906. In 1913-1914, the Lewises moved the Snyder build-ing back from the lakefront and turned it into a general store. They built a Swiss-style hotel on the original site of Snyder's Hotel and named it the Glacier Hotel (right). Lewis' Glacier Hotel was sold to the Great Northern Railway in 1930, then to Glacier National Park in 1932, becoming Lake McDonald Lodge. LEFT, MORTON J. ELROD, RIGHT, R. E. MARBLE, BOTH COURTESY OF GLACIER NATIONAL PARK ARCHIVES.

The F. I. Whitney docks at the foot of Lake McDonald, circa 1907. COURTESY OF GLACIER NATIONAL PARK ARCHIVES.

who aided in the rescue, they knew that Libby's heft would make it impossible to pull her into a rowboat without it capsizing. So they boarded the steamboat *F. I. Whitney*, which was tied to the dock, and went to the rescue. When they reached the overturned rowboat, McPartland had disappeared under water. Chan was helped into the *Whitney*, but Libby was too heavy to pull up and into the boat. Instead, they tied a rope under her armpits and towed her back to the dock where they managed to get her out of the water.

The next day, they dropped dynamite into the lake to bring up McPartland's body, but he never surfaced. His body was never found.

Libby returned to cattle ranching in Choteau, Montana, and Chan moved to Columbia Falls, eventually becoming somewhat of a local character.

DAD WALKER AND THE BRUTE

In 1910, two months after Glacier became a national park, Norton Pearl, a young man born and raised in Eastport, Michigan, who later worked as a Butte, Montana, school principal, came to vacation in the new park. He must have enjoyed his adventure because in November

1912 he began employment as a Glacier National Park ranger at Lower Two Medicine. Pearl kept detailed journals and diaries of his time in the park, which were later published by his granddaughter, Leslie Lee, in *Backcountry Ranger in Glacier National Park, 1910-1913.* Pearl became friends with many of the old-timers and included his experiences with them in his journals. We have included some of those events in later chapters, such as the story of Joe Prince freezing to death. Pearl also wrote up old-timers' accounts of the times before Glacier became a park.

Prospector "Dad" Walker came in 1899 to try his luck and stake mineral claims when the mining boomtown of Altyn sprang up near Swiftcurrent Falls in the flats below what is now the Many Glacier Hotel. The boomtown of Altyn busted in 1902, and prospectors and mining investors headed elsewhere but Dad Walker stayed. The old prospector got to know Pearl and Pearl's hiking friend Mark Markley from Butte, who came on Pearl's vacation trek through the park in 1910. Pearl wrote in his journal:

> The Divide here is called the Garden Wall and it's very pretty. We went up until we found the old prospect cabin all fallen in. We helped Dad put up the roof logs before coming away this morn & also cut him some wood. His roof blew off awhile back & he is afraid of getting drowned out by mud & water with his dirt roof if he doesn't put the boards back on before long. He told us many of his ups & downs and I should take a day off putting em down & also a description of his hut. We came by a grave. Miss Pritchard who died of child birth. Dad said her husband made her cook supper for his men the night she died & then the child had been dead nine days & putrefied. They had no doctor & when one came he could do nothing & a fine little French woman she was. The man got his legs cut off in a saw mill & died. He probably deserved it. There is a daughter & dad wants me to find her. She is a teacher. The brute sold all & went away even leaving a little family bible & the marriage certificate in the house. The cer. Is in a little pot/box & dad has it & wants the girl to get it.

Unfortunately we don't know if the girl ever got the bible and the marriage certificate.

ROGERS MEADOW

In 1896, twenty-six-year-old Josiah Rogers filed his homestead

Josiah Rogers homesteaded up the North Fork beginning in 1896. COURTESY OF LUCI YEATS.

claim in the North Fork near the Camas Creek Trail where the trail opens onto what is now known as Rogers Meadow. Joe Rogers and his neighbor on Camas Creek, Ernest Christensen, were the earliest long-term settlers to take up homestead claims.

Both young men went off to fight during the Spanish-American War in 1898, and Rogers returned to the North Fork in the summer of 1899. He packed for oil exploration companies and U.S. Geological Survey crews while developing his homestead into a working ranch. In 1902, he married Mary "Mollie" Miller of Columbia Falls, and the newlyweds settled into life in the wilderness. He built a cabin and an eighteen-by-fifty-two-foot log barn, put in fifty acres of timothy, cleared ten acres of brush from a large natural meadow, and put in a mile and a half of fencing. Rogers ran horses and beef cattle on his ranch. Homesteading was never-

Mary and Josiah Rogers risked an arduous life in the wilds before Glacier became a park. COURTESY OF LUCI YEATS.

ceasing hard work, and winters were brutally cold. Sadly, Mary wasn't up to it. In the winter of 1908, twenty-nine-year-old Mary fell ill. The cause was unknown and her condition gradually worsened over the next several months. By June, she was so sick that Josiah decided to take her to the hospital in Columbia Falls. Three miles into the journey Mary died. According to all accounts, the young wife and homesteader had added to the lives and memories of all who knew her, and she was deeply mourned.

Josiah Rogers went on to become one of the icons of early Glacier National Park. A natural-born entrepreneur, he had already begun a packing concession for tourists at Lake McDonald well before the park was established. He ran 70 to 100 horses and used a trail over Howe Ridge to go between his Camas Creek Ranch and Lake McDonald. In 1910, he married Marie Kuhr of Chinook and built a house on Lake McDonald. In 1912, Rogers paid half the cost of constructing a road along the east side of Lake McDonald to the Lewis Glacier Hotel. He kept his pack strings there and took groups of fifteen to twenty people on camping trips of up to thirty days.

TRAPPER SLIM LINK, A BEAR, AND A DOG

In 1908, Slim Link ran his trap lines from a log cabin on Kishenehn Creek on the east side of the North Fork of the Flathead River. This site was a few miles south of the U.S.-British Columbia border. It would later become the Kishenehn Ranger Station. At that time, there were a number of homesteads on both sides of the river, and an oil boom was underway at the upper end of the valley on both sides of the border.

Charles Green, who grew up in Coram, Montana, eight miles from the west entrance to the park, told the following story in *Montana Memories, Vol. I*. Green was a friend of homesteader Matt Brill, who gave him this account of the incident. Green and Brill believed this was the first recorded death by a grizzly in northwest Montana.

Green described Slim as a man of about forty who was tall, slender, and had bushy black hair; he was friendly with his few distant neighbors but never talked about himself. "Many such men roamed the country in the early days," Green wrote. "The name they went by, where they were from or where they went was no one's business but their own."

Slim made his living trapping. At that time black martens were plentiful, as were beavers, otters, mink, wolverines, and a few wolves. Slim sold his pelts each spring, and they provided him a comfortable living.

In the fall of 1907, Slim went back to civilization—what the locals called "outside"—for the winter. Where or why, no one knows, but early the next spring he stopped at Matt Brill's cabin north of Trail Creek one evening with a full packsack of groceries, his .45-90 Winchester rifle, and the small black dog that was his constant companion. Slim spent the night with Matt. Before going to bed, he told of a large grizzly prowling around his cabin the previous fall and said if it bothered him again he was going to shoot it.

When Slim left the next morning, Matt walked down to the river with him. He said Slim took off his boots and socks, tied them on his large pack and started to wade the river. It was April and the cold water was up to his knees, the little dog swimming ahead. Slim stopped in midstream, hung his rifle on his shoulder, and calmly rolled a Bull Durham cigarette. He lit it, waded on across the river, and sat down to put his boots on. Then he turned to wave goodbye and vanished in the woods with his dog in the lead.

One morning about a week later, Matt was awakened by the little dog scratching on his door. He let the famished pup in and fed him. Then the dog begged, the way that dogs do, for Matt to follow him back to the river. Matt had company due in that day and couldn't leave. He wrote a note to a trapper who lived about one mile from Slim's cabin telling him to go up to see what was wrong. He taped the note in some waterproof cloth and attached it to the dog's collar and walked down to the river. Matt said the dog seemed overjoyed, but when he realized Matt wasn't going with him the dog swam the river and raced up the trail for home.

Matt's company, two men from Columbia Falls, came in on horseback that morning and stayed overnight. The next morning they heard a whimper at the cabin door. It was the little black dog again, dejected, bushed, and famished. The note was still on its collar, which meant he had failed to find the neighbor up the valley. After some discussion, the three men decided to investigate. They fed the dog, had breakfast, saddled their horses, checked their rifles that were in scabbards, made sure they had plenty of extra ammunition, mounted their horses, and headed for the river.

The dog took the lead, urging them on. He ran up the trail ahead, swam the river, waited for them to ford across, and then scampered up the trail, urging them to hurry.

When they got to Slim's cabin they found a scene of "utter desolation." They could only surmise what had happened. They looked at the cabin first. The door was open. Slim's .45-90 rifle was leaning against the outside wall fully loaded. Inside, a grizzly had wrecked everything. The food had been eaten, stoves were upset, every container and even the stove pipe was flattened, blankets were ripped to shreds, and there were teeth and claw marks and dried blood everywhere.

In the yard in front of the cabin was a stump beside the trail and on the ground beside it an old large-bore single-shot rifle. A fine wire was attached to the trigger. There was an empty shell in the gun and one on the ground. Slim had rigged a "set gun" for the bear, with a wire stretched across the path. People sometimes used this lethal device in the early days to kill bad bears or other intruders.

Based on the evidence at the scene, Matt and his friends determined that Slim had set the trap in the evening and the bear had walked into it at night. Slim awakened and went out to see if the bear had been killed. Finding that the bear was not dead or even in sight, Slim had reloaded the gun and reset the snare. Then the bear must have charged so suddenly that Slim was unable to reach the other rifle eight feet away. Matt and his friends guessed that the bear had either pushed Slim into his own gun or the bear had been shot again before killing Slim.

The little dog was across the clearing and barking for attention. The men, with rifles ready, followed the dog to what remained of his master's body. Lying in the grass was a human skeleton with the bones picked clean. They found balls of fabric scattered from the cabin to the skeleton—parts of Slim's clothing. The bear in its fury had destroyed all evidence of the man.

The three men looked around the area, but there was no trace of the bear, alive or dead. They believed it had left the vicinity to die of its wounds.

They searched Slim's cabin. There was no clue as to his history, where he came from, or if he had any kin. Slim Link, or whoever he was, would always be a mystery. For Matt and anyone who knew him, there was no doubt that that's the way Slim wanted it. They buried his remains near the cabin and did not mark the grave.

The rifle and the dog were the only things not destroyed by the bear. Matt tied the rifle to his saddle, and the dog followed behind the horses back down the trail. Matt's friends returned home the next day and reported the tragedy to authorities. The dog stayed with Matt until it died of old age. Matt told Green that every year on the anniversary of Slim's death the dog would leave and be gone for two days. There was no doubt in Matt Brill or Charles Green's minds that the "pup would return to the cabin, hoping to find his master waiting for him at their old home."

When Glacier Park was created two years later, Slim's cabin was burned and the Kishenehn patrol cabin was built nearby.

ON THE OTHER SIDE OF THE MOUNTAINS

On the east side of what is now the park, the township of St. Mary sprang up around 1898 during the mining boom. When no rich ores were found, much of the population left the area for better prospects elsewhere, but a small community remained. The group of buildings at that site became known as "old town." These diehard residents, having abandoned the notion of becoming rich miners, centered their livelihood on raising horses, hunting, trapping, freighting, fishing, and caring for occasional travelers.

Jack Monroe arrived at St. Mary sometime after 1887. Some believe that he built the log building standing across U.S. Highway 89 from the

Park Café. Monroe cared for travelers and guided hunters, and once the park was established he bought concession permits and packed park visitors into the backcountry. Monroe was remembered for his belief that bathing nude daily in the icy waters of Divide Creek increased his hardiness. He left St. Mary sometime around 1930.

George Flowers and his wife Mary came to St. Mary soon after the area was opened to mining. He was one of the town's leading citizens, serving as the town handyman, doctor, dentist, and wheelwright. In 1912, when his mining claims were disallowed, he moved to Kalispell.

"Two Dog" Jack Harp was one of St. Mary's most colorful characters. Supposedly he was nicknamed for the number of dogs he claimed to need to sleep with on a cold night. He was a trapper and claimed to be the first cross-country skier in the area. One midwinter day, Jack took a pair of homemade skis up a hill near St. Mary. He returned that night all skinned up and without his wool stocking cap. When asked where his cap was, he muttered, "It's up in some damn tree up there!" In the 1920s, he cut ice blocks from nearby Duck Lake during the winter and stored the blocks in an ice house for summer use by the St. Mary Chalet. Two Dog Flats is named for Jack Harp.

John "Jack" Bryce filed a mining claim in 1898 and, according to Bruce Fladmark's *History of St. Mary*, Bryce "participated in the mineral exploration from its opening day." He kept a cabin at St. Mary. On February 11, 1911, Bryce was caught in a snowstorm walking between St. Mary and Babb and froze to death. Frank Harrison, who lived in St. Mary as a child and was at Bryce's burial in St. Mary, recalled that when he was buried, coyotes howled and owls hooted as one of the men solemnly gave a sermon over Bryce's body.

CHAPTER THREE

THE LAND

Becomes a

NATIONAL PARK

When Glacier National Park was officially established in 1910, there was no National Park Service and most of the existing national parks were managed by the military. Colonel Logan, assigned as the first superintendent of Glacier, did not have park visitors on his mind during the first summer that Glacier was a park. Instead, he was dealing with massive wild-

President Taft signed legislation officially establishing Glacier National Park on May 11, 1910. JACOB W. FRANK, COURTESY OF NATIONAL PARK SERVICE.

fires in the park, part of the widespread fires of 1910 that engulfed 3 million acres across the Pacific Northwest.

In addition to fighting fires, park staff had to deal with locals who lived in the park (known as in-holders), who didn't like the new park status, and other locals, both inside and outside park boundaries, who continued to treat Glacier's landscape as if it had not acquired official, protected status. Logan was also tasked with developing infrastructure, such as the first roads. It was a busy time for the new protectors of the park.

The first ranger of Glacier was Frank Liebig, who single-handedly patrolled a half million acres that are now in the park. He worked for the U.S. Bureau of Forestry (predecessor to the U.S. Forest Service), the agency responsible for this area just prior to the founding of Glacier Park. Upon starting his job, he was given a notebook, a silver badge, a double-bit axe, a one-man crosscut saw, a box of ammunition for his .45-70 rifle, and two big sheets of paper on which he was to write what he did each day and send in at the end of each month. As described in *The First Ranger*, Liebig was told, "The whole country is yours, from Belton to Canada and across the Rockies to the prairie between Waterton Lake and the foot of St. Mary Lake. You're to look for fires, timber thieves, squatters and game violators. Go to it and good luck." Although Liebig did a great job as a forest ranger protecting forest resources, he was only one man patrolling a large and mostly unpopulated landscape. Now that landscape was going to have a new management strategy; as a national park the focus was to both promote and regulate public use while also preserving the scenery, the natural and historic features, and the wildlife so that they will remain unimpaired for the enjoyment of future generations. The new national park needed more rangers on patrol, ranger stations, a system of roads and trails, and the means to enforce new rules and regulations. Originally there were six park rangers assigned, and by 1912 the number had increased to sixteen. As the fledgling Glacier Park administration grew over the next decade, it began to cope with increasing park visitation, spurred by the Great Northern Railway's successful advertising campaigns. Early on, there was recognition that most of the tourists would be coming from "back East" or from areas where they wouldn't be familiar with the dangers of a mountain wilderness. George Bird Grinnell, the prominent and influential advocate for creating Glacier, wrote on November 29, 1922, to L. O. Vaught of his concerns about "making the Glacier Park a place where men and women could leave the beaten track and fend for themselves in the real wilds. . . ." He goes on to say, ". . . so many people when they get off a beaten path are perfectly incompetent, that there is some danger in encouraging traveling by individuals. We all have supreme confidence in our ability to take care of ourselves, but I suspect that 99 out of every 100 men, women and children—if you take them a few yards from a road or a trail and turn them around two or three times—would be quite unable to get back to the road. Then somebody must be sent out to find and bring them in. I feel that it is necessary to consider this, for if a man is lost or suffers in the park, the sort of advertising the park gets from this does it harm."

As Glacier Park began to chronicle its first deaths, the concerns that Grinnell expressed led the park to begin developing resources for search and rescue and to provide cautionary language in signage or pamphlets to be handed out to visitors. Nonetheless, deaths occurred, and, with these deaths, policies and regulations changed to try to prevent them. More safety features were added at overlooks, and infrastructure was designed in hopes of averting more fatalities.

It wasn't until late in the twentieth century that anyone seriously critiqued this approach to visitor safety. Joseph Sax was one of the first to profoundly question "coddling" park visitors in his 1980 book *Mountains without Handrails: Reflections on the National Parks*. Sax questioned many of the National Park Service's management choices as it struggled to accommodate increasing throngs of visitors. In particular, he clearly felt that parks should not be "urbanized" to guide visitors away from all danger. Many others have since decried what they see as an overzealous push to safeguard park visitors, noting that a crucial part of the essence and appeal of a natural park like Glacier is its opportunities for wilderness adventure.

The tension between adventure and risk is inherent to visiting Glacier Park. People have made quite different personal decisions about that balance, and this has sometimes resulted in death. This book focuses not only on the deaths and their causes, but also on the personal decisions that led to fatalities and, in some cases, to survival, and the tough job of rescues.

PART TWO

DEATH AND SURVIVAL
ALONG THE
GOING-TO-THE-SUN ROAD

Dedicated in 1933, the Going-to-the-Sun Road was the first national park road designed to complement the scenic wonders it traversed. Park officials, landscape architects, construction engineers, and countless hard-working, dedicated men labored nearly twenty years to carve a road that blended in with the magnificent landscape of Glacier National Park. It was built to the highest standards of road construction of the times and with the least possible damage to the landscape. In 1985, it was listed as a National Historic Civil Engineering Landmark.

The road climbs from the west side of the Continental Divide from Lake McDonald Valley, hugging the Garden Wall in the alpine section. It runs across cliffs and along steep slopes. Its construction necessitated two tunnels and some amazing feats of engineering, such as the Triple Arches, to access Logan Pass and descend down to St. Mary Valley on the east side.

This amazing road heralded a new era for the park. Increasingly more visitors could now enjoy this spectacular country and access the park's hotels and numerous trailheads by driving their vehicles over the road. In 2007, the Apgar Transit Center—now known as the Apgar Visitor Center—was constructed at the T-intersection a mile north of the West Entrance station on the Going-to-the-Sun Road. The center provides visitor information and pick-up and drop-off services for the park's free shuttle system as well as for tour buses and transportation services.

Due to the steep terrain along its path over the mountains, the Going-to-the-Sun Road is stunningly scenic and breathtakingly exciting. For some, it's a white-knuckle experience. Nearly seventy percent of all park visitors tour this amazing road, and it has an impressive safety record. Nearly all the deaths along this road are out-of-vehicle deaths.

As of 2016, fifty-one people have died along the Going-to-the-Sun Road, including three deaths during its construction. On the east side of Logan Pass, only four deaths have occurred on the road below, whereas forty-seven people have died between the West Entrance station and Logan Pass. Most of the deaths on the west side of the road occurred on Upper McDonald Creek, particularly around McDonald Falls where a

The Going-to-the-Sun Road is one of the most scenic highways in the world.
TIM RAINS, COURTESY OF NATIONAL PARK SERVICE.

number of people drowned, and on the alpine section of the road above the Loop. There have been twelve drownings, fourteen deaths from falling, and ten vehicle accidents on the Going-to-the-Sun Road. The rest have been due to falling rock, avalanches, and heart attacks. Add to that tally two murders.

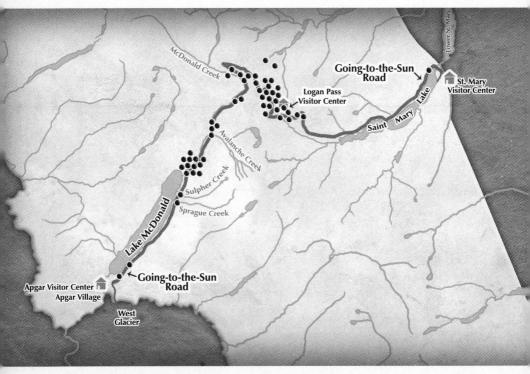

Most deaths within the park have occurred within the Going-to-the-Sun Road corridor. Markers on this map may indicate more than a single fatal incident. Deaths away from the road are not included here.

CHAPTER FOUR

FALLING
from
THE ROAD

The Going-to-the-Sun Road is a stunningly scenic byway, not least because of the jaw-droppingly steep terrain it traverses. The road provides access to alpine meadows at Logan Pass and also to the attendant hazards of roadside drop-offs and plunging slopes. The road is also the most popular drive within the park—nearly seventy percent of all park visitors tour the road each year. It's a classic case of "if you build it, they will come." And some will wander too close to the edge.

All of the falling deaths from roads within the park have occurred on the Going-to-the-Sun Road. The earliest of these was during the road's construction in 1926. In June that year, the trail crew foreman, Charles Rudberg, lost his grip and fell while descending along the route about one mile east of the Loop. As the trail crew foreman, Rudberg was likely involved in road construction because some of the Going-to-the-Sun Road was built over the existing trail to Logan Pass. The section of roadway from which he fell had been recently blasted out of steep cliffs. Additional details are available in an oral history interview with Russell Smith, a project engineer for the road's construction. In his recollections to Phillip Iversen forty-one years later on July 26, 1977, Russell describes Rudberg as a contractor's powderman. Rudberg was sent to inspect the top of a cut in the road about seventy feet above the road-

Construction of Going-to-the-Sun Road routinely exposed workers to inclement weather, rockfall, and perilous heights. Note the worker here reaching from the wooden scaffolding in the arch on the left. COURTESY OF GLACIER NATIONAL PARK ARCHIVES.

bed, which was littered with large rocks from recent blasting. There was a large stone poised at the top of the cut, about six feet in diameter, with a crack through it. Russell was concerned that it would come down on someone, so he put ropes out from the top of the cut and over the rock. The ropes hung free from the rock directly down to the roadbed. Rudberg came down the ropes, inspected the rock, and declared it safe, meaning that they didn't have to blast it to bring it down. As he started down the ropes, just as he got free of the rock and was hanging away from the cliff, he let go and fell seventy feet onto the rock debris on the road. Russell was able to get his car up to the accident site and lift Rudberg onto a cot that was quickly put into his car. They headed for Kalispell as fast as possible, but by the time they reached Avalanche Creek, Rudberg had stopped moaning and breathing. He was dead.

This incident illustrates the difficulty in obtaining accurate information on deaths, accidents, and survival in the early days of the park. Details were often not officially recorded at the time, and corroborating evidence was even scarcer, except when recollections were recorded many years or decades later. As a case in point, various records, such as the Montana Death Index, coroners' reports, and books other than this one, have described Mr. Rudberg as Charles Rudman, Charles Rudbergin, Thowald Rudberg, and Thorwald Rudberg! The most likely case is that he was legally named Thorwald Rudberg and went by Charles.

Three men died during the entire construction of the road. Two fell off the road and one died from being struck by falling rock, possibly after a dynamite blast to remove a section of rock. The latter was Carl Rosenquist, who died in 1931. The second man to fall from the road was Gust Swanson, a stonemason. He was killed near Logan Pass on July 14, 1932, when a rockslide carried him 400 feet down the mountain about one mile east of the pass.

After the Going-to-the-Sun Road was completed in 1934, no further deaths appear in the record until 1951. On August 30 that year, Samuel Insley Stokes, sixty-four, was working as a traffic flagger during road maintenance about one mile east of the Loop. The fog was heavy that day; Stokes stepped over the side of the road and fell. His body, 450 feet below the road, wasn't found until September 1.

A few years later, the *Hungry Horse News* titled an article on another falling death from the road as "Prank Sees Man Tumble to Death." The article described the July 20, 1956, incident as follows: "Apparently a dare brought death to Kenneth Matheson, 44, Calgary taxi driver, in Glacier National Park Sunday evening about 7:45 P.M. He fell over a 250 foot cliff and slope on Garden Wall with his body dropping, bouncing and rolling, according to Flathead County Coroner Sol Catron." As of that date, the alpine, or Garden Wall, section of the Going-to-the-Sun Road had not had any automobile traffic deaths, and Matheson was only the third

An early touring car passes a rock retaining wall along a vertigo-inducing stretch of Going-to-the-Sun Road.
T. J. HILEMAN, COURTESY OF GLACIER NATIONAL PARK ARCHIVES.

to fall from the road. The article indicates that the "presence of liquor in the car was evident" and that when Matheson's car stopped at a pullout a short distance above the Loop for the passengers to take in the view, Matheson stepped over the stone retaining wall, apparently on a dare. He promptly lost his balance and plunged over the cliff. According to the coroner, his body was badly broken during the fall. One of his fellow travelers hiked down to Matheson and determined that he was dead. Rather than retrieve the body from where Matheson had fallen, rescuers brought the body down to the road below the Loop.

Another Canadian, Lillian H. Mayall, fifty-two, was sightseeing along the road on a Sunday outing in late August 1960. She was traveling with her family from Moose Jaw, Saskatchewan, when they stopped at McDonald Falls on McDonald Creek above Lake McDonald. Perhaps to get a better view, Mayall stepped beyond a retaining wall out onto a narrow ledge overlooking the falls. According to the *Hungry Horse News*, "Miss Wist, who saw the accident, said she believed Mrs. Mayall either turned her ankle or slipped." Mayall fell about fifty feet over rocks to the edge of McDonald Creek below. Her watch stopped at 10:10 A.M. Coroner Sol Catron said that injuries included compound fractures of both legs, both knees were broken, and there were multiple fractures of her hands, feet, and face. He commented that "for all practical purpose she died in the fall." A responding nurse felt a slight pulse that soon stopped. Bringing the body up the cliff to the road required six men.

In nearly the same place, in 1973, another family witnessed one of their members fall to a violent death. Karl Staner, seventy-two, from Albuquerque, New Mexico, was touring the park with his family on August 21. One can imagine the family in a festive vacation mood, being awed by the scenery and anxious to get a few good photographs to show friends back home. This is what the majority of Sun Road travelers are like. Around 2 P.M., Staner stopped to take pictures just below lower McDonald Falls and then stepped over the rock wall, perhaps for a better shot. With his wife standing nearby, he slipped and fell sixty feet onto rocks, rolled into the water, and floated down the creek about 100 yards.

Shortly thereafter, Roger Witt, a visitor from Michigan, spotted the body as he was walking along the creek and notified park headquarters. Within fifteen minutes of Staner's tragic fall, authorities received numerous urgent phone calls. As in the previous case, the coroner determined that death was due to massive injuries from the fall and not by drowning. In reporting the incident, the local newspaper editor noted that Glacier has had numerous drownings or falls in this area.

On August 1, 1976, Don William Ash, twenty-nine, from Whitefish was driving along the Going-to-the-Sun Road near Haystack Creek, four miles below Logan Pass. It was around 4 P.M. He stopped his car, grabbed his canteen, and walked about ten feet below the road to fill his canteen in the stream. He slipped and then tumbled about eighty feet over the rock cliff and landed in the middle of the streambed below. Park visitor Dan Johnson of Fairfax, Virginia, happened to be in the area and was first to reach Ash. He noted that Ash had severe head injuries, no pulse, and was apparently dead. The accident was reported to the Logan Pass Visitor Center at 4:30 P.M., and ten minutes later seasonal ranger Greg Burns arrived at the scene to coordinate the recovery. At the time of the accident, foreman Curt Buchholtz and his "hot shot crew" were practicing mountain rescue techniques on Mount Cannon near Avalanche Creek. They brought their equipment, including a winch, to the scene, and by 6 P.M. they had brought Ash's body up to the road. The body was then transported to park headquarters and later to a funeral home in Columbia Falls.

More recently, Harold Addison, seventy-four, was driving the Going-to-the-Sun Road on August 13, 1999. Near the East Tunnel, not far below Logan Pass, he stopped to take a photo and stepped over a retaining wall to get a better angle for the picture. Unfortunately, this section of the road is built through a section of cliffs and Addison lost his balance. He fell 400 to 500 feet and died.

Only a few years later, Don Fogg Harris, an elderly gentleman of eighty-five, was on a family tour driving up the Going-to-the-Sun Road on June 14, 2001. From the hairpin turn known as the Loop, the road ascends into the alpine zone. The car stopped at Crystal Point turnout, not far above the Loop, so the family could enjoy the view and perhaps take some photos. Harris got out of the car, apparently stumbled over to the edge of the overlook, and momentum carried him over the low, rock retaining wall. It isn't known whether he simply lost his balance or if he suffered a medical problem at just that moment. His fall down the steep slope below the overlook caused him to eventually land on the Sun Road below. People driving up the lower part of the road toward the Loop were shocked to see a body fall onto the road right in front of them.

Another fatal fall from the Going-to-the-Sun Road is documented from stories in the *Hungry Horse News* and park press releases. Eighteen-year-old Brandon Luis Avalos, from St. Maries, Idaho, was visiting Glacier Park with three friends late in the evening of September 18, 2014. Around 10 P.M., they stopped at a pullout along the Sun Road just east of Logan Pass. In winter, the Big Drift forms here, filling the roadcut with snow between cliffs above and below the road. By September, the snow is long gone, but the dangerous cliffs remain. Avalos got out of the vehicle and wandered off in the dark. His friends waited, but Avalos did not return. After a while, the friends concluded that he might have hiked up to Logan Pass, so they drove to the parking lot on the pass and waited through the cold night. The next morning they began looking for Avalos. Back at the Big Drift pullout, they discovered that he had fallen about 100 feet down steep terrain with small bands of cliffs. Unable to safely descend to him, they notified park employees at Logan Pass. Park rangers soon arrived and rappelled down to Avalos. They determined that he was dead and used ropes to pull his body back up to the road. Avalos' death was ruled to be accidental, but his story is a strong reminder that guardrails along a mountain road are there for a reason.

Another unfortunate death occurred not by falling *off* the Sun Road but falling from *underneath* it. Lisa L. Handford, a local woman from Kalispell, was only twenty years old. She graduated from high school in Kalispell and attended Flathead Valley Community College. As reported

Haystack Creek tumbles beneath Going-to-the-Sun Road and through a culvert to plunge down the cliff below.
T. J. HILEMAN, COURTESY OF GLACIER NATIONAL PARK ARCHIVES.

in the August 12, 1982, issue of the *Hungry Horse News*, she was enjoying a Friday evening in Glacier National Park with her friend, Curtis Reber. After they stopped along the road next to Haystack Creek on August 6, they decided to take off their shoes and wade into the creek from the uphill side of the road where the water goes through a large culvert underneath the road. Inside the culvert, wet moss, running water, and bare feet made for a slippery situation and Handford fell. Reber grabbed her but was unable to hold on as the water swept her through the culvert and out the opening on the other side of the road, sending her plunging to the rocks below. Responding rangers pronounced her dead at the scene.

The Sun Road corridor has had many deaths and close calls along its fifty-mile length. When drownings, falls, murders, and vehicle accidents are combined, this road accounts for the largest concentration of fatalities in the park. Many deaths are well publicized, and park press releases consistently caution people about the dangers along this scenic route. Thus, it is surprising that people still act blissfully unaware of the risk to themselves while enjoying the views and heights along the road. A recent story serves to illustrate.

While driving the Sun Road on Saturday, July 16, 2016, Kathleen Marshall could not believe what she was seeing. It was astonishing. An attractive young woman in striped yoga pants was atop the rock guard wall in the alpine section of the Going-to-the-Sun Road, posing in various yoga positions.

It was a beautiful day for driving the road and a beautiful day for taking pictures, which Marshall loved to do. She worked in the park and knew it well. Her grandfather had been bringing her to the park since she was six months old. She instinctively knew that the girl posing on the stone guard walls, which are there for a reason, was risking a fall into an abyss of sky followed by bouncing off boulders, sliding through loose rock, and tumbling hundreds of feet down the mountain. The girl on the guard wall was being coached by another woman who was instructing her on various positions to take while photographing the yoga poses. The coach then asked the girl to go over to a tree on the other side of the wall that overhung the edge of the mountain, grab a low-hanging branch, get into the tree, and strike a yoga pose.

Meanwhile a tall young man, about twenty-five, had pulled into the turnout. Just as the girl grabbed for the branch, he jumped over the guard wall, grabbed the girl, lifted her out of the tree, and brought her back to the turnout side of the guard wall, scolding her all the while. "This isn't Yellowstone," he said. "We don't do this in Glacier." Then he added, "I just didn't want you to die."

He put her in the coach's van. He said he was going to contact a ranger, then he got in his vehicle and left. He most likely saved the girl's life, but the two women appeared visibly angry or perhaps dazed as they began to realize what they had almost done. The women drove away without saying anything. Marshall, still in shock at the utter foolishness of the two women, also got in her vehicle and drove down the road thinking how fortunate the women were that the brave young man came by when he did.

CHAPTER FIVE

DROWNING—
It Can
HAPPEN TO ANYONE

Who doesn't love to splash in the water, hop from rock to rock, or take a photograph of themselves or their family having fun surrounded by nature! Visitors are naturally drawn to Glacier National Park's spectacular cascading waterfalls, clear, swift-running creeks, and stress-relieving lakes. These waters drain from a glaciated landscape, and many are milky blue from glacial silt washed down from the mountains. Some lakes are nearly turquoise, such as Grinnell Lake and Cracker Lake. The brightly colored creek and lake beds created from ancient limestone and mudstone are unforgettably beautiful.

The wonders of nature that make the creeks, falls, and lakes of Glacier National Park stunningly beautiful and irresistibly inviting also make them dangerous. Even the most agile visitors have fallen on the slippery rocks. And the strongest of men have tumbled and drowned due to the tremendous force of rushing water. Expert, fit swimmers have succumbed quickly to hypothermia caused by frigid water temperatures. It can happen to anyone. Drowning is a leading cause of death in all national parks that have waterways. In Glacier, drownings are in a near tie with deaths due to natural causes (such as heart disease, respiratory failure, etc.), both of which trail closely behind falling as the number one cause.

Jane Davis, a thirty-nine-year-old nurse from Taylor, Pennsylvania, was the first person to drown in Glacier National Park. In 1916, Jane, her aunt Annie Simpson, and Annie's daughter were touring the park and staying at the Glacier Park Hotel on the east side. On June 25, Davis arranged with the Park Saddle Horse Company to provide a horse and guide to visit Two Medicine Lake. After visiting the lake and enjoying the view, Davis decided she wanted to visit Trick Falls (now known as Running Eagle Falls) and asked the guide to take her there. On the way to Trick Falls they had to cross a tributary of Two Medicine Lake known as Dry Fork Creek. In summer, Dry Fork is indeed dry. In spring, it carries water, and on this June day the creek was about fifteen to twenty feet

Standing on the shores of the mountain-mirroring lakes in Glacier National Park is one of life's greatest pleasures. It is, as early 1900s Glacier advertising claimed, "the best West of worry, care-killing, stress quieting scenery in the world." And so it is, but deep below many of these waters are the ghosts of the drowned. Cold lakes seldom give up their dead. Bodies are slow to decay and bloat and don't produce the gases that carry them to the surface. Eventually some bodies come to the surface and are delivered to their families. Some never do. JACOB W. FRANK, COURTESY OF NATIONAL PARK SERVICE.

wide and thirty inches deep. Davis was riding a small horse, but the water level did not reach its belly. Her guide, Ed Swingley, was on the lead horse with Davis following shortly behind. While they were crossing, he called back to her, asking if she was afraid of water, and she answered no. When he reached the opposite bank, he turned to see how Davis was doing and saw her in the water. He jumped from his horse to try to grab her, but somewhat hampered by his chaps, he could not get to her before the swift water took her downstream.

Swingley notified rangers at their camp and they responded. Davis' body was found lodged against a fallen tree. The water was running so swiftly that it was necessary to attach a rope to the ranger to keep him from being dragged downstream while he walked the creek to where the body was lodged to free it and bring it to shore.

Davis' aunt told the rangers and the acting county coroner that Davis was subject to fainting spells. After a routine inquiry, it was decided that Davis had fainted while crossing the creek and fell from her horse. There was no indication of foul play and no blame was attached to her death.

STORM WARNING

In July 1923, University of Wisconsin student Samantha "Sammie" Jones of Chicago, Illinois, and Columbia University student Fred W. Huber Jr. of New York City came to the park with a party from the University of Wisconsin on a geological trip. Dr. A. K. Lobeck, Professor of Geology at Columbia University and the University of Wisconsin, accompanied the students. The parties arrived on July 1 and stayed at the Lewis Hotel at the head of Lake McDonald. After a short lecture about Sperry Glacier and the hike to get there, Professor Lobeck instructed the students to retire at 9:30 P.M. so they could get an early start the next morning. Two boys and two girls decided that the hike to Sperry Glacier would be too strenuous for them and told the professor. He excused them from the hike and said they did not have to observe the 9:30 P.M. curfew. Around 9 P.M. Jones, Huber, and two unnamed students rented two canoes from the Lewis Hotel and went canoeing on Lake McDonald. A sudden, severe storm came up, blowing from the northeast. During the storm, the unnamed couple was blown down the lake and landed some distance south of the hotel. They were unharmed and able to walk back to the hotel. It appears that Jones and Huber had gone straight across the lake from the Lewis Hotel and then toward the foot of the lake. Their canoe was found about six miles down the lake overturned on the opposite shore. Paddles and cushions were found floating near the shore of the lake, but there was no trace of the young students. At first, it was hoped that the couple had got to shore, become confused, took a wrong trail, and were lost in the woods. Search parties combed the area and finally concluded that they had drowned. Park officials dragged the lake continuously for several days, finally advising the family that it was unlikely that the bodies would ever be found. The deep cold of Lake McDonald seldom gives up its dead.

That 1923 canoeing incident fostered a good deal of controversy over whether canoes should be allowed on lakes in Glacier where sudden storms are prevalent. At that time, life vests and personal flotation devices (PFDs) were not in common use. The park wrestled with the issue off

Glacier's lakes are beautiful, but also deep and cold. JACOB W. FRANK, COURTESY OF NATIONAL PARK SERVICE.

and on over the years. Park officials finally decided that yes, they are allowed. Today, children are required to wear a personal flotation device, and there must be a PFD in the boat for each adult. All boaters, including people in canoes and kayaks, are encouraged to follow water safety rules, check the weather, and be prepared for sudden storms.

PERISH IN THE ATTEMPT

It's in our DNA to try to save someone in peril. Sadly, some people perish in the attempt. Glacier has recorded six deaths when a family member jumped into the water to save another from drowning and died trying. At least one incident occurred when a rescue diver died trying to recover the body of a little boy for his parents. The following are their stories.

In 1925, twenty-year-old Lena Longini and her eleven-year-old brother Henry were visiting the park on a Burlington Tour. The tour group had hiked through the forest to the spectacular St. Mary Falls where the rushing waters drop about thirty-five feet in three separate tiers. Henry was photographing the falls, perhaps trying to get a shot of a water ouzel (also known as the American dipper), which are often seen here diving under the waterfalls for food. Henry, engrossed in his task, fell into the falls. In an instinctive attempt to grab her brother, Lena slipped and also fell into the turbulent waters of the falls. It all happened in an instant. They both drowned in the cascades below St. Mary Falls. The other members of the tour group were stunned and reported that there was no possibility of rescuing the heroic Lena or young Henry. The rushing waters were too turbulent and running too swiftly.

On June 28, 1962, Alberta Dickman, her husband Francis, and their two teenage daughters, Kathleen Ann and Mary Jo, had stopped at the overlook above McDonald Creek Falls to take in the view of the surrounding mountains and the cascading waters. Mary Jo somehow fell into the creek. Alberta tried to help her daughter, lost her balance, and fell into the water, striking her head on a rock. Apparently unconscious,

At twenty-six miles, Upper McDonald Creek is the longest of the 563 creeks in the park. COURTESY OF GLACIER NATIONAL PARK.

WILD RUSHING WATER

The Going-to-the-Sun Road follows water drainages east and west of Logan Pass as they rise to their source high in the mountains. Engineers laid out the road that way for the best of reasons—the breathtaking scenery. Waterfalls occur or are visible all along the road, including the Weeping Wall, Lunch Creek, Sunrift Gorge, McDonald Falls, and Bird Woman Falls. Along the way, park visitors pull into viewing turnouts just to enjoy the sights and sounds of the wild rushing waters and spectacular waterfalls. Some hike to a trailhead leading to other backcountry features and to creeks and incredible waterfalls such as St. Mary Falls and Virginia Falls. While basking in the pleasure of their surroundings and the joy of the moment, or absorbed in the task of getting a good photograph, some people become careless and ignore posted warning signs. Perhaps they don't realize how incredibly powerful cold, rushing water can be. For some it's a fatal mistake.

she was swept downstream. A passerby got word to Ranger Fred Wood at the Lake McDonald Ranger Station. Wood rushed to the scene, found Alberta, and tried artificial respiration for a while. He then brought in a resuscitator. They tried for another hour to revive her, but there were no signs of life. Mary Jo survived; her mother didn't.

On June 26, 1963, the Trenor family from Seattle, Washington—Cameron, his wife, their three sons, Douglas, Melvin, and Gregory, and a young playmate—were enjoying the spectacular views of an early evening in Glacier National Park. Gregory, six years old, was playing on the rocks just below the Horse Trail Bridge upstream of McDonald Falls. Suddenly he slipped. Cameron jumped in to rescue his son from the snow-cold water but could not reach him in time. The turbulent waters of Upper McDonald Creek were already pulling Gregory over slippery boulders, through whirling pools, until he was out of sight, rushing toward Lake McDonald.

Park officials called in the Flathead Lifesaving and Rescue Association. Almost immediately, Bud Darling, head of the Columbia Falls unit, arrived with a boat and rescue team including SCUBA divers. They quickly began search and diving operations along McDonald Creek and at the head of Lake McDonald. They searched for Gregory until 10:30 P.M. By then there was little chance that Gregory was still alive. But until a body is recovered there is always hope, and either way the searchers wanted to find the boy. They resumed the search at daylight.

Tom Dumay, twenty-one, was one of eight divers working to find Gregory. Dumay was an honor student, athlete, and senior in physical education and biological science at Montana State University. He planned to be a teacher. Tom and his girlfriend, Sandra Westre, a nursing student, were to be married in two months on August 31.

Lake McDonald bottoms out at 464 feet. Tom and his SCUBA partner, twenty-year-old Ron Koppang, went down to forty feet on their first dive. When they surfaced, they reported that at that depth McDonald Creek water flowing into the lake created an underwater current. On their second dive they went down to ninety feet. Tom ran out of air and used the buddy system to share air from Ron's tank. Then both ran out of air.

Ron Koppang came to the surface fast—too fast. He was in intense pain from air embolisms and the bends (air bubbles in the bloodstream). He was also grief stricken: all was lost. They had not found the boy, and Tom Dumay was still down there, drowned.

Meanwhile, the grieving Trenors had started back to Seattle and heard over the radio that a diver had been lost trying to find their son. Cameron Trenor phoned park authorities, saying, "Please discontinue the search for our son and look for the diver."

At 11:25 A.M. there was a call for fresh divers, and the search for Tom Dumay and Gregory Trenor resumed. Sam Ellman, president of the Flathead Lifesaving and Rescue Association, and Columbia Falls Police Chief Darvin Lundstrom monitored the time the divers could safely be down at various depths. They pulled on the rope attached to the divers when their allowable time at that depth was up. Bill Walterskirchen coordinated the sequence of relief divers going down with additional air.

By 3:46 P.M. all the divers had used up their allowable time down at depths, and Sam Ellman was tugging on the 150-foot rope to signal up the last divers, Don Elgin and Jack Von Lindern, who were at the end of their allowable ten minutes down. At 3:49 P.M. Elgin and Von Lindern surfaced with Tom Dumay's body.

The search for Gregory's body continued, but as Glacier's Chief Ranger Lyle H. McDowell reported ". . . the cold lakes of Glacier seldom give up their bodies."

About two months later, the lake did give up Gregory Trenor. North-shore summer resident Eugene Fox of Chicago had been "keeping an eye out for the boy's body." On August 23, his attention was drawn to a white object under a large boulder adjacent to a sunken log at the confluence of McDonald Creek and the lake. He notified Chief Ranger McDowell. It was Gregory; his body was shipped to Seattle for burial.

Another sad day in the park was June 23, 1977, when two seasonal employees died while saving their friends.

Randy Hill, a twenty-two-year-old student from Mount Morris, Michigan, who attended Michigan State University, and David Barry, a twenty-year-old student from Falls Church, Virginia, who attended Syracuse University in New York, had recently met park visitors Tarisa and Mary Ann Guderian of Covington, Louisiana. Tarisa and Mary Ann were staying with their parents at Many Glacier Hotel. The four hiked during the day. In the early evening they applied for a fire permit at the Pow Wow Campsite on Wilbur Creek and then went swimming. According to the girls, as reported in the *Hungry Horse News* by Mel Ruder, the four youths planned to jump into the swift waters of Wilbur Creek and be carried down the fast-moving stream into a shallow pool.

Dave Barry jumped in first. He floated down the creek to the shallows without any problems. Randy jumped next, came out opposite of where Dave landed and stood up. Tarisa was next and a little hesitant, but she jumped in. She had difficulty but made it to Randy and then called out to Mary Ann to discourage her from jumping into the cold, swirling waters. But Mary Ann had already jumped and was in trouble.

Randy saw Mary Ann struggling and jumped in to help her. So did Dave. Together, they briefly held her up and then they all disappeared. Suddenly Mary Ann "popped out" of the water and Tarisa grabbed her. Randy and Dave did not surface.

Mary Ann yelled for help and Tarisa ran down the trail to Swiftcurrent, asking visitors at the laundromat to call for help. Rangers Penttila, Isdahl, and Reese, and District Ranger Robert Frauson responded. Gary Hicks and Nashashi Harada of Swiftcurrent helped the rangers search. They found Dave Barry face up in the pool below the rapids, pulled him to shore, and gave him artificial respiration, but it was too late.

Rangers searched the creek and the surrounding area for Randy Hill with flashlights. Other park personnel assisted at the water's edge, using ropes to secure the rangers from falling into the creek. They searched until 2 A.M. At daylight they continued searching. Ranger Lloyd Kortge of St. Mary spotted a flash of color showing in the white waters above Wilbur Falls. Hill's body was in a deep hole. Kortge searched the area, using an eighteen-foot aluminum probe to feel for the body, being careful not to nudge the body over the falls or fall over himself. The body was recovered at 3:40 P.M. The bodies of the two boys were sent to their families.

On July 27, 1981, Donald and Betty Danielowski from Minnesota and Betty's sister and her family were enjoying the sights and sounds of McDonald Creek while vacationing in Glacier Park. The two families were traveling in the Danielowski's motor home and stopped at a pullout about one mile northeast of the "moose country" interpretive area on the Going-to-the-Sun Road. Donald was taking videos of Betty and her nine-year-old nephew, Dale Dahl, walking along the rock boundary on the east edge of McDonald Creek. Betty and her nephew slipped on the wet rocks and fell into the water. The boy's father, Jack, and Donald jumped into the water to save Dale and Betty.

Jack Dahl managed to pull his son from the creek unharmed. Donald caught Betty by her shirt and was trying to pull her to shore, but both he and Betty were tumbled downstream by the force of rushing water. About thirty yards downstream, Donald struck his head on a large rock and was apparently rendered unconscious. He let go of Betty. Her body was found about 150 yards downstream, and Donald's body was found one tenth of a mile farther down. Jack flagged down a passing vehicle for help, and park personnel and a doctor and nurse who were visiting the park administered CPR. Their attempts to revive Betty and Donald failed.

What can you do if someone is drowning in turbulent, swift-running waters? Trained swift-water rescuers advise against going into the water after the victim. Chances are great that you too will be injured or die. Instead, notify a park ranger or other park official as quickly as possible. They will call in rescue teams.

In July 2014, the exception to the rule occurred when a twelve-year-old boy from Georgia was playing on a log over McDonald Creek near Red Rock Point. He slipped and fell and was swept downstream about twenty yards in a steep, constricted area. A man from Wisconsin jumped into the creek and was able to get the boy to the opposite bank. They both survived without injuries. Park rangers using life jackets and an inflatable kayak brought the man and the boy back to the roadside bank of McDonald Creek.

CAPSIZED

In July 1971, Sally Boughner, twenty-two, Murdock Houghs, twenty-seven, and James Rieben, twenty-three, all of Michigan, were traveling to Oregon and visiting Glacier Park on the way. Murdock and Sally put an inflatable canoe into McDonald Creek about one mile above its confluence with Avalanche Creek. When the canoe reached the gorge in McDonald Creek upstream from the Avalanche picnic area, it capsized, spilling Sally and Murdock into the water. Neither was wearing a life jacket. Murdock managed to get onto the rocks. Sally was flailing in the water, and Murdock's attempts to reach her were unsuccessful.

A nearby fisherman notified park officials. They found Sally's body under a ledge about 100 feet downstream from where the canoe capsized. It is likely the trio of travelers from Michigan didn't recognize the almost certainty of capsizing a canoe in swift, turbulent waters such as McDonald Creek. (McDonald Creek is now closed to boating for most of the year to protect nesting and feeding harlequin ducks.)

HIS DAY TO DIE

Dennis Brooks, forty, was an avid climber and outdoorsman. He loved Glacier National Park. "It's where he wanted to be," said his mother, Snoma Meagher. Dennis grew up in nearby Hungry Horse and Whitefish. As an adult he moved to Everett, Washington, to work as an architectural welder. But his heart was always in Glacier. It was the first place he went whenever he visited his family in Montana.

In November 2005, Dennis, his sister Denise, and her husband, Cliff Willis of Hungry Horse, were in the park, standing on the viewing platform just above McDonald Falls. Dennis was feeling good—he was where he wanted to be. Possibly in an act of whimsy, he jumped over the railing and hopped from rock to rock. Then it happened—that instant, quick-as lightning, no-time-to-recover slip and fall.

McDonald Falls runs through a torrent chute and then flattens out into a pool. A few people who have fallen into the falls have been lucky enough to ride all the way through to the pool below and survive. But not this day! The strong, cold current propelled Dennis into the pool, and as in a recirculating wave, held him underwater.

As soon as his sister and brother-in-law saw him fall, one of them hurried to Lake McDonald Lodge to call for help. The Flathead County Dive Team responded. The divers had to rappel down into the gorge area to retrieve his body.

Dennis knew the park and knew McDonald Creek waters. Perhaps overconfidence or the sheer joy of being in his favorite place led him to happy-dance himself into the creek. He wasn't lucky like some who thread the falls and surface in the pool, sputtering but alive. Maybe, as those who believe in fate would say, it was simply his day to die.

Many of the victims who drowned in park waters did so under circumstances similar to what happened to Dennis Brooks: they were happy to be there, overconfident, and a little careless. Others have slipped, fallen, and drowned just trying to get the perfect photograph.

WALKING THE LOGS

One of the most popular short hikes in the park is the trail to Avalanche Lake. It starts at the Trail of the Cedars trailhead and winds along Avalanche Creek to Avalanche Lake. A short but deep and water-sculpted gorge along the creek tempts the unwise to risk walking right to the edge of its damp, slippery precipice for a photograph. Fallen logs across the creek above the gorge have also proven to be too tempting for daredevils to pass up. This rarely ends well. Think of walking such a log as *walking the plank*—you will end up in the water, and you will most likely die.

In 1941, Charles Green, a Civilian Conservation Corps supervisor in

The beauty of Avalanche Gorge lures many visitors too close for comfort.
JACOB W. FRANK, COURTESY OF NATIONAL PARK SERVICE.

Glacier National Park, wrote about his experiences in the park in *Montana Memories, Volume IV*. One of those experiences was his attempted rescue of forty-nine-year-old Alice Olson who slipped and fell into Avalanche Creek. His account is sober reading for anyone tempted to go close to the edge.

A half mile up from the campground the creek enters a gorge with solid rock walls up to thirty feet high, and the water roars down through this canyon to level out at the campground. Where the creek enters the gorge it is about eight feet wide and four feet deep and there was a wind fell tree about ten inches in diameter spanning the banks with the swift water flowing beneath it.

A lady from North Dakota was hiking with a nephew, and he claimed she walked out on the slippery log so he could take her picture. If this was true it was a case of suicide for no lumberjack would have attempted such a feat with two peaveys and shod with caulked boots. She of course fell into the swirling water, and it was our job to find her body.

When my leader and I arrived, crews were dynamiting the upper end of the gorge without results. The Chief Ranger, Elmer Fladmark, was there and I told Elmer I was sure her body was hung up on what we call a jill-poke in the lower canyon. This is an expression to describe a pole or tree sticking upstream from the bottom of a creek or river, and also for a pole sticking out into a trail to snag a pack animal.

The crew that had arrived before us had packed in several cases of dynamite, fuses and caps, so I loaded two bombs each with four sticks of powder in sacks with small rocks for sinkers, and attached thirty feet of small rope to each one. Ranger Fladmark, my leader, and I went downstream with the bombs. From high on the bank I slid the charge down the pole. The water sucked it right to the bottom of the boiling water. When the charge exploded, a woman's skirt came up and the swift water swept it down stream. Our second bomb cut the pole, the victim's *body surfaced and both were washed down the creek.*

*A quarter of a mile downstream in the campground was
a large pile of driftwood and we knew if her corpse got
under this, it would take days to recover it. We both ran
down the trail and barely won the race for, as we reached
the creek bank above the driftwood, she came around
a bend. Grasping hands, Elmer in the lead and me with a
grip on a willow, we waded out, chest deep in the icy water.
Ten feet above the logs, he caught the body by the hair.*

*We slowly made our way back to shore, laid the corpse
on a sandbar, and I called my leader to get a blanket from
our pickup to cover her. Then I sent him up to stop the
search, and we reported the death and recovery to the
coroner who came up with an ambulance. No inquest was
held, but I always believed there should have been.*

*One of the amazing things about recovering a corpse
with dynamite, it always removes all clothes when the
charge is close, but doesn't disfigure the remains. In this
case all of her clothes were gone except one shoe and
stocking.*

DEVALI WALKS A LOG

In 1982, thirteen-year-old Devali Oakes was returning from an early
morning hike to Avalanche Lake with her father, Dr. Jerry Oakes. The
Oakes family was from Durham, North Carolina, and they were staying
at Lake McDonald Lodge, with plans to move on to Many Glacier later
in the week. As they meandered down the trail from the lake, Devali
saw a log that had fallen near the creek about 100 yards from the head
of Avalanche Gorge. She stepped onto the log, slipped, and fell into the
rushing waters of Avalanche Creek. The torrent carried her downstream
until she was caught under a log jam. Her father tried to free her but
couldn't, so he ran to his car parked at Avalanche Campground and drove
to Lake McDonald Lodge to get help. Jerry Bell responded to the call,
and with the help of park personnel Steve Frye, Curt Buchholtz, Dan
O'Brien, Mike Ober, and Dave Panebaker they recovered Devali's body.

A SLIP AND A SLIDE

During the 100-plus years that Glacier has been a park, a number of people have died due to a slip on wet rocks, wet logs, or a wet bridge followed by a slide into turbulent, swift-running waters from which they couldn't escape. Over the years, a lucky few have survived the wild ride in turbulent creek waters, but don't count on it. In 1963, an unnamed woman from St. Paul, Minnesota, was walking along the rock ledge above McDonald Falls. She fell into the creek, was swept over the falls, and flushed downstream nearly 300 feet. The woman came ashore on the opposite bank from the Going-to-the-Sun Road. She had no serious injuries. Ranger Raymond Dilley, who responded to the incident, said it was a miracle that she survived. In the following incidents, there are no miracles.

Sometime after 6 P.M. on July 22, 1981, seven-year-old Kevin Dolack and his ten-year-old brother were playing on the rocks on the east bank of McDonald Creek near the wooden footbridge at Sacred Dancing Cascade. According to witnesses, the boys were clowning around as young boys will. Kevin slipped off the rocks and the rushing waters carried him downstream. A fisherman who was about fifteen feet away saw Kevin fall and saw him struggling in the water. Kevin seemed to stop on a snag that held him partly out of the water. The fisherman urged Kevin to steady himself and catch his breath and to remain quiet so that he could help him. Apparently Kevin tried to stand up and was then swept back into the current. The fisherman hurried to report the incident to the ranger station while Kevin's distraught mother frantically searched the downstream shoreline. When the rangers arrived, one offered to take Kevin's mother back to the footbridge while the other rescue personnel continued searching. Rangers called for assistance, and rescue crews and a jet boat went to the head of Lake McDonald. Other fire and rescue personnel met them there and proceeded up the creek for about 220 yards with the jet boat. They returned for a second pass up the creek and spotted young Kevin's body in five to six feet of water where the creek empties into Lake McDonald. A slip and a slide led to a sad ending to a playful moment.

On June 28, 2002, Manita Felicidad Diaz Nery, fifty-nine, of Freeland, Washington, was hiking the Avalanche Lake Trail with a friend when she stopped above the gorge to take a picture. She slipped, slid into the creek, and disappeared. The creek was swollen with rain and snowmelt and was running unusually fast and murky. Ranger Charlie Logan and more than twenty park staffers looked for Nery all day and through the night. Search dogs from Flathead Search and Rescue and the David Thompson Search and Rescue Team from Libby were brought in. Park personnel were posted along the creek to watch for Nery below small cascades that may have been holding her down. Searchers found Nery's body the next day about 100 yards downstream from the bridge that overlooks the gorge.

In the Nery incident, search and rescue dogs and teams from nearby communities in the Flathead Valley and Libby came to help. Park personnel who are trained and regularly assigned to search and rescue activities took part, and nearby park office staff also helped in the search. The people who live and work in the park and the surrounding areas have a special bond. We like to think this brotherhood of people is inherent in those who answer Glacier's "Call of the Mountains." They are dedicated to the park, the people, and nature. It's also true that in addition to park and local community people, visitors to the park—strangers to the area and to whoever is in trouble—frequently help those in danger, sometimes at their own peril. Often, however, the people who offer help have rescue or medical skills, know what to do, and intuitively work well with the rangers. There are many such incidents chronicled in this book. One such incident follows.

At about 3 P.M. on Saturday, July 12, 2014, park visitors Abigail Sylvester, thirty-three, of Buckley, Washington, and her husband were taking photos near the bridge below Upper McDonald Creek Falls. Sylvester slipped and fell into the creek, and in an instant the swift-running current swept her downstream. Her husband (whose name was not released) jumped in to save her, and he too was overcome by the cold, turbulent waters. Somehow he was able to make it to the creek bank. By then, Sylvester was out of sight. She was carried over Lower McDonald Creek Falls and was somewhere farther downstream.

A visitor on a Glacier Park interpretive tour in the area caught a glimpse of Sylvester being carried downstream. He called out to the tour's park ranger and the ranger notified park dispatch who sent rangers to the area. Meanwhile, a father, mother, and teenage son were traveling the Going-to-the-Sun Road and heard about the incident (we don't know how). They went to the bridge near Lower McDonald Creek Falls to help search for the woman. Close to where McDonald Creek flows into Lake McDonald, the father, who was a volunteer fireman, spotted Sylvester. He waded into the creek and began swimming in waist-deep cold water to retrieve her. His son helped lift her from the water onto a small island. While the father, son, and two other park visitors assisted park rangers performing CPR, the Three Rivers Ambulance and ALERT helicopter were on the way. ALERT transported Sylvester to the Kalispell Regional Medical Center. Despite gallant efforts to save her, the following day Abigail Sylvester was pronounced dead from drowning. Nonetheless, many people responded almost instinctively to the drowning woman. Their actions were noble.

IN THE BACKCOUNTRY

Most drownings in the park occur in the creeks, waterfalls, and lakes that are accessible along the Going-to-the-Sun Road because that's where most visitors congregate, but a few people have drowned in the backcountry.

In 2002, seventeen-year-old Tom Hart from Tennessee was exploring Hudson Bay Creek near Red Eagle Lake and fell into the gorge. He went over the waterfall and drowned. In 2010, Elizabeth Gray McNamara, sixty-two, slipped and fell off a footbridge into Virginia Falls. Her body was found trapped underwater 220 yards downstream.

In Kintla Lake and on the North Fork of the Flathead River, most drowning deaths have been due to rafts or boats capsizing.

In September 1950, John Provine, thirty-three, and Aubrey Olinger, thirty-eight, both of Ontario, California, were visiting their longtime friend James Pinney, thirty-five, who operated a general store in Fortine, Montana. The three men loaded an aluminum boat onto Pinney's station wagon and drove to Kintla Lake to fish.

On a Wednesday, J. L. Edwards, from Stryker (about nine miles down the road from Fortine), noticed the trio of fishermen going out on the lake. The next day he saw their partially submerged boat out on the lake and called park officials. Aubrey Olinger's legs were wedged under the middle compartment of the boat. He was face down in the water. His watch had stopped at 2:15. Fishing tackle, a gas can, and other fishing and clothing items were floating on the surface of the lake. A jacket was found with one sleeve inside out, indicating an attempt to shed clothing. The boat's motor had fallen off, which led investigators to believe that they had hit something that caused the boat to capsize. Even after an extensive search, the cold waters of Kintla Lake still hold James Pinney and John Provine.

Others who rest in peace at the bottom of the cold lakes of Glacier National Park are Frank Denney, sixty, of Cut Bank, who drowned in the cold, blue waters of St. Mary Lake in 1950, and James Krell, who disappeared after a boating accident on Lake McDonald in 1976.

In June 1970, Robert Personett, twenty-three, was home on leave from the U.S. Navy before assignment to Vietnam. He was an electrician's mate in the submarine service and had been stationed in Hawaii, Guam, Connecticut, and California. He and his buddies—Mike Ren, a Columbia Falls policeman; Robert Cluka, fifty-one, a café operator; Eugene Hallas, home on leave from the army; and seventeen-year-old Arthur Ott—planned a two-day float on the North Fork of the Flathead River. They put their fifteen-man navy surplus raft into the river at Polebridge and planned to float to Blankenship Bridge.

Fifteen minutes and one and a half miles into the voyage, they hit a log jam, rupturing the raft. Robert Personett was caught in the raft's rope boarding ladder. He struggled to free himself but couldn't. Almost immediately, the net-like ladder and Robert went into the water and under a log.

Mike Ren and Robert Cluka were swept downstream by the current. Three hundred yards downriver, Ren crawled out onto an island. He saw Cluka being carried past him by the high waters of the swollen river and managed to pull him onto the island. Arthur Ott and Eugene Hallas got off the raft when it ruptured and climbed onto the log jam. They saw Ren and Cluka had made it to the island and risked a swim to join them. They made it. It was a long night for the four men on the island. They built a fire and huddled around it. In the morning they constructed a makeshift raft, but it was caught in the current and swept downstream along with Mike Ren's only pair of boots.

Just before noon they saw Dick Michaels of Helena, Montana, fishing in his fourteen-foot aluminum boat. They fired a gun to attract his attention to their predicament. He went to the island and the four men climbed into his boat. Michaels let the men out near Moran Creek, which would be a short walk to the North Fork Road for help. The walk was short but tedious, especially for Mike Ren who was barefoot. When they reached the road, they flagged down a tourist who stopped. They asked him to call the sheriff's office and then continued walking toward Polebridge. They walked about two miles when a Montana highway patrolman on vacation came by. He took them to Polebridge and they called the sheriff's office. A search party of friends, family, and volunteers was formed, headed by Dick Walsh. Search party members felt that "no one knows the North Fork River better than Walsh." The search party quickly began searching for Personett. John and Tom Ladenburg brought in a cat and winch and removed about fifty feet of the log jam. Gear, tent poles, and pumps were found. Jack Thompson of Columbia Falls used his airboat to search, and Jim Herron of Ferndale rode his Sea-Doo (a personal watercraft), looking for Personett. Robert Colby of Kalispell flew the river daily, and the boats of family and friends worked up and down the waters looking for Robert. It wasn't until August 8 that Walsh and the family search party found Personett's body in a remote location about ten miles from where the raft sank.

LUCKY TO BE ALIVE

In the summer of 1976, Pamela Goering, twenty-one, of Clarkston, Michigan, and a student at Michigan State, was working as a switchboard operator at Glacier Park Lodge. Goering and her friends, Henry Rubio, a sophomore at California State, Fullerton, who worked at the gift shop; Diane Keyser of Miami, Florida, who worked at the front desk; and Cheryl Rowland, a reservationist, went hiking up to Iceberg Lake on their day off. Pam said, "It was beautiful with many wildflowers, and Iceberg Lake just starting to thaw." At about 2:30 P.M., they were coming back on the trail. They were rounding the curve to Ptarmigan Creek when Goering slipped and fell into the cold, swift-flowing creek. According to the *Hungry Horse News* report, she screamed and went over two small falls. Her backpack acted as a life preserver and kept bringing her up out of the water. Rowland tried to grab her, fell in, and then managed to get out. Then Rubio saw Goering's backpack in the water. She was face down. He waded into the water and pulled his half-conscious friend out. She was suffering from hypothermia. He started down the trail carrying Goering piggyback. Keyser hurried ahead to the Many Glacier Ranger Station to get help. The responders took Goering by litter to the end of the road, and she was then transported to the nearest hospital in Cardston, Alberta, Canada.

The next afternoon, Goering was back at the Glacier Park Lodge switchboard. She was a little sore, with some bruises and a sprained right leg. She had survived, she was happy, and she was grateful to Rubio, who acted quickly and saved her life.

SURVIVING THE NORTH FORK

In July 2014, park visitors in the Glacier Rim area twelve miles north of Columbia Falls reported seeing a cooler, plastic bags, and a life jacket floating down the North Fork of the Flathead River. They notified park rangers and almost immediately the Flathead County sheriff's deputies, a Two Bear Air helicopter crew, and the North Valley Search and Rescue responded. According to the July 16 *Missoulian,* a California family of two adults and two children had flipped their raft while floating downstream through rapids. Fortunately they all were wearing life jackets and were able to reach shore on the park side of the river. The helicopter crew spotted them, and rescuers in a boat returned the wet and cold family to their vehicle.

Whitewater rafters enjoy wild rivers on the borders of Glacier National Park.
JON RINER, COURTESY OF THE NATIONAL PARK SERVICE.

WATER WISE

Being water wise is simple stuff. We all know it. We just have to remember it while having fun.

As tempting as it may be don't walk, play, or climb on rocks and logs around creeks and waterfalls.

Don't lean over bridge rails.

When boating, always wear a life jacket or personal flotation device. Don't stand up or lean over the side.

Heed Glacier Park's boating rules and regulations. Doing so helps protect Glacier's waters and may save your life.

Avoid hypothermia—it's mean and quick. Exposure to the frigid temperatures of Glacier's creeks and lakes can be life threatening. Hypothermia is described as the "progressive physical collapse and reduced mental capacity resulting from the chilling of the inner core of the human body." It can occur in temperatures above freezing, especially if you get wet. Don't fall in the water.

CHAPTER SIX

HOMICIDES
and
SUICIDES

"The sun also sets."
—ERNEST HEMINGWAY

Nearly 3 million people visit Glacier National Park every year to connect with nature. Just being in the park lifts their spirits. Why then, would eight people commit suicide and three people commit murder here? However reasonless it seems, an average of twenty to thirty people commit suicide each year in our national parks. Studies by the Center for Disease Control and Prevention show that most suicidal people say they would choose a place of natural beauty to spend their last minutes on earth. They enter the parks fully prepared to die by their chosen means. They bring whatever apparatus they need: rope, guns, or hoses for asphyxiation. Park officials try to be proactive to prevent suicides, but that's easier said than done once a suicidal person enters the park.

As for the three murders that have occurred in Glacier, the lesson is "never go to a mountainous national park with strangers or someone who doesn't like you."

1913—SHOOT OUT AT SNYDER'S

In the case of this first murder, the lesson is "never go to a saloon and drink all day with a hot-head who thinks he's a gunslinger."

On August 18, 1913, at about 2 P.M., A. C. Daly, who had a poor reputation as a gunslinger, shot Montana horse trader Frank Ellis with a Colt .45

revolver at George Snyder's place by the park's west entrance.

Frank Ellis and A. C. Daly had been batching together at Snyder's saloon and hostel for several weeks. According to a Kalispell newspaper, Ellis was considered an old-timer in the area. He had lived in Kalispell, Whitefish, Columbia Falls, and Belton for the past twenty years. Ellis was well known as a shrewd horse trader who was rarely beaten in a trade. He was also well liked and known all over the county. Ellis lived by his wits more than his hands and made friends easily. He was known to be a sympathetic man and had never refused to help anyone in trouble if he had the means to do so. Daly was also an

Snyder's Saloon, shown here circa 1923, was the site of the first homicide in the park. COURTESY OF GLACIER NATIONAL PARK ARCHIVES.

old-timer in the county. He tended bar in one of the saloons in the Kalispell vice district. For the previous three years, Daly had lived in different parts of Montana. Two years earlier, he had quarreled with a man in Chinook and taken a shot at him. Until June 1913, he had been tending bar for George Snyder. When Snyder's liquor license ran out, Daly stayed around Snyder's place, as had Ellis.

On August 18, Ellis and Daly started drinking early in the day and were quarreling about a dog that Ellis had picked up. The dog had been hit by an automobile and had a broken leg. Ellis brought the dog to Snyder's place, splinted the dog's leg, and put the dog on one of the beds. Whether it was Daly's bed is not known. They continued quarreling about the dog, and a lot of drinks later the argument grew more and more intense. Whether someone asked them to leave or they took the initiative, the two men went outside to continue their fight. How long they argued after that is not known. At some point, Daly pulled out his Colt .45 revolver and shot Ellis in his left side. Ellis then staggered into Snyder's hostel and sank onto a bunk. Meanwhile A. O'Donnell, who had witnessed the shooting, "slipped down the government road towards Lake McDonald."

George Snyder, who was a short distance away, heard the shot. As soon as he realized what happened, he went to Belton to report the shooting. Along the way he "caught up" with Ora Reeves, another local resident and homesteader on Camas Creek. Reeves was not a law officer but he offered to arrest Daly. He grabbed his revolver and followed Snyder back to the saloon.

Reeves opened the saloon door. Daly was standing in a corner with his hands held behind his back. Reeves demanded to know who did the shooting, but Daly said no shot was fired. Ellis had simply fallen, broken a rib, and the jagged edge of the rib had penetrated his stomach. Reeves knew that was a bald-faced lie and went for his gun and "got the drop on Daly." He told him to raise his hands and surrender and Daly grudgingly complied. Reeves took Daly's revolver from his hip pocket, then turned him over to Ranger Vaught, who had just arrived.

While Vaught was taking Daly to Belton to wait for the sheriff to arrive, Reeves mounted his horse and took off after O'Donnell, the only eyewitness to the shooting.

O'Donnell had been seen heading toward Lake McDonald. Just as Reeves reached Fish Creek on the southwest side of the lake, he saw O'Donnell walking out of the timber where he had been hiding. O'Donnell denied witnessing the shooting. But when Reeves told him that he could be arrested for the crime, O'Donnell admitted seeing Daly shoot Ellis.

Reeves took O'Donnell to Belton where Vaught had sent a telegram to Sheriff Ingraham in Kalispell, and they waited for the sheriff to arrive. When Ingraham and Deputy Metcalf arrived on the train from Kalispell, they took Daly and O'Donnell to the Flathead County jail. Frank Ellis was taken to the Sister's Hospital in Kalispell. The bullet had lodged in Frank's liver, and he died three days later on August 21, 1913.

THE HIGH LONESOME

Assigned to the Kishenehn Ranger Station, William McAfee described the job's isolation in 1926, writing, "You know, take it all in all, there are many disadvantages to a job of this kind. You know what I mean. A fellow is shut out from the outside world too much and at times the lonesomeness is almost maddening. So I'm thinking very much of quitting the Park Service for good."

In a land of rugged mountain ranges and isolated valleys, the territory of the Kishenehn Ranger District is one of Glacier's most remote. The log cabin station on the northwest edge of the park is three miles from the U.S-Canadian border. Rangers assigned to Kishenehn were charged with monitoring the park's border with Canada and the park's western boundary along the North Fork of the Flathead River.

Life in these remote outposts was physically difficult and lonely. Some rangers took to it, enjoying the months of solitude and the peacefulness of the snow-covered wilderness. Some did not. Being a backcountry ranger was a seven-day-a-week job filled with tedious routine and the occasional park violation incident. They observed and protected wildlife, searched for poachers or other violators, patrolled their areas regularly, and were a presence in the park. Even in the 1920s and 1930s, the ranger credo was, "Protect the park from the people, the people from the park, and the people from themselves." Rangers patrolled in summer on foot or horseback and

Kishenehn Ranger Station, seen here circa 1921, is named for nearby Kishenehn Creek, which flows into the North Fork of the Flathead River. The original station was burned in 1913 and replaced in 1919. Kishenehn is the Kootenai word for "no good." Why the Kootenai thought the creek was no good is a mystery. GEORGE GRANT, COURTESY OF GLACIER NATIONAL PARK ARCHIVES.

on snowshoes in winter. They kept detailed journals of their daily patrols. An unwritten rule was to complete 300 miles of patrol every month. In early spring, they shouldered axes and saws and opened trails, got their firefighting equipment in shape, and brought the horses in from winter pasture at local ranches. In those days, rangers provided their own pack and saddle horses and saddles. They cared for their horses—trimming hooves and checking teeth and the horses' general health—mended corrals and pasture fences, and hauled food and supplies to their post for their horses and themselves.

Texan William McAfee came to Montana and settled on a homestead near Trail Creek. He took a position with the park service in the winter of 1925-1926 at Kishenehn Ranger Station. Apparently, the thirty-five-year-old McAfee had had a relationship with someone he affectionately called "the kid." For reasons he never revealed, the relationship failed, casting him into a bout of depression. The winter's isolation at Kishenehn deepened his depression, and on January 13 he wrote his friend in Kalispell that he was going to quit the park service "for good." Four weeks later on February 7, McAfee fulfilled his promise in an unexpected way. He walked outside of the Kishenehn Ranger Station, unholstered his service revolver, and shot himself in the head.

Park staff originally reported that McAfee died of a heart attack. People regarded the park rangers and forest rangers of the 1920s and 1930s with the same awe and respect as Old West sheriffs. They were tough and dedicated. They helped the law-abiding good guys and caught the bad guys. They did not kill themselves; it was unthinkable. A park ranger committing suicide was not something the park or the public were ready to face. However, sometime later, the park announced that the death was a suicide. McAfee's remains are interred in the Montana Veterans Cemetery in Columbia Falls.

As a result of the completion of the Going-to-the-Sun Road in 1933 and the subsequent increase in park visitation, the park service sharpened its focus on visitor protection and front-country services and cut back the number of backcountry rangers and stations. They staffed Kishenehn only in the summer and eventually closed it except as an overnight stop for rangers on patrol. In 1986, the station was placed on the U.S. National Register of Historic Places.

THINGS JUST WENT WRONG TOO MANY TIMES

Seven other suicides within the park were attributed to despondency over the loss of a loved one, the loss of a job, or just life gone wrong. These seven men chose to never know what their tomorrows would bring.

In May 1968, Larry Jones of Spokane was found dead in his automobile near Apgar Campground. A .22 pistol was in his hand. Larry was twenty-nine, single, and a University of Michigan graduate. He had recently dropped out of Gonzaga University law school. Friends said he was despondent. Things were just not going well.

Another Jones, Paul E., also killed himself with a .22, near the Avalanche Campground. Both suicides were in the month of May three years apart. The two Joneses were not related and there is no known connection. Coincidence? Apparently!

On April 29, 1986, park rangers received a radio call to investigate a possible injured man in a vehicle at Packers Roost. A park visitor had discovered a yellow Datsun parked in the area with a man in the vehicle bleeding from the head. The body was bloated and stiff, blood and fluids were evident in the mouth, nose, and eyes, and there was no pulse. Officials found no identification on the body, but there was a vehicle registration in the glove box. On the floor was a recently opened box of sleeping tablets, empty beer cans, and a combination vacuum cleaner and plastic hose rigged from the exhaust pipe into the passenger compartment. Twenty-four-year-old Peter Soderlund had killed himself by asphyxiation. On the dashboard was a small notebook. On the cover was the word "Mom" and inside the book was a suicide note. We don't know what was in the note, and we don't know what could have been so wrong that a twenty-four-year-old couldn't make right over time.

On October 7, 2008, Bruce Colburn, president and CEO of Kadent Corporation in Reading, Pennsylvania, flew to the Flathead Valley and checked into a hotel. He was fifty-four years old and had recently lost his job. The day after he arrived in the Flathead Valley, Colburn hired a private shuttle driver to take him to Kintla Lake. During the ride, Colburn told the driver he was leaving his suitcase and duffle bag with her and said he would return for them in one to four weeks, but if he didn't, she should donate them to charity. At the Kintla Lake Campground Colburn told the park ranger he planned to go hiking. He was advised that backcountry permits are required for overnight trips and camping is allowed only in designated backcountry sites. (The permit also serves as the reservation system for those sites. The permit process is primarily for the safety of the hiker. It lets the hiker know what trails are open and their level of difficulty and helps rangers locate a hiker who is overdue.) The next morning, Colburn left the campsite. He did not get a backcountry permit, and his direction of travel was unknown. Fifteen days later, the

Blackfeet tribal member Clinton Croff performs the Chicken Dance. "That's how I will remember him," said Maynard Kicking Woman, "as a dancer, a singer, an eagle-bone whistle carrier. From the day he was born, Clinton was connected to this culture." COURTESY OF MARK WAGNER.

shuttle driver became concerned when she had not heard from Colburn as planned. She notified park officials, and a foot search of the Kintla area began on October 25. The search eventually required thirty interagency personnel, a helicopter, a boat, and a horse. On October 29, after a grid search of several hours, searchers found a backpack and sleeping pad. The searchers called in the helicopter that was flying recon in the area, and after aerial searching for several minutes they located a body on the side of a clearing. The rescue team headed upslope and found Colburn's body. A .40 caliber Beretta semi-automatic handgun was nearby. A single bullet hole was in his chest. Colburn had made his final executive decision.

In July 2010, thirty-year-old Clinton Croff, well known throughout Indian country for his talents as a singer, drummer, and dancer and his passion as a keeper of the Blackfeet culture, died after an altercation in the Two Medicine Valley. His death brought a great sadness to the Blackfeet and to Glacier National Park.

In November 2012, Martin Crundall, forty-nine, chose to die in the Bowman Lake parking lot on the west side of Glacier National Park. The suicide was by asphyxiation from a generator running in the vehicle. As with the other suicides, Crundall's motivation remains unclear.

BEWARE THE HITCHHIKER

The second recorded murder in Glacier since it became a park occurred in July 1983. Some unidentified visitors at the park stopped about a mile from the Loop at Crystal Point turnout to take in the surrounding view and photograph Heavens Peak. Quite naturally, they looked over the edge of the 186-foot cliff. Clearly visible below was a gruesomely battered body.

U.S. Coast Guard Lieutenant Frederick H. Pongrace was honorably discharged from active duty on June 30, 1983, and was on his way to Seattle from Washington, D.C. to visit a friend. Pongrace graduated from the University of Virginia and enlisted in the Coast Guard as a lieutenant junior grade. He was involved in environmental ocean research and had been stationed in Hawaii, Alaska, and Washington, D.C. Pongrace was traveling in a camper-equipped Volkswagen van and was visiting the national parks along the way.

Meanwhile, Scott David Steel was hitchhiking from Canada to Montana with his big black Labrador-mix dog. U.S. Customs agents noted that he carried a California driver's license. At the time they had no reason to detain him, but they later discovered that the hitchhiker had robbed someone in Canada. Based on information from the FBI and included in the *Grosse Pointe News* (where Pongrace was from), park ranger Jerry Bell reported that Steel "had been in a bar, met some guys, and went with them to their place to continue drinking. Then he stole a wallet from a truck, locked the keys in the truck, and took off."

Steel caught a ride to Wolf Point and then to Havre. In or near Havre he robbed his ride, then walked back to U.S. Highway 2 and put out his thumb to catch another ride. Pongrace, on his way to Glacier National Park, picked him up.

Pongrace, Steel, and the dog went on to Cut Bank and stayed the night at the Shady Grove Campground. Sometime during the night, Steel got into a fight with some of the other campers and pulled a knife. The next day, the owner of the campground asked Steel to leave. He said Pongrace could stay but Steel would have to leave. It is not known whether Pongrace knew about the fight, but he was visibly upset that Steel was being tossed out. He told Steel, "I brought you here. I'll see you get out." He called the Havre police at 7:30 A.M. and again at 3 P.M. to complain about the camp owner. After the first call, Pongrace, Steel, and the big black dog drove sixty miles west to Glacier National Park.

The tourists who spotted the body at the bottom of Crystal Point immediately notified park officials. World War II veteran and ranger Jerry Bell responded to the call.

After investigating the scene, Bell said the body ". . . was banged up pretty bad because it's a vertical drop and it's solid rock terrain there." There were four wounds in the abdomen that did not seem to have been caused by the fall. An inch and a half of rain had fallen during the night and washed the scene clean. There was no sign of a struggle, no blood, and no evidence that there was foul play. Later, an autopsy revealed that Pongrace had been stabbed four times and evidently pushed over the edge of the cliff.

There was no identification on the body, but a vehicle registration for a 1968 Volkswagen van was found in a billfold. It was registered to Pongrace and a woman who turned out to be his sister. Ranger Bell called the number and got a positive identification that the body was that of Frederick Pongrace.

The Volkswagen van was missing. According to his parents, at the time of his murder Pongrace was carrying about $700 in cash and $1,000 in travelers' checks, and he had camping gear, a camera, and stereo equipment in the van.

Ranger Bell put out an all-points bulletin for the van. Almost immediately, the sheriff at Cut Bank called Bell and told him of the incident at the Shady Grove Campground. Now Bell had one clue about what happened—there had been a passenger in the van. Another call came in from Wolf Point identifying the passenger as Scott David Steel from California. He was described as a clean-shaven white male, around five feet seven inches tall and stocky. He carried a blue backpack.

When Steel left the park, he traveled eighty-two miles southwest on U.S. Highway 93 and got as far as Ronan on the Flathead Reservation. Somehow he got the van stuck in mud. He called a tow truck and paid the driver with Pongrace's camera. The truck driver, suspicious of the circumstances, contacted the police and the police notified Ranger Bell.

At this point Bell, police, and the FBI rightly assumed Steel was headed to California. A quick check revealed there were fifty Scott Steel's in California, although not all spelled their name the same way. The van and Steel got through the California border checkpoint without being stopped. Finding him was not going to be easy.

Sometime later Bell got a call from the California police that a van matching the description in the APB was being robbed in an alley in Los Angeles. Bell told them to call the FBI so they could get to the scene before any of the evidence in the van was disturbed.

Inside the van there were blood stains on the seat belt, visor, backseat, and rear areas of the van and a crumpled piece of paper with a number on it. The FBI called the number. A woman answered and said Scott Steel had gone downtown. The woman was Steel's sister; she and a male resident at the house were both training to be police officers and they agreed to help with the investigation. The FBI found Pongrace's gear at the residence. But Scott Steel was on the run again.

Several months later, police in St. George, Utah, called Ranger Bell. They had Steel in custody. He was transported to Missoula, Montana, and tried in U.S. District Court. He was charged with murder, felony theft, and interstate transportation of a stolen vehicle. He was convicted of all three charges and sentenced to life in prison. Steel was paroled after serving sixteen years. He later violated parole and fled to Mexico. Working with Mexican authorities, U.S. Marshals arrested Steel after six years on the run and returned him to custody in the United States.

DEARLY BELOVED

Cody Johnson was a lighthearted, loving, selfless guy with an easy manner and a perpetual smile. A longtime friend said, "He was just one of those great friends who was always a pleasure to have around. He was an overall great, good-hearted guy. He was the man every father hopes his daughter will marry."

Sometime in 2011, Johnson met the attractive brunette Jordan Linn Graham. For him it was love at first sight. Graham worked as a nanny, and according to her childhood friend, she embodied the ideal of an honest, wholesome Christian girl. They dated about one year. The two opposites—she was shy and introverted and he was gregarious and outgoing—seemingly got along very well. Johnson's friends thought she was antisocial and unfriendly and voiced their opinion on a few occasions, but he chalked up her reserved behavior toward his friends to her shyness. There was no doubt in his mind that she was the girl for him.

Shortly before Christmas 2012, Johnson proposed and the couple married June 30 the following year. He moved into a new home seven days before the wedding. His love for his fiancé and his lifetime commitment to the marriage was profoundly evident at the wedding. According to his close friends, Johnson was ecstatic. It was what he wanted.

Graham, however, was not so sure. She confided to a friend that she was having second thoughts about the marriage. She cried before the wedding and did not look at her soon-to-be new husband when they said their vows.

Seven days after the wedding, Cody Johnson disappeared.

On July 8, when the always dependable Johnson didn't show up for work at Nomad Global Communication Solutions in Kalispell, his friend and co-worker Cameron Fredrickson knew something was wrong. He called and texted the new couple and other relatives and friends, trying to find Johnson. He then called local authorities and the media seeking help in finding his friend. Neighbors rallied in the search. Concerned friends put up missing-person posters with Cody Johnson's picture all over town.

Graham initially told Fredrickson that she wasn't at the house when her husband left on a day trip with friends. Later she told authorities that Cody got into a dark-colored vehicle with Washington plates. The inconsistencies in the young woman's story troubled Fredrickson. He suspected foul play and went to the authorities with the text messages he had exchanged with Graham about Johnson's disappearance. Investigation by the Kalispell City Police Department, the Flathead County Sheriff's Office, and the FBI got underway.

During the days after Johnson disappeared, Graham was strangely calm and unemotional. Even her childhood friend, Lytaunie Blasdel, thought she was acting very peculiar for a woman whose husband of eight days was missing. She was unemotional and seemingly unconcerned about her husband's whereabouts. Blasdel said, "I just keep telling myself maybe it's a coping mechanism or maybe it's because she's around children all day and she doesn't want to upset them."

Three days later, on July 11, Graham contacted friends and family and the authorities, saying that she had found Johnson's body in Glacier Park. She led them to the bottom of the ravine near the Loop Trail where his body lay in a pool of water. The next day, park officials retrieved the body by helicopter.

The park ranger who responded to the call remarked to her that it was unusual that Graham happened to be the one who located her husband's body. She replied, "It was a place he wanted to see before he died," and then added, "he would come up here with friends to drive fast when his friends were visiting from out of state."

Authorities interviewed Graham again on July 16. During that questioning, she admitted giving false statements previously and confessed that she and her husband had driven to Glacier on July 7. They walked along a trail in the Loop area, and then walked to the other side of the trail where the terrain was very steep. Along the way, they argued over her doubts about their marriage. The argument intensified, and at one point Johnson grabbed her arm. She removed his hand from her arm. She then admitted she could have just walked away, but due to her anger, she pushed him with both hands in the back and he fell face first off the cliff.

According to later court testimony, after she pushed her husband to his death, she climbed up from the precipice, got into her husband's car with his keys and his cell phone, and drove away. In a calculated move to deceive family, friends, and the authorities about her part in what happened to her husband of eight days, she then sent text messages to friends about an upcoming church event, boasting about her dance moves.

In October, a grand jury charged Graham with first-degree and second-degree murder and a third charge of making false statements to officials. After four days of trial in December, she pleaded guilty to second-degree murder as part of a plea agreement.

During the sentencing hearing, a tearful Graham showed a rare display of emotion, saying, "It was a moment of complete shock and panic. . . . I have no other explanation. Life," she said, "is precious. It's a special gift, and I need to learn to cherish it." Then she added that it's too bad it took a tragedy for her to learn a simple lesson.

Four family members spoke at the hearing, telling of their pain at the loss of Cody Johnson. All requested life in prison for his wife. Johnson's mother, Sherry, spoke of the family moving from California to Montana, seeking a safer environment to raise him, her only son, who was a teenager at the time. Johnson's uncle Tim said he thought Graham should "rot in prison." Uncle Jerry Watson recalled a family trip to Glacier National Park, saying the family could no longer return to enjoy its magnificent beauty. For his family, Graham had turned the national treasure into "a gravesite." He then added, "Although the hanging tree is no longer acceptable in this society . . . neither is murder."

Jordan Linn Graham Johnson was sentenced to thirty years in prison. The federal public defender filed an appeal arguing that her sentence was extreme. That appeal was denied on February 17, 2016.

MYSTERIOUS SUSPECTED SUICIDE

On March 24, 2015, park dispatch received a call from three visitors driving along the Going-to-the-Sun Road. They reported a nonresponsive man who was slumped over the steering wheel in a vehicle at one of the pullouts along the road. Park rangers responded. Their investigation indicated that Robert Douglas Haetinger, forty-nine, from Virginia Beach, Virginia, drove his vehicle on the Going-to-the-Sun Road to about one mile from the foot of Lake McDonald. He pulled the car into a turnout and shot himself. Why he did so remains a mystery.

CHAPTER SEVEN

DRIVING

the

HIGH ROADS

The primary road through Glacier National Park is the world-renowned Going-to-the-Sun Road. It is well worth a trip to the park just to see the road-building craftsmanship—truly a marvel of engineering. The fifty-mile drive across the "backbone of the world" is often described

Traversing steep—even vertical—terrain (here, the cliff face at Triple Arches), the Going-to-the-Sun Road can give even seasoned drivers a case of the butterflies.
JACOB W. FRANK, COURESTY OF NATIONAL PARK SERVICE.

as the most thrilling, jaw-dropping, white-knuckle experience imaginable. The road hugs the mountains, climbing along a series of sheer cliffs as it traverses the park through its most spectacular landscapes. It was built to be a slow, scenic drive. Numerous viewpoints and turnouts along the way enable visitors to stop and photograph the breathtaking scenery, explore the area, or just sit and enjoy the wonders of nature. Rock and wooden guardrails line the outer edge of the road for added safety. Speed and caution signs are posted throughout.

Traffic cones mark a break in the rock guardrail just below Triple Arches on Going-to-the-Sun Road. COURTESY OF LIBRARY OF CONGRESS, HAER MONT,15-WEGLA,5--70.

Other roads in or bordering the park include U.S. Highway 2, a two-lane, fifty-six-mile scenic byway winding over Marias Pass and along the park's southern border connecting East Glacier with West Glacier. Portions of this road are inside the park boundary. On the east side of the park, Montana Highway 49, known as Looking Glass Hill Road, after the Nez Perce chief, starts at East Glacier, winds around miles of rolling hills with stunning views of Lower Two Medicine Lake, and then connects with U.S. Highway 89 at Kiowa Junction. The road continues north, over the Hudson Bay Divide to St Mary, then north toward Babb and the entrance road to Lake Sherburne and Many Glacier. This stretch of road is part of U.S. Highway 89 but is known locally as the Glacier-St. Mary Road.

According to traffic management studies, park roads see an average of forty to forty-five vehicle accidents each year. Roughly half occur on the Going-to-the-Sun Road, which also has the highest volume of vehicle traffic. Most are in the category of fender benders, but there have been thirty-three vehicle fatalities since park officials began keeping records of deaths in 1913. No vehicle deaths were recorded before 1922.

FIRST AUTOMOBILE IN THE PARK

Before the Going-to-the Sun Road was built, there were very few automobiles in the park. Drivers who ventured into the park found jarring dirt roads, including stretches "paved" with log corduroy. The vehicles were slow and the drivers careful. In those days, driving or riding in a "motorcar" was as much a social event as a get-to-a-destination journey. Frank Stoop drove the first automobile in Glacier National Park—his E-M-F 30 motorcar. He putted along the dirt tote road from Coram to Belton (now West Glacier) on May 2, 1911, covering the nearly eight miles in nine hours. A horse and buggy would have been faster, but Stoop intended to be the first to drive an automobile into the park. With a 30 horsepower engine, the E-M-F 30 was capable of faster speeds than it traveled on that first trip to the park.

This E-M-F 30 motorcar was the first automobile to negotiate a road within the park. COURTESY OF GLACIER NATIONAL PARK ARCHIVES.

But the bad roads, utter lack of road in places, and stops along the way to chat with onlookers slowed Stoop's journey. He was proving that an automobile could navigate the rough tote road, while also making a point about the need for paved roads from the surrounding communities into the park. Although it was yet to be paved, by the end of summer Flathead County workers had vastly improved the road from Coram to the park.

FIRST VEHICLE DEATH

The first officially listed vehicle death in Glacier National Park was twenty-three-year-old Charles Barker, who died on September 8, 1922.

He had driven a tour bus for the Glacier Park Transportation Company for the past two years and was on his last trip of the 1922 season. Barker was driving on U.S. Highway 89 (just outside the park) at his customary slow speed so that his

An early "Red Bus" picks up visitors to the park outside the Glacier Hotel in 1922. COURTESY OF GLACIER NATIONAL PARK ARCHIVES.

eight passengers could enjoy the scenery. Along the way, he pointed out various features of the landscape, punctuating his stories with Blackfeet tales about specific sites of interest such as Chief White Calf's grave. Near Divide Hill, due to heavy rains the night before, the edge of the road suddenly gave way and the bus skidded off the road and overturned. Barker's skull was crushed and his leg broken. He died instantly. Only two of the eight passengers were injured; Reverend Scudder from New York City was severely bruised, and his wife's arm was broken and her shoulder dislocated. To the credit of the "gear jammers" (tour bus drivers), there have been no tour bus fatalities since Charles Barker's accident in 1922.

THE GOING-TO-THE-SUN ROAD

Road maintenance crews are gutsy and good at what they do. Every year, opening the Going-to-the-Sun Road (aka Sun Road) in the spring and ensuring that it is safe to drive and cleared of snow is a high-risk job for the crews. There have been a few roadwork-related vehicle accidents over the years, but fortunately only four were fatal. In fact, the first vehicle death on the Sun Road was not a park visitor gazing at the scenery. It was a crane operator attached to the park's Civilian Conservation Corps (CCC) project to clean up the road right-of-way in the Logan Pass area. On August 24, 1937, thirty-four-year-old Lloyd Campbell, National Park

Service foreman and crane operator, and a CCC crew were removing a dead tree when Campbell's truck and derrick ran onto the soft road shoulder. Campbell and the rig went over the embankment. He landed about fifty feet below the road. His skull was fractured, the right side of his chest was crushed, and he had numerous other fractures and hemorrhages. Campbell died in the ambulance on the way to the hospital in Kalispell. (Two years earlier, in July 1935, eighteen-year-old Robert McCormack, a CCC employee assigned to the Sherburne Camp, was killed when the dump truck he was driving in the Many Glacier area rolled over, crushing him.)

In the early years, Going-to-the-Sun Road was much narrower than it is today, with a bed of crushed rock. The park employees and their wives in this motorcar at Crystal Point appeared to enjoy their tour of the nearly completed route in the late 1920s. COURTESY OF LIBRARY OF CONGRESS, LC-USZ62-62262.

Just opening the road every year is a challenge for the snowplow operators. The greatest dangers are avalanches and going over the edge on "borrowed snow" (plowed snow that deceptively extends the outer road edge). In 1953, an avalanche above Haystack Creek buried four workers, killing two—George Beaton and William Whitford—and scattering the rotary plow in pieces down the slope. In 1964, a tractor plow and operator went over the edge when borrowed snow broke out from under the plow. The tractor rolled down the hillside below the Big Drift. Somehow both the operator and tractor survived. During the 2005 spring road opening, a bulldozer broke through borrowed snow and slid 600 feet down the slope below the Rimrock just west of Oberlin Bend and Logan Pass. Miraculously neither the operator nor the dozer was harmed.

In September 2010, as part of a major road rehabilitation project, construction worker Wainuma Ned, from Coeur d'Alene, Idaho, and his crew were working on the stone retaining wall on the Going-to-the-Sun Road near the East Tunnel about one mile east of Logan Pass. At 9:30 A.M. Ned was operating a small excavator to move the wall's heavy stones, working near the lip of a sheer drop. "I swung over the edge and just started tipping," Ned later told reporters, "so I started to swing back and it was kind of too late, so I just sort of dropped everything and bailed out. I figured, it's a long way down, a bunch of big rocks. I didn't know if it was gonna be safe or not." Ned unfastened his seat belt and jumped clear of the excavator, falling about forty feet before landing on the mountainside and sliding headfirst down to a slope covered in talus (loose rock). He bounced off one large rock and then hit another. Ned finally stopped sliding about 100 feet below the road. The excavator had tumbled down the mountain ahead of him, falling 200 feet farther and breaking into several pieces.

A park ranger on road patrol overheard the urgent call over the radio. Once at the site of the incident, she requested the ALERT helicopter from Kalispell and aid from the Babb/St. Mary Volunteer Fire Department. The fire department responded with a rescue truck and two firefighters. The first EMT arrived within a few minutes and scrambled down the mountain. Ned was conscious, alert, and oriented, complaining of pain in his lower back. By then, the Bell 407 ALERT helicopter had arrived and was hovering above. The helicopter crew was instructed to land at Logan Pass, and park rangers provided ground transportation to the scene. When they arrived, the ALERT medic started an intravenous (IV) line to provide pain medication for Ned. The rescuers determined that the situation was not as bad as initially thought. It would not require a vertical rope rescue; a low-angle litter evacuation would do. They rigged an anchor to the heavy-duty tow hooks of a large pickup truck and attached Prusik hitches (a smaller loop of cord knotted to the main rope) and a Prusik-minding pulley. They also positioned a forklift and attached a directional (a rope with a loop knotted into it) to avoid rope friction on boulders and possible rockfall caused by the rope. Then they organized other

Ross Reed was at the wheel of his Dodge Polaris when it plunged over the edge of the Going-to-the-Sun Road, and he became the first vehicle-related visitor fatality in the park. COURTESY OF HUNGRY HORSE NEWS.

workers and responders to form a haul team to provide a direct pull of Ned and the litter up the slope. A ground ambulance transported Ned to the helicopter at Logan Pass and the helicopter took him to Kalispell Regional Medical Center. He had a fractured clavicle, bruising on his back, and facial lacerations. "The excavator was mangled," Ned noted afterward. "If I'd stayed in it, I'd have been dead."

THE SUN ROAD'S FIRST PARK VISITOR VEHICLE FATALITY

Nearly fifty years after Lloyd Campbell's 1937 death while working on the Sun Road, the first fatal vehicle accident involving a park visitor occurred. In August 1986, Ross Alden Reed of Cardston, Alberta, crashed through a steel-reinforced wooden guardrail a mile east of Haystack Creek. He was found dead on the steep slope about 350 feet below the road. His 1964 Dodge Polaris convertible was wrapped around a tree 200 feet below where Reed was found. Wreckage from the car was scattered several hundred feet down the slope. A door, seat, and the trunk lid had separated from the vehicle. The plunging car broke two sections of steel-backed guardrail, which is put up each spring in avalanche-prone areas and bolted to concrete supports on the roadside. According to

Ranger Tom Habecker, it appeared that Reed lost control after the curve, apparently due to excessive speed. No skid marks were found on the road. A car fitting the Dodge Polaris' description had forced a motorcyclist off the road just minutes earlier near Logan Pass.

Another vehicle plunged off the road in 1991. Edgar Fetter from Cardiff-by-the-Sea near San Diego, California, had been visiting relatives in Bigfork, Montana, and took the opportunity to visit Glacier National Park. He was alone and driving his SUV along the Going-to-the-Sun Road. Just east of the East Tunnel he pulled into a turnout but kept driving, plummeting over the edge. A witness said he did not see a signal or brake lights on Fetter's vehicle before it disappeared over the road. Initially it was thought that Edgar had had a heart attack, but an autopsy did not confirm that.

We can speculate that Ross Reed was deliberately speeding and that Edgar Fetter, for some undetermined reason, lost consciousness, but we don't really know why either of the two men drove their vehicles off the road. In both instances there was no indication that the drivers braked to stop before their fatal plunges. What we do know is that there was no external cause such as icy pavement or falling rock for either incident.

A crew works to retrieve Edgar Fetter's vehicle from below Going-to-the-Sun Road.
COURTESY OF *HUNGRY HORSE NEWS.*

COLLISION ON U.S. HIGHWAY 2

July 23, 1959, was a nice day. It was a Thursday, and Dwight Grist, his wife, Margaret, and their daughter, Margaret Ann, decided to go for a drive. Their son, Jimmy, stayed home in Apgar to fish in Lake McDonald.

Dwight Grist was born in Columbia Falls in 1906 and lived there most of his life. This small community, seventeen miles west of the park, is where Dwight attended school and later owned and operated the Park Theatre. He was a member of the local volunteer fire department and mayor of Columbia Falls for two terms in the 1930s. In June 1942, Dwight was working as an assistant fire guard in Glacier National Park. In August he enlisted in the U.S. Army Medical Corps and went to war. When he returned, he went to work for the National Park Service as a seasonal employee in a myriad of jobs: temporary ranger, laborer lead man, truck driver, carpenter, and maintenance man. Dwight and Margaret and their two children moved to Apgar in 1947 to be closer to his work, and in 1958 he was given an appointment as an electrician.

On that sunny summer day in July, the Grists were traveling east on U.S. Highway 2. At the same time, Robert Lynch, an aluminum siding salesman from Great Falls, and his passenger, Donald Pigg, of Davenport, Iowa, were traveling west. The road was clear and Lynch was traveling fast. About a mile and a half east of Nyack on the curve between the two Great Northern overpasses, Lynch's car veered eleven feet over the centerline and into the Grists' car. Both cars plunged over the twenty-foot bank opposite the Middle Fork of the Flathead River. Dwight Grist was pinned under his car, dead from head injuries. Lynch was partially pinned under his car and was also dead. Margaret's knee was severely cut and she had other cuts and bruises. Her daughter Margaret Ann was cut and her skull, thumb, and wrist fractured. Donald Pigg, the passenger in Lynch's car, was cut and bruised.

Truckers from Valier, Montana, were first on the wreck scene to help the survivors, and a Great Northern Railway west-bound freight train saw the wreck and sent word to authorities. The two Margarets were taken to Kalispell Regional Medical Center and eventually recovered from their injuries. Donald Pigg received a fifteen-day jail sentence for being a drunk pedestrian; it would seem that there is more to that story but the details are lost in the fog of time.

WHAT A DIFFERENCE A SEAT BELT MAKES

Nineteen-year-old Diane Neale from Wichita Falls, Texas, was one of many college students who worked as a seasonal employee at the park. Attractive and well liked, Neale had just completed her freshman year at Midwestern University and was working as a maid at Many Glacier Hotel. Neale and three other seasonals—Robert Mullins, twenty-one, from Birmingham, Alabama; Pamela Jane Norris, nineteen, from Wichita Falls, Texas; and Horace C. Phelps Jr., twenty-one, also from Wichita Falls—were on their way from St. Mary to Many Glacier. Mullins was driving and Norris was in the front passenger seat. Neale and Phelps were sitting in the backseat; she was on the right. None were wearing seat belts.

They passed Sherburne Dam and were on a surfaced stretch of highway about 100 yards inside the park boundary. The vehicle crossed the road out of control, went down the bank, rolled a number of times, and came to rest on the edge of Lake Sherburne with the bumper hanging over the water. When the car came to rest, Mullins was still at the wheel, scraped and bruised. Norris, who had been riding in the front seat, was on the floor in the backseat. She was also scraped and bruised and was later diagnosed with a minor concussion. Phelps was laying half in and half out of the car and was the most seriously hurt. He had a jagged cut on his right eye and eyelid, a hole in his right thigh, and numerous scrapes, gashes, and bruises. Neale was nowhere to be found.

Mullins, Phelps, and Norris looked around the crash area for Neale, then started walking to the Sherburne entrance station to get help. They caught a ride and reported the accident to Ranger Lawrence Faser at the entrance station. They received some first aid then returned to the accident scene with Ranger Robert Wood from Many Glacier and District Ranger Robert Frauson from St. Mary. Using a wade line, the two rangers went into the water. About twenty feet from the shore they found Diane. She had been thrown from the car and died of a broken neck.

Just how Mullins lost control of the car is not clear. They were not drinking. They were having fun, and in the carefree existence of nineteen- and twenty-year-olds they were traveling too fast for these roads. If they had only worn their seat belts, Neale would likely have survived the accident.

It is easy to judge these young folks as foolish for not wearing seat belts, but in the context of their times it is more understandable. This accident occurred in June 1968. The first national seat belt law was passed only six months earlier on January 1, 1968. Americans did not yet fully appreciate what a difference a seat belt makes. They were more concerned about not being able to unfasten the belt to escape a sinking or burning car. It took a long time, a lot of lives, and a lot of traffic tickets to convince the young and the old of America to routinely fasten their seat belts.

In 1991, seat belts saved the lives of six visitors whose van crashed through the guardrail four miles west of Logan Pass just below the Weeping Wall. The van plunged more than 600 feet down the mountain,

A vehicle zips past the Weeping Wall about four miles west of Logan Pass. COURTESY OF LIBRARY OF CONGRESS, HAER MONT,15-WEGLA,5--16.

rolling over before finally coming to a stop. The driver, Livio Tavernini, sixty-seven, of Lethbridge, Alberta, broke his neck. He would be paralyzed but he was alive. Rosa Tavernini, sixty-four, and her sister, Carla Galas, were also seriously injured but alive. The Taverninis were brought up the mountain in litters to an ambulance then transferred to an emergency helicopter and flown to the Kalispell Regional Medical Center. The other passengers—fifty-one-year-old Luigi Galas and teenagers Eric and Claudia Galas—had minor injuries and were able to climb up the mountain to the road.

Today, the youth of America have grown up in a world where seat belts are mandatory and buckling up is a way of life. Yet many, perhaps counting on their perceived invincibility, still don't buckle up even on the magnificently scary Sun Road.

In 2004, a Ford Explorer full of unbelted young people who were having a jolly time touring the Going-to-the-Sun Road plummeted off the highway. They were eastbound, a little over a mile above the Loop, near Granite Creek, when their SUV drove off the road, rolled down the mountain about 150 feet, and settled on its roof. The driver and all the passengers were ejected and scattered down the hillside. Two landed in a ravine. Two rangers made their way down to the victims. A third ranger roped up and sent down medical equipment. The driver, nineteen-year-old Angel Star Makes Cold Weather of East Glacier, was killed, and passengers Simon Chavez, nineteen, and Joseph Burdeau, twenty-three, both of Browning, and two unnamed minors were injured. The rangers managed to get all five back up to the highway. An ALERT helicopter picked them up and flew them to the hospital in Kalispell. In this case alcohol was a factor in the cause of the wreck. If the youths had been wearing seat belts, however, the fatal wreck may have been only a wild ride down the side of a mountain.

ONE TOO MANY FOR THE ROAD

John Sydney Jam, twenty-six, of Kalispell had spent three years in the U.S. Army Corps of Engineers, including duty in Korea. In 1955 he was employed as a plumber's helper in the park and was planning to return to Montana State University in the fall as a junior. On August 21, Jam left Many Glacier Hotel around midnight. About one-quarter mile east of the hotel, his car deflected off the face of a cliff, flipped completely over, and landed on its wheels. Jam's only injury was a cut on his arm. A supervisory employee at the hotel saw the accident and went to the scene. It was apparent to him that Jam was in no condition to drive. He took the keys out of the ignition and turned them over to Ranger John Higgins. While Higgins was confiscating the keys, Jam used a second set of keys to start the car and drive down the road. Minutes—maybe only seconds—later, Jam drove the car off the road, plunging into Swiftcurrent Creek about 100 feet below. At far too young an age, John Jam was dead from a fractured skull and his ill-fated decision.

BY CHANCE

Sometimes life or death hangs on chance, luck, or fate. Such was the tragic case in 1951 when a tree fell onto the Going-to-the-Sun Road just west of Sprague Creek Campground, crushing a passing car and killing infant passenger Bernida M. Byrd. In 1962, another incident took an ironic twist when car passenger Alice Jean Leckie, who was terrified of the sheer cliffs along the Going-to-the-Sun Road, avoided facing her fear only to die from another, less obvious hazard (see Chapter 10).

In the following incident, it was a tree that saved three people from almost certain death. In July 1960, Henry Engan and his wife, both in their sixties, and their son, thirty-five-year-old Henry Jr., from Park Ridge, Illinois, were on a tour of national parks. They had spent the previous night in Banff National Park in Canada and were traveling through Glacier on their way to Yellowstone National Park. The senior Henry was driving his 1959 Ford. They were moving along slowly about one-half mile below the Weeping Wall on the Garden Wall section of the Going-to-the-Sun Road. Suddenly the left front tire blew out and the car went out of control. According to the incident report, the car "cleared the low retaining wall leaving scarcely a mark" and plummeted 100 feet down the slope, lodging against a tree.

The younger Henry, who was riding in the backseat, had numerous lacerations but managed to get out of the car and crawl up the Garden Wall to the road. He flagged down a car and asked the occupants to report the accident at the Lake McDonald Ranger Station. Subdistrict Ranger James Thornson along with Charles J. Pinkepank and seasonal rangers William Brockman and Gilbert Adams hurried to the wreck site.

Henry and the rangers looked down the side of the mountain. The car was not visible, and the path the car had made on its descent through the shrubs had closed back in. They heard a faint cry from Mrs. Engan. The rangers scrambled over the cliff and down to the car. Using a rope as a guideline, they brought Mrs. Engan up, then they brought Mr. Engan up on a stretcher and took them both to Kalispell Regional Medical Center. Mr. Engan had a fractured rib, a concussion, and lung contusions. Mrs. Engan had a fractured facial bone and lacerations.

If the tree had not stopped Engan's car it would have plummeted another 500 feet, leaving little chance of survival for the three occupants.

RIDING THE HIGH ROADS—
MOTORCYCLES AND BICYCLES

The twisting turns and steep elevation changes of the Going-to-the-Sun Road offer motorcyclists and bicyclists a challenging ride through incredible scenery. It is listed among America's best fifteen motorcycling roads, and many motorcyclists refer to it as the "Holy Grail" or "Mount Everest" of motorcycle routes. Bicyclists refer to it as the "Crown Jewel." Pump your way up the 3,300-foot climb from Lake McDonald to Logan Pass and you'll know why.

Ten fatalities (roughly a third of all vehicle deaths in the park since records have been kept) have been due to motorcycle accidents. Only two bicycle deaths have occurred.

The first recorded motorcycle death in the park was in July 1951 when Charles S. Norris, nineteen, of London, Ontario, ran into a riderless horse on the Going-to-the-Sun Road about one-half mile inside the park's east boundary. The horse had strayed into the St. Mary Ridge area near the foot of St. Mary Lake from a nearby ranch outside the park. The horse died shortly after the accident. Norris died, without gaining consciousness, near Logan Pass while being transported in a park pickup to the hospital in Whitefish.

In 1987, thirty-two-year-old Bradley J. Cox of Calgary, Alberta, and a motorcycling partner were traveling thirty to thirty-five miles an hour when they approached the series of sharp turns near the Triple Arches. Cox lost control of his Yamaha motorcycle, tried to brake, and left a sixteen-foot skid mark before crashing into a rock retaining wall and catapulting over the cliff. He fell 275 feet. Ranger Loren Fredin reached him within minutes of the crash and performed CPR. Ranger Tom Habecker rappelled down the cliff with a heart monitor and relayed the medical information to Kalispell Regional Medical Center by radio. Two hours after the crash, Cox was pronounced dead. His helmet was strapped to his motorcycle. We can't know whether he would have survived if he had been wearing his helmet, but it might have made a difference.

In Montana, motorcyclists and their passengers under age eighteen must wear a helmet. If over eighteen, the decision is up to the riders. The challenges of mountain roads would seem to argue in favor of protecting your brain no matter what age you are.

In the following accident, unfortunately, the helmet did not make a difference. Motorcyclists are very aware that their bodies are not protected as well as when surrounded by steel and plastic in a car. It's part of the "feel of freedom." In 2009, a group of twenty-seven motorcyclists from Alberta, Canada, was traveling the Sun Road. When the riders were about one-half mile west of the Wild Goose Island overlook, George Zlatnik, fifty-one, riding a Honda Gold Wing, disappeared. The rider ahead of him happened to look in his rearview mirror and realized George was not in sight. He called out to the other motorcyclists and they contacted a ranger. They found Zlatnik and his Honda thirty feet below the road.

He apparently lost control on the turn and plunged over the edge. His helmet was still on, but he had died from other injuries.

Bicyclists are a regular sight on the Sun Road as they pedal up to Logan Pass. Because the upper sections of the road were designed for Model-Ts and other automobiles of the 1920s, the road is narrow and has no shoulder. It is a testament to the nerve of the cyclists and the courtesy of the drivers that no fatal accidents between a vehicle and cyclist have occurred in the history of this road in the sky. Park managers have reduced the chances of accidents and collisions by limiting cyclists to using the road early in the morning and then again late in the afternoon to avoid the crush of automobiles surging to Logan Pass from mid-morning to late afternoon. Despite these restrictions, the challenge of climbing to Logan Pass under one's own pedal power is irresistible to many cyclists, so drivers need to be alert for cyclists on the road.

The two bicycle deaths occurred thirty-seven years apart. The first one was in the park headquarters area, not on the Sun Road. In 1964, Glacier Park road foreman Paul W. Gerrish, his wife Mary Ann, and their two children were living in park housing near park headquarters in West Glacier. On July 15, Paul's five-year-old son Paul Jeffery Gerrish, known in the neighborhood as P. J., was just starting to ride without training wheels. P. J. was proudly pedaling his bike around his home in the park headquarters community housing area when he was hit by a delivery truck driven by Tom Jones of Kalispell. P. J. was mortally injured in the accident and died the next day. Tom Jones was known to be a careful driver, and after an investigation by the coroner no inquest was required. The *Hungry Horse News* reported that "Park Headquarters has something of a big family feeling toward all children of the community." The community mourned the loss of the little boy as one of their own.

Thirty-seven years later, a bicyclist was enjoying a "full moon" bicycle ride down the west side of the Going-to-the Sun Road from Logan Pass. This popular cycling activity involves transporting a bicycle to Logan Pass on a vehicle and then, after the restricted time is past in the late afternoon, coasting down the west side of the Going-to-the-Sun Road to Avalanche Creek. Swooping down through the curves in the road in stunning mountain scenery is a thrill. It also can be fatal. On August 5, 2001, thirty-year-old cyclist David Olseth, of Whitefish, waited at Logan Pass on a full moon night. Riding down the road under the full moon had become a local custom, and there were generally more than a few night riders on each of the summer's full moon nights. David, an experienced cyclist, began his descent but at some point lost control and hit a rock retaining wall at sufficient speed to launch him and his bicycle over the wall and out into the night. David's body and bike were found almost 300 feet below the road. Although the slope below the point where he flipped over the wall was very steep, the distance he fell suggested that his speed and momentum must have been considerable when he hit the wall and went over. It also was speculated that he may not have braked. A possible scenario is that he was racing around one of the bends in the road and was blinded by an oncoming car's headlights unexpectedly. If so, that inability to see where the road or wall was, even for an instant, was enough to cause this tragic death.

Glacier National Park shuttles provide free rides to many stops along Going-to-the-Sun Road, including *Logan Pass.* JACOB W. FRANK, COURTESY OF NATIONAL PARK SERVICE.

The popular full moon bicycle ride is usually safe. On a clear night, the full moon provides enough light to see by, and cyclists use tail and headlights (as required by park regulations) so that others can see them. According to park officials, Olseth apparently was not using a headlight. A small flashlight was found where he left the road. He was not wearing a helmet (it's doubtful that a helmet would have saved him). Speed and loss of control were factors in the accident. Park rangers were notified of the accident at 2 A.M. and ALERT rescuers were on the scene shortly afterward. At approximately 5:30 A.M. the ALERT nurse pronounced Olseth dead at the scene. A park boom truck was used to recover the body.

"LEAVE THE DRIVING TO US"

Driving the roads in Glacier is a unique and enjoyable experience. If you'd prefer to relax and more fully enjoy the scenery while helping to reduce traffic, consider taking an interpretive tour on one of Glacier's historic Red Buses or on a Sun Tour bus. Also, Glacier's free shuttle system is a wonderful way to travel the Going-to-the-Sun Road, with a dozen stops between Apgar and the St. Mary Visitor Center. West of Logan Pass, shuttles run every fifteen to thirty minutes, and east-side shuttles run every thirty to sixty minutes. The air-conditioned shuttles are ADA accessible, seat twelve to twenty passengers, and feature large windows for sightseeing.

Sun Tours, a Blackfeet Tribal chartered business, provides interpretive tours emphasizing park history and the spiritual and philosophical stories of the Blackfeet people. COURTESY OF SUN TOURS AND GLACIER NATIONAL PARK.

CHAPTER EIGHT

NATURAL CAUSES
and other
DEADLY INCIDENTS

Falling is the leading cause of death in Glacier National Park, followed closely by drowning. But heart attacks and other cardiovascular troubles are not far behind. In fact, if we lump those together with other "natural" causes, such as respiratory failure and undiagnosed deaths (mostly at a later age), then deaths from natural causes take the number two spot in the ranking (see the table on page 299). Such deaths occur naturally in humans and are not necessarily related to or caused by being in the park. Most of the heart and respiratory-related deaths in the park occurred among people in their later years. Exceptions to this are concession employee Jean Jensen, twenty-three, who died at Lake McDonald Lodge of an unknown natural cause in 1958; one-year-old Harry Culp, who died in his sleep at the Many Glacier Hotel in 1962; and eight-month-old Christine Pettee, who died of respiratory problems at Lake McDonald Lodge in 1965. Seventy-five percent of the deaths from natural causes were visitors to the park; the other twenty-five percent were park residents or employees.

Being in a new environment such as the park and taking part in different activities can trigger underlying health issues, but in most of these cases the natural deaths could have happened anywhere and were not attributed to being in the mountains. The sixty-three incidents of deaths from natural causes are listed in the List of Deaths in Glacier National Park (see page 290), but we present here only those that provide a powerful cautionary lesson or, as in the case of these first six incidents, those that are particularly relevant to life and times in Glacier National Park.

Among the "other deadly incidents" described in this chapter are two deaths due to intoxication, another death when a house burned, and one victim who died from falling off a runaway horse.

HOMESTEADER DAN DOVERSPIKE

In 1907, Dan Doverspike established residency on his homestead claim at the north end of Big Prairie along the western edge of what would become Glacier National Park. The 1862 Homestead Act as later amended in 1912 required a claimant to live on the land for three years, build a home, make improvements, and farm the land. At the time Doverspike filed, he was fifty-six years old, the father of nine children, and separated from his wife. Doverspike had worked for the oil companies exploring in the North Fork during the early 1900s and also had packed for the U.S. Geological Survey crews when they re-surveyed the U.S.-Canadian boundary in 1907.

Sometime around 1912, Dan's two sons, Earl and Harry, joined him. By 1913, when Dan "proved up" (met the requirements of the Homestead Act) on his homestead claim, the three men had seeded twenty acres in hay, had a one-half-acre garden, and, with the help of Big Prairie neighbor Charlie Schoenberger, had erected a two-story log house with a double shake roof, a large log barn, a shed, a root cellar, a chicken house, a hog house, and a mile and a half of fencing. During the winter of 1918, the house burned to the ground and Dan rebuilt it the next spring.

On October 12, 1922, Dan's neighbor Ike Chance stopped by for a visit and later reported that Dan seemed in his usual good health. The following Friday, Chance made a trip down to the post office and as was his custom picked up Dan's mail. On the homeward trip he went to Dan's place and knocked at the door. He did not receive an answer so he opened the door and went in. According to Chance, Dan was lying in bed and looked as though he had passed away in peaceful sleep not many hours earlier. His dog was in the room and a clock was ticking. The coroner was notified and investigated the case. It appeared that the seventy-year-old homesteader died of heart failure.

THE KELLYS OF LAKE MCDONALD

Frank Kelly came into the country that would later become Glacier National Park in 1892 when the Great Northern Railway was laying track westward from Cut Bank to the Flathead Valley. Born in Dubuque, Iowa, in 1855, Kelly was a natural-born jack-of-all-trades—he worked as a carpenter, a timberman, and a raft man. He was a man who knew boats and was good at reading water. When he was nineteen, he went to Minnesota and rafted logs down the Mississippi. He first came to Montana in 1883 while working for the Northern Pacific Railroad. Then, while going from one job to another, Kelly traveled to Oregon and California, then back to Oregon, took a sailing vessel loaded with lumber around Cape Horn, then went to France, England, New York, and Wisconsin. He came back to Montana in 1892 to run a portable sawmill for the Great Northern Railway.

Kelly staked his homestead claim on the west shore of Lake McDonald in March 1894. Three years later, at forty-two, Kelly married

This May 23, 1915, photograph shows the Emeline listing to starboard with a full complement of happy passengers. COURTESY OF GLACIER NATIONAL PARK ARCHIVES.

twenty-year-old Emeline Haworth, the widow of the Great Northern Railway's section foreman at Belton. She had a three-year-old son, Vern. Kelly adopted the boy, whether formally or not we don't know, but he did give Vern his last name.

About this time, tourism at Lake McDonald was picking up due to the grand advertising of the Great Northern Railway. Brochures of the time proclaimed the country as the "Swiss Alps of America" and Lake McDonald as "where God sat when he made America." Guest cabins were built at the foot of the lake near the Apgar's, and at the head of the lake George

Emeline and Frank Kelly posed for this image on their wedding day in 1897.
J. L. PHELPS, COURTESY OF GLACIER NATIONAL PARK ARCHIVES.

Snyder built his hotel and launched the steamer *F. I. Whitney* to provide transportation for guests from the foot of the lake to his hotel at the head of the lake. In 1906, although the tourism business was booming, the *F. I. Whitney* was decommissioned. To fill the gap, Kelly built a thirty-five-foot gas-powered launch to transport guests and residents up and down the lake. He christened it the *Emeline* in honor of his wife. He then went into the boat business with Orville Denny when Denny brought the *Cassie D* to the lake and set up a dock in Apgar. John E. Lewis, then owner of the Glacier Hotel, bought out Denny's share. Kelly and Lewis built the *Ethel* at Apgar and launched her. A year later, they jointly bought a third boat, the *City of Polson*, from Flathead Lake and renamed her *Lewtana*. They ran all four boats until 1918. Then Kelly bought out Lewis, and he and Vern continued running the boats until 1921.

In the 1920s, Kelly built a string of log resort cabins on his homestead lands, which would be known as Kelly's Camp. For the next fifteen years, the Kellys continued to be an important part of the Lake McDonald community.

In January 1935, both Frank and Emeline became very sick. They were later diagnosed as having pneumonia. Lake McDonald ranger Ray Newberry wrote of their situation in his station log book:

> **Thursday, January 10, 1935.** Made two trips to Belton at night getting a doctor for Kelly.
>
> **Friday, January 11, 1935.** Cloudy—North wind. Temp. High 33 degrees. Low 10 degrees. Calm and warm most of the day but late afternoon wind swung into the north and a howling blizzard blowing at night with three feet of snow-fall at 11:00 P.M. Made two trips to Kelly's today on webs [snowshoes]. Second trip to help Vern [Frank and Emeline's son] carry stuff. He had been to Kalispell to get drugs and a trained nurse but the wind made it impossible for him to cross the lake from the hotel. He drove to station and we went in on webs. Frank Kelly and his wife both very sick.
>
> **Saturday, January 12, 1935.** Part cloudy—N Wind Temperature High 10 degrees Low 0 degrees. Went to Kelly's. 4 of them under the weather and two quite sick. Vern & the nurse have their hands full. Didn't prove to be of much value myself but the Mrs. [Newberry's wife] was useful. Rankin attempted to drive out but didn't get far. Word received by telegram to Rankin that Frank Geduhn died Thurs. Jan 10 in California. 4" of snow last night.
>
> **Sunday, January 13, 1935.** Partly cloudy. Slight N Wind Temperature High 10 degrees Low -2 degrees. The Mrs. left for Kelly's in the morning. Whitecraft called wanting me to meet Dr. at Apgar with a boat. Wished that job on to Rankin as he has Chadbourne's outfit, a faster motor and more sea worthy boat. Gave him 4 gallons of gas oil mix. Dr. McKenzie of CCC Camp 1 stopped at Kelly's tonight. Hiked toward Kelly's and met Mrs. enroute home.

Monday, January 14, 1935. *Snow plow arrived about midnight. The bulldozer started on the Kelly road but got into trouble in ¼ mile and went back. Roy and Ray Haworth and a priest from Whitefish arrived by car early and went to Kelly's on webs. After feeding deer, went over. The Dr. came back with me and I drove him to Camp 1. One stop at hotel. Sackness [?] has a bad boil and another at Apgar where Cal Sibley had a rupture and was sent to Kalispell Hospital. Talked with Whitecraft about the necessity of plowing the Kelly road. He says the dozer will be up tonight and plow out tomorrow. At night, packed some groceries to Kelly's and came back by boat which Haworth had used in bringing in another nurse. Travel 7 miles by webs, 2 by boat and 28 by car.*

Tuesday, January 15, 1935. *Frank Kelly died at 2:25 A.M. Haworth stopped in at 4:40 A.M. wanting me to go to Kelly's. Hiked over on webs. Road plow first showed up at 8:30 and car came in at 1 P.M. Sherman and son took the body to Kalispell. Burial will probably be at Columbia Falls. Henry Hutchings drove up to notarize some papers. Rode back to station with him and drove back at night. The Mrs. returned with me at 11:00 P.M. Mrs. Kelly is very sick tonight.*

Wednesday, January 16, 1935. *Blizzard N. Wind Temperature High 18 degrees Low 3 degrees. After feeding deer, drove to Kelly's. Kennick went with us. Broke the transmission shaft in the Ford in backing into the parking place. Shoveled some snow. Mrs. Frank Kelly died at 2:30 P.M. Did considerable phoning to Hdq and CCC 1 in an effort to get the road plowed for the hearse from Kalispell. Attempt was made but hearse broke down and was towed back to Belton. Word received at night that bulldozer will start at day break with truck following to hand the body to Belton. Haworth brought Helen, Stanley and me home. Vern came along and took his Ford home. Snow depth at station 34".*

Thursday, January 17, 1935. Blizzard. Strong N Wind Snow 5" Temperature High 3 degrees low -15 degrees. Stayed at station today. Weather conditions made it impossible to get up to Kelly's from the lower country. Nothing we can do but wait. Promise is now that a cat will bring up a sleigh since it is a slow job to open the road.

Friday, January 18, 1935. Cloudy. Blizzard. N. Wind Snow 4" Temp-High -11 degrees, Low -16 degrees. Tractor manned by 4 men and towing a covered logging sleigh came up this afternoon. Vern Kelly, Roy Haworth, Helen Collins and the two nurses rode out with them. The body of Mrs. Frank Kelly taken down for shipment to Kalispell. It took the tractor 5 hours to come up and 2½ hours from here to Apgar. Both Haworth's and Kelly's cars left at Kelly's alongside my broken down Ford. Kennick and I went to Kelly's on webs and returned on the sleigh. Travel 2 miles on webs, 2 by sleigh.

Monday, January 21, 1935. Cloudy—Snowing Temp High 8 degrees Low -9 degrees. Hiked to Belton. Asked Mr. Scoyen [park supervisor] for leave for today but he said it was unnecessary. Rode to Kalispell and return in Geo. Slack's car. Attended the double funeral of Frank Kelly and his wife.

APGAR 1941

Most of the deaths reported in this chapter were due to natural causes—primarily heart attacks—but on February 17, 1941, at CCC Camp 15, Apgar Flats, another deadly incident occurred when Antone Shiller, forty-five, died of alcohol poisoning. Two days after Christmas in 1941, another kind of deadly incident took the life of twenty-three-year-old Cal Irvin Sibley. Cal and his wife, Juanita Claire Sibley, lived in Apgar at the foot of Lake McDonald. On the cold night of December 27, the furnace in their home overheated, setting the house on fire. Cal and Juanita escaped. Then Cal went back into the burning house to the bedroom to try to save property or a pet, we're not sure which. He was caught in the smoke and flames, suffocated, and burned to death. The house burned to the ground.

1951 NORTH FORK FIDDLERS—
JESSE BEMIS AND UNCLE HENRY COVEY

The November 30, 1951, edition of the *Hungry Horse News* featured an item on the passing of Jesse Bemis. "There's an old uncle, Henry Covey, 76, two old horses, Whitey, 30, and Queen, 24, two dogs Buck, 15 (part husky), Chubb, 12, and some good friends to mourn the loss of Covey's nephew, Jesse Bemis, 68, who died with his boots on last Sunday," the paper noted. "Home for these well respected gentlemen of the Flathead River's North Fork was on Bowman Creek above Polebridge. It was in the park, but the land was theirs, before there was a Glacier National Park. The Covey-Bemis place remained frontier."

Henry Covey and Jesse Bemis were both born in Little Falls, Wisconsin—Henry in 1875 and Jesse in 1883. Henry was Jesse's uncle. They went to North Dakota in 1897, then to Alberta, Canada, to raise horses and trap for furs. In 1908, Henry moved to Columbia Falls, Montana, and Jesse landed in northern Idaho. The next year, Jesse came over from Idaho and he and Henry went up the North Fork of the Flathead River to Bowman Creek. Jesse bought a one-room log cabin from an earlier squatter named William J. Doney in August 1909 and filed for a homestead claim on the land that same year.

Jesse and Henry were soon joined by Henry's two brothers, George and Bob. The four bachelors lived together on the homestead during the 1910s and 1920s. According to interviews by Cindy Mish with North Fork residents for *Homesteading on the North Fork in Glacier National Park*, the four men were well-liked, colorful characters of the North Fork. Jesse, Uncle Henry, and Bob were the principal local musicians; their fiddle tunes kept the North Fork folks dancing through many all-night winter parties.

Homesteaders almost never made a living raising hay and livestock alone. Instead, they took odd jobs at whatever they could get to provide subsistence and "prove up" their lands. The men were independent in the way of frontiersmen. If you did them a favor, they'd make sure that a favor was returned, and most refused to accept public assistance. Jesse, Henry, Bob, and George occasionally got work with the U.S. Forest Service. They did a little hunting, trapping, and bootlegging to provide basic necessities. They also tried raising chinchilla rabbits. They started with four or five pairs, but transportation costs made the venture unprofitable and they turned the bunnies loose. In 1910 when the census taker came by, both Henry and Jesse listed their occupations as "none."

By the time Jesse "proved up" on his homestead in 1914, the four men had constructed a two-story log house with a hewn log interior, a large log barn, a log tool house (which may have been the original log cabin), two miles of fencing, eighty rods (1,320 feet) of ditch work, and a half-acre garden, and they had eleven and one-half acres in timothy hay. There was one cow, two dozen chickens, and a lot of rabbits.

Henry Covey's brother George left the North Fork in the 1920s. His other brother Bob died of diabetes. Jesse and Henry continued to live on the homestead. They made do with occasional outside work. In an interview with Cindy Mish, Frank Humor said, "When groceries would run low, they would cook up a batch [of moonshine] and take it down to Kalispell and sell it, 'til they got enough money to buy groceries. Then they'd loaf around again until they needed more groceries."

On November 25, 1951, Jesse went to get a load of wood. When he finished, he was taking the harness off Whitey and Queen and apparently had a heart attack. When Henry found him he was dead. Henry went to the Polebridge Ranger Station to report the death to Ranger Ed Olmstead. Olmstead and Ben Rover at the Polebridge Store brought Jesse out. He was buried in the Conrad Memorial Cemetery. A few months later, park rangers helped take Henry to the hospital where he later died. The heirs of the Covey-Bemis estate sold the land to the park in 1959.

THE POWELLS AND CHARLIE RUSSELL
AT LAKE MCDONALD

A second-generation Montana cowboy, Asa August Powell worked on several horse ranches around the country. He eventually married a school-teacher and settled down to homesteading. As with other homesteaders in northwest Montana, there was little money for making the necessary improvements. After a few hard years homesteading, Asa went to work for the National Park Service and moved to Apgar. In a relatively short time, he acquired a saddle horse outfit and went into the business of guiding tourists through the park. The affable Asa worked as a horse wrangler, stable boss, guide, and packer in the park. In 1912, Asa's son Asa Lynn Powell was born. Young Asa was soon known as Ace. He grew up around horses and the mountains and streams of Glacier National Park. By age ten, young Ace Powell was a working wrangler and a want-to-be artist. It was his good fortune that his father, the elder Asa, was a friend, guide, and cook on hunting trips for cowboy artist Charles M. Russell, who had built a cabin near Lake McDonald. Young Ace Powell often accompanied Charlie Russell on morning rides, watching Russell sketch and draw. When Ace was fourteen years old, Charlie Russell died in Great Falls on October 24, 1926. While in his early twenties, Ace got a job as a wrangler on the Bar X6 Ranch and handled horses for the park. Ace liked being a cowboy, enjoyed commiserating with tourists, had four wives (not at the same time), possessed a wicked sense of humor, and drank a lot. But Ace never gave up his ambition to be an artist.

In addition to the artistic influ-ence that Charlie Russell had on

During his lifetime, Ace Powell produced nearly 15,000 works of art, including this 1940 portrait of a Blackfeet man. COURTESY OF TED SOLDOWSKI COLLECTION.

his work, Ace also had contact with other artists around Glacier Park—Olaf Seltzer, Hans and Winold Reiss, and John Clarke. Ace eventually became a well-known artist; his painted signature was the ace of diamonds card. He produced thousands of works of art—paintings, sculptures, and wood carvings—and is considered one of the finest painters of American western art.

Ace's father died of a heart attack at sixty-five years old in his home in Apgar on August 22, 1952. After a career as a successful western artist, Ace passed away on January 25, 1978, in Kalispell.

CAUTION: COLD WATER AND HIGH ALTITUDES

In July 1965, Henry M. Noldan from Syracuse, New York, was traveling with his son Henry Jr. (a fire control officer with the U.S. Bureau of Land Management in Dillon), his daughter-in-law, and her two children. They had camped at Seeley Lake the day before and arrived at Fish Creek Campground Sunday afternoon on July 25. The elder Noldan, sixty-five, was known as a good swimmer and went for a dip in Lake McDonald. He swam out about fifty yards in the 48-degree water and was back on shore when his son noticed that his father appeared in pain and was breathing heavily. He called for help and responders gave first aid, but Henry soon died.

According to the National Center for Cold Water Safety, plunging into cold water during hot weather can cause heart attacks, even in young, fit, healthy individuals. The temperature of the water in Lake McDonald was 48 degrees F on that July day, which may not sound particularly cold or dangerous if you are comparing it with a 48 degrees F air temperature. But water temperatures as warm as 50 to 60 degrees F are cold and can throw you into what's known as cold shock. This speeds up the heart rate, raises blood pressure, may cause hyperventilation, and may also cause the heart to beat in abnormal rhythms. It can be fatal. Scientists contend that acclimation and body fat makes the difference on how someone responds to cold water. If you plan to swim in the cold waters of the park, it is strongly recommended that you acclimate to cold water through a series of gradual, repeated exposures before coming to the park.

GLACIER CALLED TO HIM

In 1936, nineteen-year-old Hans Jungster, his parents, and other family members immigrated to New York from Germany to escape Nazi oppression. As a boy, Hans had gone to school in Switzerland where he became an excellent skier and acquired a lifelong love for the mountains. During World War II, he joined the U.S. Army's 10th Mountain Division, a specialized outfit trained for fighting in mountainous and arctic conditions. Hans was a reconnaissance scout in the battles in the North

Antoinette and Hans Jungster opened Montana House, an arts and crafts store, in Apgar Village in 1959. COURTESY OF MONICA JUNGSTER.

Apennines, Po Valley, and Aleutian Islands, receiving the Bronze Star and Purple Heart with one Oak Leaf.

After the war, Hans came west. He enrolled at the University of Washington, majoring in forestry. He met his future wife, Antoinette "Toni" Stanton, a botanist, while on a field trip to Montana. Hans and Toni married and moved to Rocky Mountain National Park where Hans worked as a park ranger teaching mountain rescue. In 1953, at the young age of thirty-six, Hans had a heart attack and left the park service. He and Toni moved back to New York so that he could be near his father, who was a doctor, and his family while he recovered. Two years later, in 1955, Hans and Toni and their daughter Monica came west again, moving to

Bigfork, Montana. They started a crafts and tea house in a log cabin named Forest and Fireside. In 1957, the Jungsters had another daughter— Leslie. Two years later, the call of Glacier brought Hans and Toni and their daughters to Apgar. They purchased a parcel of land that was part of Milo Apgar's original homestead and built a retail store, Montana House.

The Jungsters had a great love for the mountains, valleys, lakes, and streams that were now in their backyard. Montana House was a way to make a living by displaying and selling art and crafts, but for the Jungsters it was more than that. They built Montana House to encourage Native Americans and local Montanans whose personal insight and various forms of art portrayed the park's history and timeless beauty in a unique way.

Hans and Toni were also active in the Montana Institute of the Arts. According to Corinne Lundgren (one of the founders of the Hockaday Center for the Arts), the couple enthusiastically supported the Flathead Valley Art Association's efforts to acquire the Carnegie Library building in Kalispell and convert it into the Hockaday Museum. Unfortunately, Hans did not live to see the opening.

In 1967, eight years after establishing Montana House and thirteen years after his first heart attack, Hans Jungster, at age forty-nine, had a second heart attack and died at his home in Apgar. Toni and her daughters —Monica and Leslie—continued to operate Montana House. When Monica finished college, she returned to Apgar to work in the store, and in 1994 she took over the business.

Monica and her husband Chuck Brasen continue to operate Montana House to "celebrate and promote creativity of Montana and Native American artists for our mutual benefit" and to share the history of the park and the lessons of the past in a series of "Look, Listen, and Learn" events by artists, authors, photographers, scientists, and park rangers.

THE OVER THE HILL GANG

"Nothing can stop these gentlemen from conquering the mountain tops. Not snow nor water. Not blindness nor heart attacks," wrote Myers Reece in his July 8, 2009, Columbia Falls Community News & Features article "In Glacier, No Trail Left Untouched." Reece was writing about Glacier Park's Over the Hill Gang.

In 1976, Ivan O'Neil, Ambrose Measure, Spencer Ryder, Hi Gibson, and Harry Isch decided to hike once each week. At that time, their average age was sixty years old. They chose Thursday as their hiking day, and as Reece said, they "put on their boots and gave birth to a tradition." Eight years later, they invited Ivan O'Neil's best friend from high school, author and Flathead radio personality George Ostrom, to join their hiking group. "We made a mistake when we invited George," O'Neil joked. "His gift of gab brought a lot of people along." The Over the Hill Gang became locally famous, and their numbers grew to twenty and even forty at times.

On July 21, 1988, a group of ten Over the Hillers hiked to the Hidden Lake Overlook at Logan Pass and were climbing 8,952-foot Mount Cannon. Ostrom was one of the hikers, as was Isch, one of the original Over the Hill Gang members. Isch was sixty-nine years old. He was born in Kalispell in 1918 and graduated from Flathead County High School in 1936. He worked for the Nash Finch Company until 1942 when he joined the U.S. Army. Isch served in the Pacific Theater until receiving his honorable discharge in 1945. He went to the University of Montana and graduated with a degree in business administration and accounting. He then went to work for Richards Accounting Service in Kalispell and in 1951 established his own accounting business.

On the trail, Harry complained of not feeling well and joked about somebody having to take his pack. One of the hikers, retired physician Dr. Harry "Hi" Gibson, seventy-five, turned and saw Harry sitting down. Harry told him he was feeling dizzy. Gibson checked Isch's pulse; it was erratic. Isch was in atrial fibrillation. Gibson and fellow hiker, Frederick A. "Pat" Gyrion, decided to take Isch back to the cars. They considered calling for a helicopter, but winds and the steep location made it too risky. Gibson picked the easiest way down. He kept checking Isch's pulse and it was normal. "Harry was doing okay," Gibson said. "Then we happened to run into a friend. I stopped to talk briefly, and when I turned around again Harry was down on the trail." A passing hiker located a ranger who radioed for ALERT. Park employee Penny Latham and two doctors who happened to be on the trail took turns administering CPR. "But it was no use," Gibson said. Harry Isch had died.

Another incident of the Over the Hillers looking out for each other occurred on May 26, 2005. This one had a happier outcome. Myers Reece reported it in his 2009 article.

Jim Folston, of Somers, had fallen far behind the rest of the guys on a trail after conversing with a friend in the parking lot. Folston, seventy at the time, set out in pursuit at a swift pace. He quickly grew tired and slightly ill. "Floaters" began flashing in front of his eyes and he took a seat, still alone. "Then this big elephant came along and stood on my chest and I knew I was in trouble then," Folston said. That big elephant, he later learned, was the failure of his right coronary artery—a heart attack in the wilderness. Folston took a couple of Advil, lay down, and dwelled on his family history of heart attack deaths. "I looked around and saw how beautiful it was and thought: 'Well, if this is my time, what could be a better way to go?'"

But it wasn't his time. Hiking partner Elmer Searle (who passed away in 2009 at age ninety) found him and used his two-way radio to contact another member of the group, Jack Klovstad. Klovstad then radioed O'Neil, who just happened to be cross-country skiing nearby. O'Neil then signaled another friend back in the parking lot who was able to contact a ranger.

An ALERT helicopter was called from Kalispell. Folston was carried on a stretcher across backcountry terrain to the waiting helicopter. By the time Klovstad made it back to his car and drove to the hospital, Folston had already undergone surgery and was on the road to recovery. After extensive rehabilitation and fitness programs, Folston made it back to the woods. "I made it through because of these great guys and a great ALERT crew," Folston said. "I'm very thankful."

In a 2013 "Over the Hill Gang update," George Ostrom wrote that the Over the Hill Gang is still very active, with new people joining.

Some make one climb and decide to seek a different form of recreation, but for others it gets in their blood and they learn from the older hands. Although Ivan O'Neil and Walter Bahr were close to eighty-five in 2013, they were still active. The oldest active members the group ever had were Ambrose Measure and Elmer Searle, who both "enjoyed climbs up to their nineties." Ostrom also added that the Over the Hill Gang spans "near half a century." During that time, "we've had one very serious injury from a fall and two deaths from heart attacks," he noted, "but that's a good record for so many wonderful adventures, and I might add, Luck had very little to do with it. Guys on Social Security are more careful."

WILD GALLOP

In August 1986, Geraldine Jacobsen, sixty-four, of Hopkins, Minnesota, and four friends and family members were vacationing in Whitefish. They came to the park and were riding horses near the head of Lake McDonald. Tod Twist of Rocky Mountain Outfitters was guiding the visitors and riding the lead horse. As the riders came near the Going-to-the-Sun Road, for some unknown reason—possibly the scent of a bear—the horses spooked and began to gallop out of control. Tod Twist was thrown, dragged a short way, and kicked in the chest by a runaway horse. Jennifer Gustafson managed to jump off her galloping horse, but the other riders didn't try or couldn't. Ranger Tom Habecker and the *Hungry Horse News* reported that the horses galloped down the access road at the head of Lake McDonald toward the ranger station. Kerri Gustafson, age twelve, fell off her horse near the McDonald Creek Bridge, and Karen Hardy, eighteen, and Geraldine Jacobsen fell off their horses two hundred yards farther along. Jacobsen hit her head when she fell. The horses continued their wild gallop until they reached the Trout Lake trailhead, several yards farther, and then slowed down. Charlene Gustafson, the mother of two of the girls, managed to stay on her horse until they stopped running. She dismounted.

Ranger Michael Ober was unhooking a horse trailer near the trail when he heard the horses gallop by. He was first on the scene, followed by Dr. Howard Steele, chief of surgery at a children's hospital in Philadelphia and a Lake McDonald summer resident. He attended to the most seriously hurt and did what he could for Geraldine Jacobsen, who had head injuries. She was taken to Lake McDonald Lodge where the ALERT helicopter picked her up. She was flown to Kalispell Regional Hospital where she died from her head injuries.

HIKING HEART ATTACKS

Various studies list cardiac arrest (heart attack) as the number three killer in the outdoors and responsible for half of all mountain-climbing fatalities. That hasn't been the case in Glacier Park; only a little over a fourth of fatal heart attacks in the park occurred while the victims were hiking or climbing. According to the *International Journal of Sports Medicine*, regular hiking actually lowers the risk of heart attack in men. The trick is to adjust your hiking goals to your age and fitness level. Also, ease into your hiking day with frequent rests, especially if you're gaining elevation. Drink and eat often to avoid dehydration. Avoid hiking in the hottest part of the day or choose shaded hikes. If you are hiking into the higher elevations or camping overnight, be sure you have adequate cold weather gear.

LOVELY LAST WALK

We close this chapter with the following incident. It is neither a powerful cautionary lesson nor particularly relevant to Glacier Park. In this book about deaths and near deaths, it's a one-sentence treatise on living. In 1987, Sue Grace Williams, at the lovely age of ninety-two, was making her way along the beautiful Trail of the Cedars in Glacier National Park when she died of natural causes.

PART THREE

CALL OF THE BACKCOUNTRY: ADVENTUROUS SPIRITS, PERILOUS DECISIONS

Climb if you will, but remember that courage and strength are naught without prudence, and that a momentary negligence may destroy the happiness of a lifetime. Do nothing in haste; look well to each step, and from the beginning think what may be the end.

—EDWARD WHYMPER, *Scrambles Amongst the Alps*

Grinnell Glacier from the summit of Mount Grinnell. COURTESY OF DAN FAGRE.

CHAPTER NINE

GRAVITY IS ABSOLUTE: FALLING WHILE HIKING *and* CLIMBING

Sculpted by ancient glaciers, the sheer verticality of Glacier Park's steep slopes, cliffs, sawtooth ridges, and pyramidal peaks is the powerfully inspiring scenery that draws tourists, photographers, and artists. It also draws adventurous hikers, backcountry explorers, and mountaineers.

The exploration of the mountain landscape was strongly encouraged by the Great Northern Railway. Their workers built the early trail system and constructed numerous backcountry chalets and shelters in the park. In some places they constructed summertime wall-tent camps that could accommodate hiking and horse-riding tourists. The network of back-country lodging was designed so that each accommodation was about a day's horse ride apart; a group could travel in a grand loop through the mountains from either East Glacier or Belton (now West Glacier) from Great Northern train stations. Early tourism focused on horseback riding. Mary Roberts Rinehart described baccountry camps in her book *Through Glacier Park in 1915,* a colorful travelogue of touring the backcountry in the early years, noting that some camps had as many as eighty or more horses.

Hiking was also encouraged. Early travel posters and booklets by the Great Northern Railway featured romanticized scenes of delighted hikers on trails and posing in front of Glacier's iconic mountains. Early

These hardy horseback riders pause for a rest atop Piegan Pass. T. J. HILEMAN, COURTESY OF GLACIER NATIONAL PARK ARCHIVES.

photographers, such as T. J. Hileman, highlighted people striding through meadows lush with wildflowers and peering over cliffs. There was a Glacier Park Hiking Society that encouraged organized hiking activities and even awarded badges for different accomplishments. Glacier Park became known as a hiker's paradise with over 700 miles of trails winding through dramatic scenery.

Today, Glacier is not only routinely featured as a top national park in magazines such as *Outside* and *Backpacker* but gets specific coverage for its hiking and backpacking opportunities.

Except for the single Going-to-the-Sun Road that crosses the park and a few roads that dead-end in valleys around the perimeter, the vast majority of the 1 million–plus acres of park land is accessible only by foot or horse. National Park Service officials estimate that there are about 33,000 backcountry camper nights each year, mostly in July and August. There are many, many more visitors who do long backcountry day hikes, loops, and traverses, but their trips are not tracked. A 1988 study estimated the number of day users entering the backcountry at 200,000. Today, overall visitation to Glacier has increased sixty percent over 1988 levels, so it's likely that trail use has grown correspondingly.

HIKING ACCIDENTS AND DEATHS: YOU ARE NOT NECESSARILY SAFE ON THE TRAILS

Trails in Glacier National Park are well planned and well constructed but often wind through steep terrain and cliffs high above the valley floor. With only a few exceptions, there are no stone retaining walls, handrails, or cables for people to use even on sections of trail where there is some risk of injury or death from falling. With appropriate attention to where you are hiking, these trails are very safe. Deaths from falling off park trails have largely been due to human error and not the safety of the trails.

The first recorded death of a trail hiker was twenty-year-old Ester Peterson on June 29, 1924. A concession employee, she fell while hiking on Mount Altyn in the Many Glacier area. A year later, on July 13, 1925, Ben J. Cushing also fell while hiking. A visitor to the park, Cushing fell to his death from the trail leading to Sperry Chalet. The exact cause of these falling deaths is not recorded.

In 1960, a local newspaper documented the fate of another young man, Frederick Robert "Bob" Steinmetz, eighteen, from Detroit, Michigan, who was working as a clerk at the Swiftcurrent store. He was an art student, described as a courteous, clean-cut boy who went to church every Sunday. He joined Tom Linnerooth, nineteen, on July 28, 1960, to hike an ambitious twenty-three-mile loop from Swiftcurrent to Redgap Pass and back to Many Glacier via the Ptarmigan Tunnel. At about 1 P.M., Steinmetz and Linnerooth stopped for a drink at a waterfall, and, it appears, Linnerooth got his drink on the uphill side of the trail, whereas Steinmetz went to the other side. Linnerooth heard Steinmetz yell and turned to see him fall 100 feet to the rocks below and land in shallow water. Still alive, Steinmetz was unconscious and bleeding from cuts on his head. Linnerooth cleaned the blood off with his T-shirt that he soaked in the stream and then headed for help, reaching the Many Glacier Ranger Station at 5:30 P.M. The initial rescue team was put together quickly and hiked the eight miles to the accident scene with Linnerooth guiding them. They arrived at 9 P.M. to find Steinmetz dead. Rescue personnel concluded that he had probably died within an hour of the accident. Numerous rescuers were needed in shifts to carry Steinmetz out by stretcher, arriving at the road at 1:40 A.M.

It should be noted here that body recoveries in the backcountry, when helicopters are unavailable or inappropriate, need a lot of people and are tremendously hard work. Carrying out a victim or body has been described as a sweat fest and one that often extends into and through the night. The allure of search and rescue work for those heroically inclined often wears out quickly when the reality sinks in that it is one percent thrill and ninety-nine percent hard labor.

The newspaper story on Steinmetz continued, "This is the first mountain death we've reported in Glacier where there appears to be no particular violation of general safety precautions. Steinmetz stopped at the side of the trail to get a drink and wash his face in the stream. He slipped on a wet rock and tumbled. Other deaths of this type involved instances of young people climbing off trails and taking extreme risks, and there was a case where one young man was sliding down a snowfield and couldn't stop. These young people are the pick of the nation, healthy, happy, and promising much for the future. Our thoughts are with the parents who had to receive a message: 'Mr. and Mrs. Steinmetz, your son is dead.'"

In 1976, another hiker fell along this same spot on the trail near Redgap Pass, suffering a serious injury. Jack Potter, now retired after a forty-two-year career in the park, was one of the response team that provided care until the injured person was evacuated by helicopter.

Another case of falling off a trail may be attributable to an inattentive moment and a slip with tragic consequences. Kenneth Gelston, twenty-two, was an honor student at Stanford University law school and was working for his fifth year at Rising Sun Inn on the east side of the park near St. Mary Lake. He was regarded as a "careful" individual and a "wonderful fellow" by the current and previous managers. On a Saturday afternoon, July 25, 1964, he was hiking with a fellow employee near the top of St. Mary Falls, which cascades fifty feet down to a pool at the base. His companion, Virginia Finney, was ahead but not too far ahead to hear him yell "Oh, no." When she turned around, he was gone. She did not see him fall, but the only place he could have fallen was into the St. Mary River, which was still swollen from snowmelt. Because there was moss near the point of his fall, it was assumed that he had slipped and plunged into the river below. His body was not found despite a multiday search of the swirling waters. SCUBA divers were brought in to search the pool, estimated to be fifteen feet deep and twenty feet across, but visibility was poor in the frothy and turbulent water. Nonetheless, the searchers were pretty sure that the body was not in the pool, and it was unlikely to have floated downriver where the river spreads out and is shallow. The searchers even used block and tackle to pull a large log out to see if Gelston's body was trapped underneath. They used grapple hooks and brought in small boats. All to no avail. Gelston's body was never found.

Another incident in the same vicinity occurred in July 2007. Matthew Kohn had recently returned from Costa Rica and was working for an educational institute that led field trips into the park. He was leading a group of students from Texas that had hiked about two miles on the trail to St. Mary Falls, and, where the trail was next to the river, one boy decided to show off with an attention-getting stunt by "falling" into the water somewhat intentionally. Young and rambunctious boys are well known for such horseplay, but it is unlikely he knew what he was getting into. Kohn recalled that the shock of cold water had an immediate effect on the boy, who started to helplessly float downriver in the current. Kohn yelled at him from shore and walked downstream parallel to the student, commanding him to swim, which he did. After the young boy got himself to a sandy bank, Kohn waded in to get the student, who was shaking with cold after mere minutes in the water. With the help of other students who donated dry clothes, they dried and warmed him and then hiked him back to their van. The boy's impulsive action as the joker of the class came close to being his last. He had no idea that swift and very cold water could leave you gasping immediately, slowing movements needed for swimming. In fact, a person has as little as five minutes in cold water before effective swimming is diminished, even less if fully clothed. People in cold water without a life jacket eventually just sink because they can't kick or swim with their arms. What seemed like a trivial prank came scarily close to being a tragedy.

In August 1965, an accident occurred at Trick Falls (now renamed Running Eagle Falls) in the Two Medicine Valley. The "trick" to Trick Falls is that most of the water emerges from a channel about halfway up a cliff, but there is enough flow in the creek above for a second cascade to flow from the top of the cliff, especially in spring and early summer. Thus, two waterfalls are formed that join halfway down to plunge into the pool at the bottom. The falls are along a maintained trail not far from the road, and it is a popular place to stop. Laurie Jean Van Mun, six, was with her father, two brothers, and a friend, exploring off the trail near the top of the falls. They had been camping at Two Medicine on their way to Idaho from Wisconsin. About 1 P.M. she lost her footing and plunged about ninety feet onto rocks. Two shocked park visitors who were at the base of the waterfalls retrieved her body and attempted CPR but without success. The little girl was dead. The county coroner, William Riddle, stated that Van Mun received severe neck and head injuries and multiple fractures of arms and legs. He believed she was dead when her broken body reached the pool of water at the bottom of the waterfall. An August 6, 1965, *Hungry Horse News* article reported that "District Ranger Robert Frauson noted that there have been seven serious injuries or deaths in the past five years from persons being off maintained park trails near water-falls and falling."

Very similar tragedies occurred about thirty years later. Twice more, hikers slipped while trying to fill water bottles along the trail to Redgap Pass in 1998, one fatally. In mid-July 1998, Brian Donald-Nelson, twenty-seven, of Seattle was hiking the trail to Redgap Pass with his wife and two other companions. Along the way, they stopped near a waterfall and rested. Donald-Nelson decided to replenish their water and went to the stream above the waterfall to fill up. (Wet rocks at the edge of streams or in streams are often coated with algae and are extremely slippery. One of the authors of this book took a fifty-foot slide down a stream when he tried to get water. The rocks in the shallow stream were so slippery that he was helpless to stop himself for several long seconds.) Donald-Nelson may not have been aware of how slippery such footing can be, and he slipped on the wet rocks and fell about 150 feet to his death.

A month later, a second hiker slipped and fell down the same water-fall. This cascade is one and one-half miles southeast of Redgap Pass and is almost certainly the same waterfall that Steinmetz fell down in 1960, thirty-eight years earlier. Erik Von Ranson, thirty-two, of Manhattan, New York, was with a hiking party and, while trying to filter water, went over the waterfall and fractured his skull and ribs, as well as fracturing and dislocating his hip in an estimated forty-foot fall. Although severely injured, he didn't die from this fall. His fellow hikers did what they could to keep him as comfortable as possible while one of the hikers went for help. A group of Boy Scouts from Redmond, Washington, happened upon the scene and provided first-aid care, stabilizing Von Ranson's hip and rib injuries. It took eight hours from the time of the accident for help to arrive. Because of the accident location, a Canadian helicopter and team was called in to extract him from the ravine below the waterfall. They lowered a rescuer from the hovering helicopter. Von Ranson was secured in a special rescue bag and flown to a second helicopter that took him to a hospital in Kalispell. He eventually recovered from his injuries. After this second recent accident, the park placed a warning sign at the spot along the trail. However, many other unsigned sections of trails pose the same hazard for hikers. All hikers should exercise care and vigilance to recognize slipping hazards near water.

In May 2016, another death occurred at Running Eagle Falls in the Two Medicine area of the park, fifty-one years after the little girl fell to her death there. This time, a twenty-six-year-old Blackfeet man, Clint Cory Not Afraid, from Browning, Montana, was fatally injured when he jumped from the cliff and landed feet first in the shallow pool below the waterfall. National Park Service authorities reported no suspicious circumstances to this leap such as suicide or foul play. It appeared to be of his own volition and, given the likely height of his jump, suggests that he was living up to his name by taking this daring leap. Unfortunately, the pool was not deep enough to accommodate his momentum and he was severely injured. Park rangers responded to an emergency call and were there in minutes to perform CPR on Not Afraid but to no avail. Emergency medical personnel who arrived on the scene an hour later declared that he was dead.

Mel Ruder, the editor of the *Hungry Horse News*, frequently used the report of another death in Glacier National Park to lament the trend he saw of nearly annual deaths of young people who venture off-trail. In 1966, an exception to that trend was the deaths of two clergy who were not young. On July 29, a Friday morning, a Catholic priest, Rev. Father Joseph H. DeVaney, fifty-two, was hiking up the slope of Mount Oberlin west of Logan Pass. He was more than a mile away from maintained trails at Logan Pass and was wearing canvas sneakers. A member of the Audubon Society, DeVaney was out early to bird-watch and was on a fairly steep slope with many small, crumbly cliff bands. At some point while watching birds, he slipped and fell about twenty-five feet over one of these cliff bands and then rolled another seventy feet. Although no one witnessed the fall, coroner Sol Catron said that his death was caused during the fall based on DeVaney's massive head injuries. DeVaney had been traveling alone and was not reported missing, but the day after his fall, a U.S. Forest Service employee, hiking with a friend up Mount Oberlin, stumbled across his body. The clergyman was still holding a bird guide in his hand.

Mel Ruder reported, "Glacier averages nearly one death a year from falls on mountains. Almost always it is a person from age 18 to 22, not walking on established trails. Frequently they lack adequate shoes, as did Father DeVaney."

Exactly two weeks later, a second priest fell to his death near Logan Pass only a half mile from where Father DeVaney died. A somewhat dramatic headline by Ruder proclaimed, "History of Glacier National Park will tell of the death by falls of two priests in the summer of 1966." Father Paul F. Schreiber, thirty-seven, was a chaplain at St. Anthony's Hospital in Fort Dodge, Kansas, and chancellor of the diocese there. On August 13, 1966, he was traveling through Glacier Park with a young man, Marlin Werner, also of Dodge City. Schreiber parked his car along the Going-to-the-Sun Road near Logan Pass in the Oberlin Bend area. He got out of his car and left the road to get a view of the Garden Wall, hiking a short distance toward the edge of the cliff. This spot is where Logan Creek, draining waters from the pass area, goes under the road and emerges to plunge down cliffs to the valley below. Werner, nineteen, admonished Schreiber to be careful as he was admiring the view on a slope near the edge of the cliff. Then, disaster struck. According to the *Hungry Horse News,* "A rock gave way from under his right foot. The priest fell backward toward the sloping edge of the cliff and tried desperately to arrest his fall with his hands." Despite clawing at the loose rocky debris, Schreiber slid thirty feet and over the cliff edge even as Werner scrambled down to assist him. "The young man saw the priest strike a lower ledge and disappear from sight." Werner then urgently called (likely screamed) over the cliff without receiving any answer. Schreiber fell over 150 feet and was killed, his body later being found under a small waterfall. The ensuing body recovery took advantage of a helicopter being used in another part of the park for construction of a telephone system. Schreiber's body was carried farther down the rugged terrain from where it was found until a relatively flat place was reached where the helicopter could land. Although Schreiber's death was not while hiking per se, his unfortunate fate underscores the consequences of small events (a rock giving way underfoot) turning into fatal outcomes when they occur above cliffs and steep terrain.

One last story serves to illustrate how seemingly small decisions while hiking on trails can lead to big consequences. Nicholas Ryan, thirty, of Omaha, Nebraska, was hiking with friends on a summer's day on the trail to Grinnell Glacier, which winds up steep slopes and through cliff bands as it climbs from Lake Josephine to Upper Grinnell Lake and the glacier. This trail in the Many Glacier area is one that opens all the way to the glacier somewhat later than other trails in the park due to late-lying snowfields that cover the trail and block the way forward. Some years, the trail crew has to use explosives to blow up part of the last snowfield that covers the trail. They then hand-shovel a tread for hikers to use across the snowfield. Without this extra effort, the path to Grinnell might not otherwise open until nearly August. And this trail is very popular since it is one of the few that takes hikers to a glacier and back in a single day's hike. At these elevations, the nights can still be cold enough to reach freezing, making the snowfields hard and slippery in the mornings. This likely isn't on the mind of a hiker seeking to get to their destination up the trail. On June 28, park officials had posted a "snow hazard" sign at the trailhead advising against travel on this trail. The trail was not scheduled for clearing until the end of July. But many park visitors want to get up close to a glacier, and their frustration is understandable when, on a warm midsummer day, they encounter a sign warning of snow hazards. That might have been the case with Nicholas and his friends when they went beyond the sign at the trailhead and began their hike. On the morning of July 18, 2011, Nicholas was crossing a steep snowfield when he slid 50 to 100 feet, stopping where the snow ended in rocks and boulders at the bottom. He sustained severe injuries, including to his head. The fall was reported just before noon to an interpretive park ranger leading a hike elsewhere along the trail. The ranger called in the incident by radio, mobilizing other rangers and personnel from the Kalispell Regional Medical Center's ALERT helicopter. Little could be done, and Nicholas died of his injuries from the fall and was pronounced dead at 1:53 P.M., barely two hours after his slide. Eric Ryan, Nicholas' brother, was told that he died instantly from the fall, but this was not verified.

To many people, this unfortunate death may have seemed more poignant because friends described Ryan as a great family man, leaving behind a wife and two young daughters. He owned a fitness facility in Omaha, which his family described as a dream of his. A statement from Ryan's family said, "Nick lived life with adventure and no regrets, lived each day to the fullest with a contagious smile for all people he came in contact with. Nick never found an obstacle too large or big and never did anything half way, always with excellence. Nick was a caring loving example that was rare and precious to his family and friends."

The dangers of snowfields were very clear in another incident involving a park service employee. The Highline Trail begins at Logan Pass and traverses steep slopes and subalpine meadows above and parallel to the Going-to-the-Sun Road on the west side of the park. It is very popular because of the terrific scenery, but the trail is exposed in a number of places. Efforts are made to open it to the public as early as possible because of its popularity. Trail crews deal with the remaining snow patches that cover the trail in early summer, shoveling or blasting them out with explosives before they are deemed safe to cross.

Morgan Bell, thirty-one, was a veteran member of a Glacier National Park trail crew and was on a five-member team working to clear sections of debris and make trail repairs on the Highline Trail, which was not yet opened. On July 3, 2012, as they were returning to Logan Pass, Bell slipped on a snowbank that covered the trail and immediately slid about 200 feet. Although trained to self-arrest under these circumstances, Bell dropped her tools and was left to slow her descent with only her hands and boots furiously scrabbling in the snow. But the snow was too firm and, unable to stop herself, she quickly reached the end of the snowfield. Previously, snowplows had cut through the snow while clearing the road, leaving a vertical drop of twelve to fifteen feet at the end of the snowfield. Bell flew off the end of the snowfield and dropped onto rocky debris by the side of the road as carloads of tourists were wending their way to the pass. She was severely injured and was initially stabilized by responding park rangers, then treated by an ambulance crew before being airlifted from the park by the ALERT helicopter to Kalispell Regional Medical Center. Despite some head injuries, which are always of grave concern, she was listed in stable condition. Undoubtedly, Bell's attempts to use her boots, arms, and legs slowed her enough to prevent even worse injuries and helped her survive. Four days later, in the intensive care unit, she was making remarkable improvements in her recovery. The park temporarily suspended all employee travel over snowfields immediately following the accident until a full investigation was completed.

The *Missoulian* reported that "this is the second incident this year where a hiker has been injured after sliding down a snowfield. In June, a 21-year-old female climber fell on a snowfield and was unable to self-arrest with an ice ax while climbing Mount Sinopah in Two Medicine. The woman slid about 200 feet across the snow and down a 10-foot cliff band. She received only minor injuries, although she required medical attention."

One of this book's authors also slipped several times while crossing snowfields at the base of Swiftcurrent Glacier after summiting Mount Grinnell. She was wearing light trail shoes without aggressive lugs or treads, and the snow was too firm to kick good steps. She was carrying an ice axe. Each time she slipped she was able to perform quick self-arrests because of her ice axe training. And that's a good thing, because the snowfields ended above a 1,000-foot cliff! This unnerving incident and the others described earlier serve to emphasize how potentially deadly snow crossings can be. Hikers need to assess them carefully, have good footwear, carry an ice axe, and possess the practiced skill to use it.

The very attributes that make Glacier visually compelling also make it deadly.

There are numerous ways that park managers attempt to alert visitors to the risks. Ranger Charlie Logan (no relation to Colonel Logan, the first park superintendent and for whom Logan Pass is named) analyzed the data and found that a high percentage of the search and rescues were for national park employees and park concession employees. He then

Ranger Charlie Logan's blaze orange "Deadly Beauty" bandanna features survival tips and lists essential items hikers should carry on every outing on Glacier's trails. COURTESY OF DAN FAGRE.

devised and promoted a "Deadly Beauty" bandanna that was given to employees. A blaze orange color, similar to hunter's orange, the bandanna had useful backcountry hiking and rescue advice printed on it. Its color made it easy to spot by rescuers, and the bandanna's purpose was to remind people that the backcountry can be dangerous as well as beautiful.

After a few years of handing out the bandannas (and similarly themed posters), the cost of search and rescue operations in the park declined. Charlie's inspiration and successful campaign earned a safety award and accolades from the National Park Service community.

Not all deaths from falling off a trail involve hiking. Glacier Park has a long history of horseback riding, and this was the primary mode of travel when the park was founded. Reputedly, the park's stables had 1,000 horses and transported 10,000 people per year in the early years after Glacier's founding in 1910. That seems like a lot of horses and riders, but consider that at that time the park had no roads except around the boundaries and in the lower valleys. Although much less common now, horseback riders still explore the high country by trail.

Joe Cosley was one of Glacier's first rangers, surviving close calls with Mother Nature and, later as a poacher, the law. COURTESY OF GLACIER NATIONAL PARK ARCHIVES.

An early close call while traveling by horse in Glacier occurred while Joe Cosley was on duty as one of the first rangers. Cosley is most well-known for later becoming a poacher and making a daring escape from the law. As described in *Man in Glacier*, acting superintendent R. H. Chapman wrote in 1912, "Ranger Cosley . . . when returning to his station after a conference at headquarters, attempted Ahern Pass. While crossing the pass a snow-covered ledge broke off and he narrowly escaped with his life. The horse he was riding and his pack horse were instantly killed, falling hundreds of feet into the canyon beneath."

One horse rider wasn't as lucky as Cosley. In July 1998, Connie Lindsey, forty-seven, of Polson, Montana, was riding her horse up the trail to Ptarmigan Tunnel from Many Glacier on the east side of the park.

Lindsey was in a small group of horse riders that included her husband and two others. The trail offers a dramatic view as it ascends and then goes through the tunnel. This tunnel was necessary because trail builders could find no safe route along the cliffs to the ridgetop and over to the other side. Once through the tunnel, a person steps outs onto a small, flat area rimmed with a low, stone wall. Beyond is a sheer cliff. Almost everyone pauses there to take photos. What happened next is described by *The Inside Trail* fall 1998 newsletter (published by the Glacier National Park Foundation) and has to be one of the most freakish incidents in the history of Glacier Park. When the group reached the tunnel, they dismounted and led their horses through the dark, 250-foot passage. On the other side, overlooking Elizabeth Lake, they remained dismounted. A little way down the trail from the tunnel, Lindsey stopped to take a picture. Her horse was close by, eating snow from a snowbank, when it suddenly jerked. As reported in *The Inside Trail*, "It knocked Lindsay [*sic*] onto the retaining wall, then lost its footing and fell on top of her. Horse and rider both rolled over the wall and fell for hundreds of feet. Lindsay's [*sic*] husband rode to Many Glacier to get help. Rangers helicoptered to an area below the cliffs. They climbed up dangerous pitches of scree and snow to recover Lindsay's [*sic*] body from a chimney in the rocks." Later, the trail crew dynamited the horse's carcass to prevent it from attracting grizzlies to the area near the trail.

DEATHS AND ACCIDENTS DUE TO CLIMBING

Falling deaths, accidents, and rescues are major events in Glacier and receive a lot of attention because they often involve spectacular rescue efforts and body recoveries. It makes sense that falling is a major source of fatalities and accidents because of the inspiring terrain with a combination of high verticality (courtesy of the work of glaciers and uplifting) and crumbly rock (courtesy of the ancient sea where the rocks were formed). These factors make Glacier's mountains more challenging from a safety standpoint than other mountains where the rock is firmer. Combine these factors with the nearly 3 million people who enter the

When she came to Glacier in 1926, British climber Dorothy Pilley bagged twenty-five peaks in nineteen days, here with Hans Reiss, leading, and I. A. Richard, below.
T. J. HILEMAN, COURTESY OF GLACIER NATIONAL PARK ARCHIVES.

park each year, many of whom take to the hills with a relative dearth of experience, and you have obvious potential for trouble and tragedy.

In addition to the natural tendency of people to climb and be drawn to mountain summits, a culture of climbing was specifically encouraged here by the Great Northern Railway and later entrepreneurs. The railway commissioned artists and photographers to create images of the mountains and to include apparently happy and carefree people in dramatic scenery. "The Call of the Mountains" was basically an advertising campaign using sponsored artists to draw people to the park for mountain adventure. Campaign sponsors even hired Swiss guides to take clients up mountains in much the same way as was done in Europe. They also brought Dorothy Pilley, a prominent female climber, to the park from England in 1926. She spent time scaling dramatic cliffs while roped to a Swiss guide, Hans Reiss, and being photographed by Ray Bell for maximum dramatic effect. Pilley climbed twenty-five peaks in nineteen days. Her book, *Climbing Days*, describes her adventures in Glacier Park and elsewhere in the western United States and undoubtedly provided inspiration for other young women to heed "the call of the mountains."

Early explorers, working for either the U.S. government or Great Northern Railway, climbed many of the park's mountains to conduct surveys for mapping or to photograph the landscape. Recreational climbers also came to Glacier in the park's early years, with many first ascents notched by Norman Clyde and groups he led. However, it was after World War II that climbing by amateurs really took off, and the number of climbers in the park increased dramatically. The U.S. Army's 10th Mountain Division, which was formed during the war for conducting mountain warfare, introduced many Americans to climbing concepts and techniques that weren't as common in the United States before that. In addition, a great deal of surplus clothing and gear from the war was available, inexpensive, and suitable for climbing. The first published climbing guide to Glacier was published in 1960 by J. Gordon Edwards, an entomology professor from California, who began documenting climbing routes while he spent his summers working as a naturalist ranger in the park and also collected insects for research. Many of the book's editions recorded the increasing number of climbing routes and variations, and Gordon provided many colorful anecdotes of first ascents and other adventures. As more people began climbing recreationally, the need for climbers to socialize, exchange information, find climbing partners, and introduce people to climbing became obvious. To meet this need, Denis and Shirley Twohig and Gordon Edwards formed the Glacier Mountaineering Society in 1981. This society has organized climbs that members can sign up for and encourages less experienced people to gain the knowledge and confidence to climb on their own. So-called gravity sports are inherently dangerous and can only be made safer up to a point. However, by mentoring climbers and imparting insights on good judgment in the mountains, the Glacier Mountaineering Society is a helpful counterpoint to blissfully unaware tourists, people who ignore warnings, and those who take deliberate risks above their abilities. (Edwards himself collapsed and died just outside the park boundary on July 19, 2004, at the age of eighty-four while starting to climb Divide Mountain.)

There are several categories of climbing that are important to distinguish. The first is going off-trail to scramble and explore terrain, whether to get to a remote lake or ascend to a ridge for a photographic opportunity. There are numerous appealing traverses in Glacier, such as the Floral Park traverse, that link various basins over unmarked passes and through notches. Another category is climbing on glaciers, which are a destination for many people who find these ice masses to be charismatic. With 175 peaks and summits in Glacier Park, it is not surprising that mountain climbing, or "peak bagging," is one of the first things that adventurous souls want to do when they visit. This type of climbing does not involve highly technical climbing or extensive climbing gear beyond a helmet to thwart loose rocks and an ice axe for the occasional snow crossing. The last type of climbing, relatively uncommon in Glacier, is full-on technical climbing with ropes and hardware. This latter category includes an increasingly popular sport—ice climbing, usually on frozen waterfalls.

OFF-TRAIL HIKING, SCRAMBLING, AND CLIMBING INCIDENTS

On July 29, 1955, after a spate of young people had recently died by either scrambling off trails and falling or dying while climbing, the following editorial appeared in the *Hungry Horse News*.

> *Prayer in Glacier National Park is for the Lord to help keep venturesome 20-year-olds alive and well. We know no better place in the world for a 20-year-old to spend a summer. When we meet these youngsters on the trails, bronzed and quick to step, we can't help but think there is improvement in the human race. Then every summer, almost without exception, one of our grim jobs is to telephone wire services and daily newspapers telling them of the death or serious injury to one of these young people, usually summer employees. They went off trails and ventured dangerous slopes.*

This editorial was paired with an article describing the death of June Johnson, twenty, from South Euclid, Ohio. This was the mountain tragedy of 1955 in Glacier National Park. Johnson was killed when she slipped and plunged 1,000 feet from high on the slopes of Mount Altyn in Many Glacier Valley. The newspaper's editor, Mel Ruder, goes on to note the deaths of Peter Kasen, eighteen, Robert Dion, seventeen, and Robert Stokes, eighteen, in the past few years (1950-1954) and concludes, "They died and their stories differ from that of Miss Johnson's only in the details." The pattern of climbing deaths occurring among concession employees was noted in the local paper many more times.

As a twenty-year-old, George Bristol arrived in Glacier National Park in 1961 from Texas. Now in his seventies, Bristol allowed us to interview him about his early experiences. He was hired onto one of the early summer trail crews that year; it was his first time in Glacier National Park. After a week of paperwork and settling in, Bristol attended a week of dynamite school. On June 21, he and the other men who had started work thus far in the season were asked to go up Mount Henkel to look for two missing young men, James F. Moylan and Douglas L. Krueger, who both worked at Swiftcurrent Motor Inn for Glacier Park, Inc., the park's concessioner. Bristol recalled that he had shown up with an old pair of slip-on motorcycle boots and had been so busy that he'd had no chance to get to town to buy sturdy trail boots. They all started up in the morning, searching from the bottom and working their way up with great effort. Because of his inadequate footwear, Bristol struggled while trying to hike over the mountain slope that was very slippery with fine shale scree. About noon they found one young man. He was alive but delirious and kept insisting that his friend had fallen below him. The search continued with a renewed effort below where this man was found. Late in the afternoon, around 4 P.M., Bristol happened to look up and saw some large birds circling high above a section of the slope. He got on the radio and said in his fine Texan accent, "Have y'all got any buzzard-like birds here in the park?" Somebody replied, "Well yes there is." Bristol responded, "Well then, I know where that boy is." When they reached him, he was dead from the fall that had occurred the night before. As they prepared to bring the body off the mountain, they looked down and a huge crowd had formed at the Swiftcurrent parking lot, "gawkers" who "were ready to look at dead bodies." So they filled a litter with blankets to make it look like there was a body under the covers and sent the decoy litter with one team down the mountain to the parking lot. The second team descended in relative obscurity with all the focus on the first team. They then slipped away on the trail that leads away from Swiftcurrent parallel to the road and reached a waiting vehicle before the crowd got wise to the trick. The consideration and dignity afforded the dead man by this ruse was appreciated by all who have heard the tale.

George Bristol also colorfully described District Ranger Bob Frauson's warning that you never leave the trail if you want to live. Bob Frauson had recently transferred from Rocky Mountain National Park, where he had been responsible for climbing rescues on Longs Peak. According to Bristol, Frauson was already quite famous as a mountaineer and had been in the 10th Mountain Division during World War II. During the training and orientation of the trail crew, concession employees, and others new to the park the week before the death on Mount Henkel, Frauson told them not to get off the trail and if you *do* get off the trail—at that point Frauson dramatically threw a body bag onto the table so that it rolled out with a snap. Bristol chuckled that it was such effective high drama that "girls cried and boys weeped," but apparently the lesson lasted only a week for Moylan and Krueger.

TRAVERSES

In addition to off-trail scrambling, exploring, and climbing, many hikers attempt to traverse ridges and difficult terrain to link one basin to another or one peak climb to another. Toma Jercinovic was doing just that in July 1996 when he extended an intended solo day hike up Mount Jackson (although his name was not found in the summit register) and continued hiking past Lake Ellen Wilson in a twenty-mile traverse toward Edwards Mountain near Sperry Glacier. He was later reported missing. After a five-day intensive search, Jack Potter, one of the searchers in a helicopter, spotted his body on the last flight of the last day of the search operation. Jercinovic was at the base of a waterfall, in the water, above upper Snyder Lake. Potter, ranger Charlie Logan, and others evacuated the body.

Jercinovic, twenty-two, was an avid mountaineer; his friend, Jeff Vick, said that Jercinovic generously shared his skills and knowledge with others. In a *Hungry Horse News* article of August 20, Vick said, "It's hard to lose your teacher, someone whose primary focus was on safety, to an accident." Although there is much speculation about Jercinovic's thinking and plans, Vick thinks that Jercinovic decided to find his way down the steep cirque at the head of the Snyder Lake drainage that comes off Edwards Mountain very close to the Little Matterhorn. This is a fairly technical route, and Jercinovic would have been exhausted after a presumed ascent of Mount Jackson and the long hike to Edwards Mountain. Vick believes that Jercinovic had almost finished the difficult part when he fell 150 feet to his death. Ironically, one of the authors was climbing Mount Brown that same evening with his oldest daughter, and they were directly across Snyder Basin when they clearly heard someone give a single yell or cry in the distance. This could have been the time Jercinovic was descending and when he got into trouble. Was it Jercinovic? We will never know. In any event, Jercinovic's death was particularly poignant for his friends because of his clear love of mountains and climbing and the special efforts he made to help others enjoy mountains through mentoring and teaching. Perhaps he underestimated the risks, especially of climbing alone, though he had talked to Vick about the risk of dying in the mountains.

One of the more popular off-trail traverses in the park is the Floral Park traverse. This ramble in alpine country starts at Logan Pass, descends past Hidden Lake, then climbs up to a divide and angles across slopes to Sperry Glacier. Continuing past the glacier, hikers gain Comeau Pass and a trail that descends past Sperry Chalet to Lake McDonald. It's a long day, and hikers need some navigational skills even under sunny skies. But sunny skies cannot be counted on in Glacier Park. In the mid-1990s, Samantha (Sam to her friends), a Glacier National Park seasonal ranger and an experienced mountaineer, was solo hiking the Floral Park traverse when dense fog enveloped her. Sam wisely waited for the fog to clear because she knew that with no visual clues, it was easy to convince yourself of a way through the fog only to end up in trouble. The fog settled in and so did Sam. She had to wait it out through the night, and by that time she was reported missing. Charlie Logan recalled that by the next morning the fog began to lift and searchers aboard a helicopter found her, cold and exhausted from an unplanned night's exposure. She was already moving under her own power but accepted the rescuer's offer to fly out. The wise choices made by Sam stand in contrast to the more common responses of people to get more lost in an attempt to solve their problem, but Sam avoided that folly well.

MISSING PERSON

- Yi-Jien Hwa
- 27 year old male
- 6' 1" 170 lbs
- Blue Kelty Backpack
- Treking Poles
- Thought to have left Logan Pass 8/11/2008: Last Known Point St. Mary
- Possible Routes:
  - Floral Park
  - Gunsight Pass Trail
  - Highline to Goat Haunt
  - Goat Haunt to Kintla Lake

If you have any information or have seen Mr. Hwa please contact Glacier National Park at 406-888-7801

Despite a massive initial search, three years passed between Yi-Jien Hwa's disappearance and the discovery of his remains. COURTESY OF GLACIER NATIONAL PARK.

The Floral Park traverse was one of the first objectives of Yi-Jien Hwa, twenty-seven, who had planned a long and taxing backpack trip through some of Glacier Park's most stunning terrain during August 2008. Hwa was originally from Malaysia and was a seminary student in Kentucky. He was an avid and experienced backpacker with trips to such places as Kentucky's Red River Gorge, Michigan's Isle Royale National Park, Hawaii's Big Island, the Smoky Mountains in North Carolina and Tennessee, and the Appalachian Trail to his credit. Hwa planned his itinerary carefully for his weeklong, ninety-seven-mile hike. When his wife had to back out of the hike for health reasons, he decided to do this trek solo. He left Logan Pass on August 11, 2008, and expected to reach the Sperry backcountry campground that same day. Because of his multiday itinerary ending on August 18, it wasn't until August 21 that his family called the park to report that he was overdue and missing. No one rec-ollected seeing him at the backcountry campground on the evening of August 11, and his mid-trip resupply was still in his parked car at Logan Pass. It seemed he had vanished on the Floral Park traverse. One of the longer and more intense searches in park history was initiated as search and rescue personnel scoured the rugged terrain along the traverse.

Despite rigorous efforts by personnel from several agencies and more than 2,500 hours spent on the search, no sign of Hwa was found. There were many theories about what happened. Because Hwa seemed to vanish without a trace, some people speculated that he had ventured onto Sperry Glacier and fallen into a crevasse. In 2008, the crevasses were deep enough that their blue-black depths could have easily hidden a body; it could be many years before the glacier's relentless forward creep would deliver any remains at the bottom of the glacier. The unsuccessful search was scaled back in September, and rangers continued to follow up on leads as they arose.

Finally, three years later on July 3, 2011, hikers John and Christopher Wagner were exploring a remote part of the Avalanche Lake basin off the Floral Park traverse and came across some clothing in a section of steep cliffs. They reported their finding to rangers. Investigating rangers recovered some human bone fragments that they shipped to a lab for DNA analysis. Other found items at the site matched the equipment that Hwa had started out with. His wife and mother were contacted.

In June 2012, the results came back: the bone fragments were all that was left of Mr. Hwa. The investigation was closed and part of the mystery was solved. What had gone wrong? There was one unconfirmed report of other hikers seeing a small light on August 11 on the cliffs above where Hwa's remains were found. These cliffs were not part of the Floral Park traverse. Had he gotten off course and continued to downclimb dangerous terrain until he fell? Those details will never be known, but it was the unfortunate end for Hwa. His would not be the last death along the Floral Park traverse.

The same trouble in route finding that was fatal for Hwa also occurred in 2015 when two female employees of the park attempted the Floral Park traverse and wandered into the steep, cliffy terrain above Avalanche Lake. Following is the press release from Glacier National Park, which also serves as an example of the primary way in which most accidents are conveyed to the press and to the public.

TWO MISSING HIKERS LOCATED

Date: September 1, 2015
Contact: Michelle Fidler
Contact: Katie Liming

WEST GLACIER, MONT. – Two missing hikers have been located at Glacier National Park. The two female hikers are employees in the Science and Resource Management Division at Glacier National Park. A friend of one employee and a family member of the other employee both contacted park staff to report the overdue hikers early Monday morning, August 31, after the two had not returned from a personal day hike Sunday night as planned.

Search efforts were launched Monday morning. Based on their planned itinerary, the search area was focused in the area between Logan Pass and Sperry Chalet. This high alpine area includes treacherous country filled with rock cliffs, waterfalls, wet and slippery rocks and boulders, and dense vegetation. A storm had moved through the area Sunday evening, resulting in inclement weather and limited visibility.

Several National Park Service ground search teams responded. The Flathead County Sheriff's Office and US Forest Service provided valuable aerial support. A park incident management team was organized to manage the search and rescue. More than 40 park staff and cooperators assisted.

Aerial search efforts were hampered Monday afternoon due to high winds and low visibility. However the two missing hikers were located late Monday on a cliff face above Avalanche Lake. The Flathead County Sheriff's Office's Two Bear Air Rescue helicopter hoisted the two injured hikers out of the area at approximately 7 am on Tuesday morning August 1, once daylight had arrived and the weather had improved. Both hikers had sustained a leg injury as a result of a fall. Park staff provided initial treatment. The hikers were then transported to the hospital for more definitive care.

The following factors contributed to the success of this rescue operation. The hikers had planned ahead and were prepared with proper footwear, clothing and equipment. They travelled as a pair. They were experienced hikers and were prepared for the challenging terrain. They also left their planned itinerary with someone, which greatly aided in timely search and rescue response.

Risk is inherent with backcountry travel in Glacier National Park and there is no guarantee for visitor safety. Significant hazards include stream and river crossings, steep snowfields, precipitous cliffs and ledges, unstable sedimentary rock, dangerous wildlife, and ever-changing weather, including sudden snowstorms and lightning. The best insurance for a safe and enjoyable trip rests with your ability to exercise good judgment, avoid unnecessary risks, and assume responsibility for your own safety while visiting Glacier's backcountry.

All visitors are encouraged to use a voluntary day trip plan form, available on www.nps.gov/glac/planyourvisit/hikingthetrails.htm, which can be used to help search personnel concentrate search efforts along your intended route, saving critical time and possibly reducing risks to responders. Additional backcountry planning tips are available in the Glacier National Park Backcountry Guide, available on www.nps.gov/glac/planyourvisit/backcountry.htm.

GLACIERS

Although the glaciers in Glacier Park are quite small by global standards, people are still fascinated by them. This was true even during the period before the park was established when Lyman Sperry explored the glacier later to bear his name and George Bird Grinnell explored his namesake glacier. "Expeditions" were organized and led by guides in the 1920s, with many historic photographs showing a crowd roped together, peering into the depths of a glacial crevasse. Later in the century, National Park Service interpreters largely took over the role of helping people discover the park's glaciers. Despite the many thousands of people who have ventured onto the ice in the last century, only a few deaths and survival stories are documented.

One of the earliest glacier incidents was reported on Sperry Glacier before the park was established, in 1905 or 1906. Frank Liebig was working as a forest ranger, covering the western half of what would become the park. In 1910, Liebig was the first ranger appointed by then Glacier National Park superintendent, Colonel Logan. In both roles, Liebig was spread pretty thin and was on patrol much of the time. The following account appears in the book *The First Ranger*, which was compiled from journals, correspondence, and stories of Frank's life. Liebig often returned to Lake McDonald from St. Mary Lake by going over Gunsight Pass and the Sperry Glacier basin.

> On one of these trips coming in across Gunsight Pass,
> I came in late one evening into Sperry Glacier basin with
> my horses, ready to set up my tent for the night. I saw a
> crowd of people a little ways off and heard someone saying
> "There is the ranger now." And soon people came run-
> ning over and said a woman had fallen into a crevasse in
> Sperry Glacier and they didn't know how to get her out. In
> the meanwhile they had sent a man down to the hotel ten
> miles away to get some ropes. No telephone on the Forest
> yet. The first telephone was installed from Belton to the
> hotel in 1910.

When the people told me about the woman falling into the crevasse, I turned the horses loose in a hurry and grabbed two lash ropes and the axe, and told the men to "come on."

The place was a quarter of a mile to the edge of the glacier, and about 250 yards across the ice to the crevasse. I cut a stunted green fir tree four or five inches across and five feet long, and had the men pack it along. When we got to the glacier three or four men stood at the place where the woman slid in. Two women and three more men came along, with them a minister of the gospel by the name of Falls—a real mountaineer. He died in Seattle two years later. I selected a place on the lower side of the crevasse and chopped a deep hole in the ice and set the green post into the hole and packed ice all around to make it fairly solid. I tied the two lash ropes together and tied a number of knots into the rope for a good hand hold. Then I tied the rope to the post sticking above the ice and told a couple of men to hang onto the post so it couldn't slip out and threw the rope into the crevasse.

I could see the woman lying almost horizontal in the ice. The crevasse was about four or five feet wide on the top and came together to a knife edge on the bottom, about 35 feet down. She was wedged in at about 30 feet, and dead as a door nail. I slid down the rope, and had some sweat worked up, and when I got down into the crevasse was it cold! I tried to hang onto the rope and pull the woman loose but couldn't budge her. We thought she was dead anyway, so I stepped on her body to rest my feet and told the men to haul up the rope and send the axe down, which they did. Then I chopped a hole on each side of the ice big enough to put my feet in for a hold, then sent the axe up again to the top. When the rope came down again I started to pull the woman loose, and nearly pulled her arm out she was wedged in so tight. But I finally got her loose and managed to get the rope around her waist and the men pulled her up to the surface and then let the rope down again.

I was so frozen by this time I was in doubt that I could climb the rope so I put it under my arms and was hauled out by the men too. When I got out I could hardly stand up I was so cold and had to stamp around a bit to get my blood in circulation again.

We had plenty of help by this time. Someone brought a lantern and candles from the camp as it was getting dark. There was no stretcher so four men got hold of the woman, one on each leg and one on each arm, and one man went ahead with the lantern. When we got to the edge of the ice there was a narrow trail leading down through the rocks and around some cliffs, one cliff over twenty feet high. We thought it would be safer for all of us to let the body down on our rope over the cliff. Someone went ahead to receive the body below. They had a palouser going and we could see the light below. When the body was half-way down, the woman began to spin around and hit her head on the rocks, cutting quite a gash, which must have brought her to her senses because she let out an awful yell. Her terrible yell scared us half to death as we had all thought she was a goner for sure. Then she fainted again.

We finally got her to the camp where they had a big fire going and lots of hot coffee and lots more of hot drinks, and we all had our share of the hot brandy. Even the minister of the gospel and yours truly, even if I was on the water wagon. I had my share and don't know today how I got into my sleeping bag only half undressed. I think someone else must have helped me.

A doctor came up towards morning and pronounced the woman O.K. Some men and women filled her up all night with hot brandy until she was glorious drunk. We sure had a late breakfast next day.

Despite this somewhat quixotic tale and "glorious" outcome, crevasses are not to be trifled with. The ice surrounding them often slopes inward so that people wanting to lean over and look into the depths are increasingly likely to slip in. Crevasses are fairly vertical, depending on what part of the glacier you are on, and they narrow with depth so that people falling into them become wedged. Crevasses have claimed several lives in Glacier Park.

One incident involved very accomplished and competent skiers, which underscores the significant danger of crevasses. Ronald Bruce Matthews, thirty-two, and three friends decided to do a ski trip to Gunsight Mountain in August 1971. Ron was accompanied by Cliff Persons, thirty-four, Gene Evans, twenty-nine, and Edmund "Ed" Roy, twenty-three, all of whom were ski instructors or on the ski patrol at nearby Big Mountain Ski Area (now Whitefish Mountain Resort). According to an August 20 *Hungry Horse News* article, they hiked to the Sperry Chalet campground on Saturday, August 14, and were joined by Ron's wife and little daughter Sarah, who was just three. After camping overnight, Ron's wife and daughter started back down the trail to the Going-to-the-Sun Road and the men hiked up through Comeau Pass and climbed Gunsight Mountain. They had lunch a little before noon and enjoyed the sun and glacier vistas. They then skied the ridge from the summit to the top of Sperry Glacier with the intent that they would ski down the top portion, take skis off to negotiate the bergschrund—a large crevasse that forms when a glacier breaks over an underlying rock outcrop—near the top of the glacier, and then resume skiing below. They considered the snow conditions to be "good." Cliff Persons was in the lead with Ron Matthews behind him. Cliff stated, "It wasn't difficult going for an expert skier like Ron. However, Ron's skis slipped. It was near the top of the snow ridge. Ron slipped about six feet. Then he arrested himself with skis and poles, setting them hard." Unfortunately, Ron continued sliding down the steep slope and fell straight into the dark and cold crevasse, landing about forty feet below. Cliff immediately skied down and saw Ron below; he could hear him breathing. Ed Roy had watched from above and, after seeing the situation, took off to get help by skiing furiously down the glacier and then running four miles over rugged rocky terrain to the trail leading to Sperry Chalet. Using a radio at Sperry Chalet, he got a message to park headquarters at 2:08 P.M., probably only an hour after the fall—a remarkable physical feat. Meanwhile, Cliff and Gene Evans began chopping steps in the ice to reach Ron, who was still breathing.

By chance, helicopter pilot Bob Schellinger was working a fire on the Flathead National Forest, ferrying men to fight the fire, and Glacier National Park officials were able to redirect him to the rescue. Bob skillfully landed the helicopter on the narrow, snowy summit ridge of Gunsight carrying Rangers Jack Fewlass and Arthur Sedlack, both mountain rescue trained, with ropes and equipment by 3 P.M. Fewlass and Sedlack roped up and lowered themselves from the ridge to the lip of the crevasse where Evans and Persons had been waiting since the fall. There were no longer any sounds coming from Ron. The rangers rappelled into the crevasse, cut Ron's pack loose so they could work on him, and started performing CPR at about 4 P.M. Ranger Sedlack said, "It looked like he was dead, but how could we be sure?" The rangers described the intense cold, saying, "We were shivering even though wearing winter clothes. Our bodies against the glacier ice would create melt and wet." They also had the risk of ice and snow collapsing on them from above, and it was difficult to move in the tight space.

More aid arrived on subsequent helicopter flights, including Dr. Wade Covill, a Columbia Falls physician who had previously been an Air Force paramedic. He was able to descend into the crevasse at about 6 P.M. and confirm Ron Matthew's demise due to a skull fracture, other body fractures, and lengthy exposure to the cold. The body recovery began. Because of the constriction of the crevasse, it was difficult to get the stretcher in, retrieve gear, and haul the body out.

Meanwhile, Ron's wife and small daughter were still descending the Sperry trail. Two rangers intercepted them at about 3:40 P.M. and informed them of Ron's accident, not knowing at that time that Ron had died. Mrs. Matthews immediately rushed out and to the hospital in Kalispell hoping that the helicopter would be bringing her husband in alive, but, alas, it was Ron's body that arrived from the mountain that evening. The two skiers that had remained at the crevasse expressed surprise and high praise for the efficiency and skill of the helicopter pilot and responding rangers. They had expected much longer delays and were relieved at the relatively swift and knowledgeable response. One was quoted as saying, "These park men really know what to do on a glacier."

Before the accident, Ron and his family had planned to leave Montana to teach ceramics and metal arts at Rosary College in Forest, Illinois. Ron had attended school in Chicago, the University of Montana, Brooklyn Museum of Arts in New York, University of California at Berkeley, and Northern Illinois University. Even while working trails during the summer at Glacier National Park and being a ski instructor, he had found time to teach at Flathead Valley Community College. His likely successful career as an artist was cut short on a glorious day in the mountains with an errant slip on steep snow.

Another accident involving a bergschrund occurred on October 12, 1983, on Swiftcurrent Glacier. Ken Lynch and Steven Fernekes had been hiking and climbing in Glacier Park for a few days. They obtained a backcountry permit when they set out on the Highline Trail from Logan Pass on October 11—a fine day with fresh snow covering the higher elevations of the park. Ken, twenty-eight, and Steven, twenty-seven, both from Danbury, Connecticut, were having a grand time climbing and hiking in many parts of the park, and they hiked to Granite Park campground that day. They hiked to the Grinnell Glacier overlook the next day and saw eagles soaring above Grinnell Mountain and the ridge that divides the Swiftcurrent and Grinnell glacier basins. They climbed the long ridge to the 8,479-foot summit of Grinnell to view the eagle migration and then hiked north, thinking they could descend back to Swiftcurrent Pass. However, as they tried to descend, they encountered snow and ice plastered on the rocks. Armed only with ice axes, Fernekes was helping Lynch negotiate a ledge as they sought a route down and Lynch slid briefly before rocks stopped him. Fernekes reached for him but also fell, tumbling twenty-five feet, pausing briefly on rocks, and then falling out of sight. Lynch couldn't see or contact him and retreated back the way they had come, eventually hiking back to Granite Park Chalet where Lynch found park maintenance workers to radio the accident to park headquarters. An attempt was made to find Fernekes that night, but it became too dark to search. The next day, helicopter pilot Jim Kruger and park rangers saw that Fernekes' body was in the bergschrund and that he had fallen directly from the ridge into this icy chasm. A rescue team was flown in to the base of the glacier where it flattens somewhat, and the team extricated Fernekes' body from about twenty feet below the lip of the bergschrund. It was estimated that he fell about 600 feet from the ridgetop into the bergschrund. Fernekes' parents flew from Connecticut to accompany their son's body back home. Lynch suffered minor head injuries and was hospitalized for several days but was also able to accompany his friend's body back home.

In the previous two cases, it is likely that falling into the bergschrunds was the primary cause of death. In this next case, however, the fall itself wasn't fatal. On Tuesday, July 27, 2004, Howard Frederick Cohn, forty-six, and a friend hiked to Grinnell Glacier. This is a very popular hike because it crosses spectacular alpine terrain on a good trail and allows the easiest access for people who want to get near a glacier. Once a hiker has reached the glacier basin, he or she can scramble along the margin of upper Grinnell Lake to the point where the glacier meets the lake. Cohn crossed onto the glacier at that spot while his friend stayed off the ice. Cohn was from Columbia, Maryland, and it is not known what experience he had on glaciers but, nonetheless, he set off across the glacier to explore. When he didn't return after a half hour, his friend ventured onto the ice to look for him and heard Cohn calling for help from a crevasse. A nearby park ranger with a radio was alerted and a rescue team was mobilized. Gary Moses was one of the responding rangers, and he found that Cohn was about forty feet down and tightly wedged in the narrowing ice near the bottom. Cohn was still verbal but not very coherent and was obviously slipping away. When he fell in, he brought surrounding snow with him and was not only wedged in at the bottom of the crevasse but also packed in with dense snow. Wearing summer hiking clothing and having been there at least a few hours, he was chilled completely. Moses was lowered down to Cohn and set to work, trying to chip ice and snow from around Cohn's body so that ropes or a harness could be fit around Cohn to haul him up. There was almost no room to swing an ice axe, and Moses was also tightly wedged in between the walls of ice. Although clad in winter clothing and a parka and working hard, Moses and other rangers had to take turns down in the tight crevasse as they got too chilled and wet to work effectively. After a miserable and desperate few hours, they were able to get Cohn up and immediately began CPR. The ALERT helicopter flew Cohn to the hospital but he was pronounced dead. Unfortunately, a sunny and warm walk on a glacier on a summer day led to a chilling death in an icy confine.

On September 3, 2013, Ted Porter set out alone to do some climbing on the flanks of Mount Jackson on the east side of the park and to explore Jackson Glacier. This thirty-six-year-old man from Los Angeles was well equipped for the climb and had appropriate experience, having spent family vacations in Glacier Park since he was an infant. Porter and his father had both worked at the Many Glacier Hotel, and Porter had attended the University of Montana in Missoula. As he stated in a *Hungry Horse News* interview, "So I'm definitely familiar with the Park, and I'm not just some Angeleno who rolled up here and didn't know what was going on." He hiked from the Going-to-the-Sun Road to Gunsight Lake and took the Jackson Glacier Overlook Trail to the bottom of the glacier. According to the *Hungry Horse News* interview, "From there, he headed up toward a col between Mount Jackson and Blackfoot Mountain for a view of Harrison Glacier, on Mount Jackson's south side. Rain began falling, making the rock ledges he was following slick and dangerous. By 4:30 P.M., he decided to head down. Making his way down a different route, he encountered a large bergschrund. He found a way around the bergschrund but neglected to put his crampons back on or get out his ice axe." "That proved to be a huge mistake," he said. "I was just standing on the glacier, and my thought was I could just kind of 'boot-ski' out."

Instead, Porter slipped, gaining speed as he approached a large crevasse below. "I just dropped right into the crevasse," he said. "From what I remember, it was violent and fast. I hit the front side, the far wall, and bounced back, and I must have dropped straight down, and I ended up on my butt with a broken back. I just knew something was severely wrong. The pain was unbelievable."

The park service press release on this incident states that he fell about forty feet into the crevasse, more than enough to kill someone. Having survived, despite the intense pain, Porter knew he had to self-rescue and started to assess possible exits from the crevasse. Understanding the gravity of his injuries and dire situation, he had the presence of mind to shoot a thirty-five-second "good-bye video" for his parents, who were back home in Kansas City. Just in case.

"I said, 'If I don't see you again, I want you to know I love you very much,'" Porter said. It took him about twenty-five minutes to find a way out of the crevasse. After strapping on his crampons, he used these and his ice axe to climb a less steep wall of ice and emerge onto the surface of the glacier, all with a broken back. From there, leaning on his ice axe, it was still an enormous struggle of several hours to descend the glacier, contend with slippery slopes and loose talus, and reach the Gunsight Lake backcountry campground three miles away. "I slipped and hit my hip really hard, which was terrible," he said.

Once Porter reached Gunsight Lake backcountry campground, campers who were staying there swung into action to care for him as best they could. Porter was grateful and gave full credit to them for the food, water, and shelter they provided. The campers attempted to immobilize him and assess his injuries. The next morning, three of them took off for the Going-to-the-Sun Road five miles away to get help since it was obvious Porter couldn't make the hike. Glacier Park dispatch received a call from a backcountry ranger who was patrolling the area and had met the hikers about 8:50 A.M. The ALERT helicopter was notified, and Porter was soon airlifted to Kalispell Regional Medical Center. "It's a miracle he's alive," his mother Cindy Porter said. "If he had broken his legs or his arms, he wouldn't have been able to climb out, or if he had been knocked unconscious."

Porter spent the next week in a back brace and, when interviewed in the hospital, said he felt fortunate his injuries weren't much worse. One vertebra in his lower back was "totally crushed," he said, and another was damaged. A doctor told him that his spinal cord was only a few millimeters away from being injured enough to cause partial or total paralysis of his legs. It is amazing that Porter was able to rescue himself and make his way to help with such severe injuries, but he made the right choice given that a search for him would likely have been too late.

The park's press release on this incident ends with this advice: "Park officials do not recommend travel on and around glaciers. Mountaineering books typically recommend that climbers on glaciers travel in groups, with each person carrying an ice ax they are trained in using, and with groups roped together and equipped with proper self-rescue devices and training in their use."

SUMMIT MOUNTAINEERING AND PEAK BAGGING

In contrast to the people who are rambling and exploring off-trail, or attempting specific traverses, other mountaineers have their sights set on getting to summits. These so-called "peak baggers" like to get up to the tops of mountains as often as possible to savor the physical challenge, the stunning scenery, and, perhaps, the high perspective that can make you feel that you are above the world's, and your own, problems. Many people come to Glacier National Park for the express purpose of climbing mountains, while others are inspired once they arrive. But, like the stories already told of falling from roads, trails, and traverses, people have died, survived accidents, and had plenty of close calls on their way to and from peaks.

The earliest summit climbers weren't climbing for pleasure but had work to do. Surveyors and map makers ascended many mountains in the park with their instruments because there were no aircraft back then from which to get high perspectives. The Wright brothers had not yet launched their glider at Kitty Hawk when some of the first maps were made of the area to become Glacier Park. A map made in 1895 is a surprisingly accurate depiction of Glacier National Park's mountains and lakes; this was achieved by climbing many of the peaks. These early mountaineers also named many of the summits and peaks at that time. Given that the surveyors wore hob-nailed boots, bulky woolen trousers or knickers, and heavy coats, and then carried heavy oaken tripods, brass surveying instruments, or large cameras for exposing images on glass plate negatives, it is amazing that there are no records of early deaths due to climbing with such encumbrances. They were strong and sure-footed explorers!

One of the earliest deaths reported after Glacier National Park was established, and also the first recorded climbing fatality, was that of Dr. Frank B. Wynn. His death occurred while climbing Mount Siyeh on July 27, 1922. Wynn was sixty-two.

Dr. Wynn was an active and early climber of peaks in the park. David Walters reported discovering in 2001 a small canister near the summit of Mount Cleveland and inside was a register with Dr. Wynn's name as the first to record a summiting of Cleveland on August 12, 1920. Wynn may have had other first ascents, as he frequently led groups from the Nature Study Club of Indiana to the summits of several of the major peaks in the park; he left behind thin metal boxes with the registers. Wynn was active in the Indiana Audubon Club and a member of the Committee to Collect Data on the Archeology of Indiana. His early advocacy for the environment, conservation, and history led to his success in creating a state park in Indiana on the site of the log cabin farm where Abraham Lincoln spent his boyhood years. It was later made a national park by President John F. Kennedy in 1962. Mount Wynn, near Mount Siyeh where Dr. Wynn died, is named in his honor. This was done to recognize his efforts to establish state parks and preserve natural areas in the United States.

Dr. Wynn was born May 28, 1860, in Springfield, Indiana, and received his medical degree from the Medical College of Ohio in 1885. After stints studying in Berlin and Vienna, he joined the faculty of the Indiana University School of Medics. He also served as captain in the U.S. Army Medical Corps during World War I.

According to a July 27, 1922, *New York Times* article, Dr. Wynn was president of the American Alpine Club and "one of the country's fore-

Dr. Frank B. Wynn, president of the American Alpine Club, died in a fall from a cliff on Mount Siyeh in 1922. COURTESY OF LIBRARY OF CONGRESS, LC-B2-1058-11.

most mountain climbers." He spent numerous vacations in the Rocky Mountains of the United States and Canada. *The Times* also reported that he had "gained considerable fame as a mountain climber in Switzerland while with Dr. Stone, former president of Purdue University, who was killed in the Canadian Rockies last Summer." Dr. Wynn had

been cautioned by his friends and family about the danger of mountain climbing, but "he replied that he had long experience, and it was improbable that he would meet with any accident." Dr. Wynn fell 300 feet from a cliff near the summit of Mount Siyeh while climbing with Dr. H. Goddard, who was a few minutes behind Wynn. "They had just neared an unusually steep place on the trail, Dr. Goddard said, when Dr. Wynn, who was leading, turned and opened his mouth as if to speak. Then, without uttering a word, he pitched forward. Before Dr. Goddard could cover the intervening distance, the body had rolled over the rocky ledge and disappeared." The article goes on to describe Dr. Goddard's speculation that Dr. Wynn had an apoplectic stroke, possibly induced by the exertion of climbing at nearly 10,000 feet.

Sixty-nine years later, another death occurred on Mount Siyeh, this time during a descent from the summit. Gordon Ochenrider, forty-six, climbed Mount Siyeh alone on August 14, 1991, and had lunch with a man and a woman on the summit about 1:30 P.M. While visiting with them, he said he was going to descend the mountain's southwest ridge toward Piegan Pass instead of returning down the route he came up. Around 3 P.M., Dr. Kenneth Barrick, a researcher from the University of Alaska-Fairbanks hiking near Piegan Pass, heard rockfall and, while scanning the mountain for its source, saw "bright colors falling down the slope." Ochenrider came to rest below a band of cliffs that skirts Mount Siyeh toward Piegan Pass. A nearby trail crew rushed to Ochenrider, but he had died from head trauma.

Ochenrider was on a leave of absence from a Whitefish bank where he was vice president. He had recently been indicted on charges of drug money laundering and was going to stand trial later in the year. Consequently, in addition to the National Park Service, both the Federal Bureau of Investigation and the U.S. Customs Service investigated the apparent mishap.

Apparently, officials thought that such a death under the cloud of serious legal problems could be something other than an accident, such as suicide or murder. But a local chiropractor and friend of Ochenrider, Dr. Doug Pitman of Columbia Falls, described him as being in good spirits. Ochenrider's daughter had been married on August 11 in Whitefish, and he had seemed very positive at that time as well. The park's chief ranger, Bob Andrew, was careful to note that witnesses said Ochenrider was climbing apart from others and no one else was nearby. An August 22 *Hungry Horse News* article stated that "Glacier National Park authorities say foul play is not suspected in the death of Gordon Ochenrider." In the same article, Dr. Pitman said, "He wasn't wimpy up there . . . but he was not foolish either. He had bad knees and they may have given him trouble coming down the other day." Despite the natural suspicions of people hearing of this incident, Ochenrider probably fell in the most innocent of ways: stumbling on a loose rock, a turned ankle, or a hand-hold that gave way.

The very next summer, another fatal fall occurred when the victim was climbing alone. Josh Skibsrud, twenty, was a local young man from nearby Kalispell who had graduated in 1990 from Flathead High School. He was an avid climber and in the previous week had summited two challenging mountains, 10,101-foot Kintla Peak and 9,944-foot Kinnerly Peak. Skibsrud was climbing 9,553-foot Mount Gould from the west side on July 19, 1992. The climbing route takes off from the Highline Trail that runs parallel to and above the Going-to-the-Sun Road. It is a popular route because it is not technical and offers fantastic views from the summit down to Grinnell Glacier, which sits at the base of a 3,000-foot face on the other side of the Continental Divide. Weather in July can still be unsettled despite the calendar saying it is summer. Clouds, mist, rain, and even snow are possible at high elevations. The visibility was variable that day with clouds spilling over the Continental Divide at various times, which would have put a fine sheen of moisture on the rocks.

Despite his youth, Skibsrud was an experienced and knowledgeable peak bagger who was "well-equipped" according to the park officials cited in a *Hungry Horse News* article of July 23. He was trailing two other climbers on the route as he ascended but was not part of their group. These climbers, Don Scharfe and Doug Compton, both of Kalispell, encountered wet rock in a gully near the summit. Scharfe and Compton reached the summit shortly before noon. Puzzled when Skibsrud didn't join them soon, they began to reverse their route and look for him. Eventually, they found his body far below in scree, having fallen a minimum of 200 feet. Skibsrud died of massive trauma despite wearing a climbing helmet. Although no one witnessed the fall, based on his whereabouts at the time of the fall, the wet rocks are likely to have been the cause of this fatal accident.

In honor of Skibsrud's life and love of mountains, the family and a local fitness facility, the Kalispell Athletic Club, sponsored an annual event called the Josh Skibsrud Memorial Duathlon and, for those six years old and under, the Skibsrud Scramble. The duathlon was a 5k run followed by jumping on your bicycle and riding 30k and finishing with another 5k run. For the younger crowd, a shorter version was held the same day, and the Fagre sisters (daughters of two of this book's authors) participated in this. Held each year, this is a fitting event to celebrate the life of an athletic and exuberant young man. The Glacier Mountaineering Society also placed a metal plaque on Mount Gould in Josh's memory.

Another fall on Mount Gould had a better outcome when Kim Taylor, a twenty-six-year-old seasonal ranger-naturalist, was also climbing near the summit on August 17, 1998. Afterward, she recalled that she was feeling adventurous and ventured up a rock face confident in her climbing skills. Taylor fell off the vertical rock but was stopped on the steep scree and didn't plummet hundreds and even thousands of feet like others have done. But she was injured, and a major rescue ensued. Climbing rangers got ready to lower her by ropes to an evacuation point. The incident commander for this rescue, Charlie Logan, was struck by the difficulty in placing reliable anchors into the rock for the rope-lowering operation because the rock was fractured and weak and the descent would mean negotiating a long series of short cliffs. Logan had previously been a climbing rescue ranger in Rocky Mountain National Park at Longs Peak, where the solid rock provided much better anchoring options. Having a large party of rescuers working on loose, steep rock was another source of stress for the rescue leader. Logan was immensely relieved when a military helicopter from Malmstrom Air Force Base arrived to complete the rescue.

In the incidents above, all the people had climbing experience and were familiar with Glacier Park. But that is not always the case. Visitors and seasonal employees are often inspired to tackle climbs for which they are ill-prepared. One such example is the case of Robert Stokes, eighteen, of Tulsa, Oklahoma. Robert was camping with three friends at the Swiftcurrent Campground in Many Glacier Valley in July 1950. They were drawn by the beauty of 9,321-foot Mount Wilbur, a massive prow of rock with a knife-edged summit at the head of Swiftcurrent Valley. Mount Wilbur is a steep and serious climb. None of these young men had equipment, or likely experience for such a climb, and the mountain held more ice and snow than usual for July. On July 12, Stokes and his friends set off on the climb and somehow made it to near the top. There Stokes slipped on some ice and plunged more than 200 feet down the mountain. His three friends were able to reach him after carefully descending and determined that he was dead. They were able to safely climb down Mount Wilbur and report the accident. A rescue party of twelve men started climbing at 3:30 A.M. and retrieved Stokes' body from high on the steep slopes about twelve hours later.

Seasonal employees are also inspired to climb and have adventures during their summer in the park, and those who work at Many Glacier Hotel are surrounded by an awesome array of mountains and climbing opportunities just minutes from their summer lodging. During summer 2013, two young men working at Many Glacier Hotel died in separate incidents. In the first case, Cesar Flores, twenty-one, from Florida, and three other employees began climbing Apikuni Mountain on the morning of July 9, 2013. Only three and a half hours later, park dispatch received a call from one of the climbers saying that one of them had fallen and the others could not see or reach the victim nor was he responding to their calls. It was later determined that Flores had fallen 1,000 feet to his death. Apikuni Mountain is very steep and has many cliffs, so rangers brought in a helicopter to search for his body, which they found about 6 P.M. in difficult terrain. A Parks Canada short-haul rescue team retrieved the body.

In the second case, just over two weeks later, a very similar chain of events led to the death of Matthew Needham, twenty-one, from California. With two companions, Matthew was climbing near Grinnell Point just a few miles from Many Glacier Hotel where all three worked. While climbing, Matthew fell at least sixty feet to his death. The accident was reported to park rangers by an employee of the Glacier Park Boat Company, which operates tour boats on Swiftcurrent and Josephine Lakes. Before rangers arrived, a group of eight hikers found Matthew and determined he was dead. Because of the steep and dangerous terrain, a helicopter used a 100-foot line to recover his body.

TECHNICAL

One of the most spectacular and well-known climbing accidents in Glacier occurred during an attempted first ascent of Mount Cleveland in winter. It is also widely viewed as one of the most tragic incidents in the park's climbing history. Some of the most enthusiastic and competent local mountaineers—who had already climbed many of the park's peaks —thought up this ambitious and audacious plan. This event and its aftermath was thoroughly covered in local and national news, has been the subject of in-depth reporting in newspapers years after the event, and was capably chronicled in an excellent book, *The White Death: Terror and Heroism in an Avalanche Zone* by McKay Jenkins, which should be referred to for an in-depth discussion beyond the outline described here.

On December 26, 1969, five young men arrived in Glacier National Park and met with District Ranger Robert Frauson to explain their plan to scale the mile-high north face of Mount Cleveland, the tallest peak in the park at 10,488 feet, near the border with Canada. Ranger Frauson, an experienced mountaineer who had served in the 10th Mountain Division during World War II and was familiar with the grand north faces of Europe's Alps, had a strong reaction. He cautioned them not to attempt the climb. Three of the climbers were from Montana State University in Bozeman and two were from Montana Tech in Butte. James Anderson, eighteen, Mark Levitan, twenty, and Clare Pogreba, twenty-two, had just recently climbed Mount Wilbur, a prominent peak above Swiftcurrent Lake, under wintry conditions with three other climbers, including Jurg Hofer, a climber from Switzerland. For the Mount Cleveland attempt they were joined by Jerry Kanzler, eighteen, and Ray Martin, twenty-two.

The expedition, for that is what it was, had been planned for some time and was not a spontaneous venture. Against Frauson's advice, the five young men were transported by boat south on Waterton Lake from the Canadian side; Alf Baker, the boatman, was the last person to see the party, about 11 A.M. on Saturday, December 27. He apparently commented that they were well clothed for a Montana winter. Tracks showed that the men then went up Cleveland Creek to the base of the north face.

For climbers, the north face of 10,488-foot Mount Cleveland is a daunting prospect even in summer. COURTESY OF U.S. GEOLOGICAL SURVEY.

Bud Anderson, a civilian pilot, tried to fly along the north face to check on their progress on December 29 and 30, but cloud cover obscured any views. He was able to get a view on December 31 and did not see them, but he wasn't too concerned since the climb was expected to take at least five days. On January 1, Anderson went to the head of the lake in a boat to pick up the climbers as previously arranged. No one was there. He saw no signs of any sort, so he alerted officials about the overdue climbers.

Chief Ranger Ruben Hart requested the use of a helicopter from Malmstrom Air Force Base. A pilot in a private plane was also able to get over Mount Cleveland one afternoon for a scouting mission, and the spotter saw climber ski tracks that ended where the men had left their skis at the base of the face. The next day, searchers found the men's base camp, which included tents, food supplies, and hard hats. As the search expanded, tracks revealed that the climbers had separated into one group of three and one group of two. Three snow caves were found where the men had sheltered on the climb, and these contained candy wrappers. More teams began arriving from other parts of the United States in addition to increasing efforts from Waterton Lakes National Park rangers and climbers from Banff and Jasper. In addition to the international rescue efforts, the media began to arrive with increasing press and radio coverage.

A helicopter from Johnson Flying Service arrived, and the helicopters eventually took over surveillance and ferrying in the bad weather; the area was closed to fixed-wing planes. Then Waterton Lake froze over and boats could not be used. Rescuers also used snowmobiles to try to get partway up Mount Cleveland's slopes.

The young men had left the names of other climbers to be called in case of emergency when they had checked in, and these climbers were called to the escalating search and rescue scene the day after the missing climbers alert was issued. Dr. Pat Callis and Pete Lev from Montana State University arrived and did a climbing search, along with Jim Kanzler, the brother of one of the missing climbers. It was dangerous and hard work, and it was Jim who found the first packsack of one of the climbers in the debris of a large avalanche that had come off the face. This did not portend a good outcome. Then a parka with a camera in the pocket was located below the snow surface using a probe, and this was found at the lower part of the avalanche debris. The film was quickly developed and showed broad views of the north face as the men were approaching it. At this point the rescue became a body recovery, as it was assumed that all the climbers had been swept from the face and were buried in the avalanche debris.

Conditions were very cold, with temperatures of -10 degrees F, and very dangerous, with a continuing threat of avalanches. The men's parents were kept continuously informed, but the costs and dangers of the on-going efforts now weighed on everyone. The search ended on January 8. Officials planned to recover the bodies when weather conditions would allow at the start of summer. There were only a few clues from the parka and the pack, but all evidence suggested that a large avalanche had engulfed the men in the west bowl near the summit. Ranger Frauson said, "You could hide an army up there."

Meanwhile, parents of the young men expressed their gratitude for the herculean efforts that had been made to rescue and find their sons. Jim Anderson's mother recognized the huge effort put forth by the Canadians, saying, "When the bodies are found, maybe a living memorial—a fountain or something for Canadians as well as for Americans, because they all helped." She went on to say that Jim had "wanted his ashes spread over the park if anything happened. That's how much he loved the park." She said he was "a searcher who has found his answers."

A very accomplished Austrian mountaineer, Helmuth Matdies, who lived in Whitefish, vigorously defended the young men in their attempt, pointing out the extensive experience and challenging climbs they had between them. He believed them to be very qualified despite their youth and said that their awareness of the potential dangers was appropriate. "It is too bad that it had to happen, but I am sure that if any of the boys would have had a choice of which cemetery to be buried, they would be happier to be buried on Cleveland than anywhere else."

As warm weather gradually returned, searchers made regular efforts to find the bodies of the young men. Finally, on June 29, 1970, the bodies of Ray Martin and James Anderson were found. Interestingly, Jim Anderson's watch had stopped on December 30 but began running again when picked up by the rescue crew. Crews were airlifted partway up the mountain to the avalanche debris, and a hydraulic operation using 400 feet of hose brought water down from above to cut through ice and snow and gravel. Using this technique, the bodies of the others were found by July 3, with Jerry Kanzler's body being the last to be brought down. An investigation of the likely area where the young men were caught in the avalanche showed that they had made it into the upper west bowl near the north face right before the final steep cliffs leading to the 10,488-foot summit. The avalanche then swept them down to about the 7,500-foot elevation.

Another technical climb that went awry and ended in the deaths of two promising climbers occurred on Rainbow Peak in the North Fork region of the park on July 3, 1997. Mark Robison, twenty-four, and Chris Foster, twenty-three, were attempting what was a likely first ascent of a snow gully that aimed for the summit. They were probably very close to the top, perhaps with only a few hundred feet to go after a long climb, when they fell an estimated 1,100 feet and died. Both climbers worked for Glacier National Park as trail crew members and had undoubtedly been eyeing this climb during their work. Mark's brother, Mason, said that

Mark had been eager for the climb and that the climbing conditions with firm snow were good. As with other climbing accidents, the climbers had talked about death and risk, sometimes often. In a *Hungry Horse News* interview, Mason said, "We knew it would be harder for the guy who lived. We couldn't imagine how it would be for the one who didn't go. It was not so much a question of 'if' but 'when,' but we both expected we would be together when it happened, in each other's arms when one of us died. That's not how it turned out." Despite their relative youth, the climbers were experienced and outstanding athletes. *Hungry Horse News* editor Brian Kennedy described Mark's considerable exploits as a local high school athlete and later ventures in the mountains of Montana, such as the time Mark and Rob Macal climbed ten summits in Glacier Park in twenty-seven hours, covering twenty miles and scaling more than 20,000 vertical feet. Perhaps most poignant in a loss like this is when the fallen climber is described as Mark was, as "a very complete person, completely good."

BASE JUMPING: FALLING ON PURPOSE

In the last several decades, the sport of BASE jumping has become more popular and has also caused conflict with park managers. BASE stands for Bridge, Antenna, Span, and Earth. Basically, the jumper leaps from fixed points like skyscrapers or cliffs and deploys a parachute before hitting the ground. The margin of error is less than with traditional parachuting from aircraft because the distances to the ground are less. Thus the thrill. BASE jumping has been banned at all national parks including Glacier.

On September 24, 1997, a BASE jumper from Marion, Montana, attempted a jump from the summit of Mount Siyeh. At 10,014 feet, Mount Siyeh is one of six summits in the park over 10,000 feet, but from a BASE jumper's perspective, there is more to the peak's attraction than mere elevation. Mount Siyeh's 3,000-foot sheer north face is slightly undercut in places, making it a safer and more alluring location for a massive jump. Perhaps the wilderness setting and the added thrill of a forbidden undertaking makes its allure stronger. In any event, James Kaufman, forty, made his way to the summit of Mount Siyeh, prepared his kit, and flung himself into the void. Unfortunately, he immediately (and ignominiously) got hung up. After he pulled his chute, his trajectory brought him back into the cliffs and he snagged on rocks about 400 feet below the summit. There he hung on the sheer north face of Siyeh for several hours as park rangers were mobilized and flown in by helicopter. Park ranger Charlie Logan had to rappel down to Kaufman, secure and stabilize him, and then a crew of rangers laboriously raised them both 400 feet back up to the summit. From there, Kaufman was transferred to the helicopter and ultimately flown to the regional hospital for treatment of soft tissue injuries to his lower leg and other scrapes. "We were home for dinner by 8:15 P.M.," Logan recalled. "That guy was really lucky."

Because the jump was illegal, charges were filed in federal court against Kaufman. He pleaded no contest to the charges against him and was ordered to pay a $9,000 fine for the costs associated with the rescue. He was also put on probation for two years during which he was not to violate any federal, state, or local laws and not enter Glacier National Park. Most ironically, he was required to sell his parachute and apply the proceeds to the cost of rescue. Was this appropriate? As Chief Ranger Steve Frye stated at the time, "This conviction sends a message to anyone considering such activities. Parachuting is not allowed at Glacier National Park for good reason. Inherent risks and obstacles make such activity inappropriate in a setting such as Glacier. Not only did his illegal parachuting place himself at great risk, but also the lives of those rangers charged with rescuing him."

Any lessons learned by BASE jumpers did not change the behavior of Beau Weiher. By all accounts, the twenty-two-year-old man from Missoula was an accomplished BASE jumper, reveling in the thrills and intense adrenaline generated by aerial adventures. Weiher had apparently made previous illicit trips into Glacier National Park to leap from summits and paraglide to the valleys below. He had traveled globally to make jumps, and the BASE-jumping lifestyle was one he embraced. However, on September 13, 2014, Weiher was reported missing by family and friends when he didn't return or contact them after a "hike" into the park in the vicinity of Piegan Pass and Mount Siyeh. The reporting family said the hike might involve a BASE jump. Weiher had gone in alone and no one will ever know exactly what went wrong, but the next day searchers found him dead far below the summit of Mount Siyeh after a ground and aerial search; his parachute was spotted by helicopter on Sunday evening. Investigators estimated that he had fallen about 2,000 feet of the 3,000 feet from the summit to the surface of Siyeh Glacier. He was attached to his parachute, which had deployed, when his body was found. Park rangers found tracks in the snow below the summit of Mount Siyeh, which suggested that Weiher had been at the summit. Rangers recovered the body. It wasn't entirely clear if Weiher had fallen before being able to deploy his chute as planned or whether he was prepared when he made the attempt, but something went wrong. He was not wearing a camera for his jump, which many jumpers do to record their feat.

Deaths due to falling continue in Glacier Park despite the improvements in equipment, rescue technologies, and ample warnings from the park service. Some people innately want to challenge themselves, seek adventure, and feel a sense of accomplishment by climbing and exploring mountains. As this book was being written, a recent death underscored the reality that climbing, surviving, and dying will be part of Glacier Park's history into the future.

Dann R. Pilipow, fifty-six, was from Portage, Indiana. Known to friends and family as "Scrappy," Pilipow visited Glacier often, starting in 1984, to hike and climb in the park's mountains; he was a longtime member of the Glacier Mountaineering Society. In August 2016, he came to the park and climbed Mount Jackson with his twenty-seven-year-old son, Chris. Mount Jackson is one of six summits in the park over 10,000 feet, and its classic pyramid shape beckons many climbers. However, it is a big undertaking, and climbers have died on its flanks before. The *Flathead Beacon* described Mount Jackson as "one of the tallest peaks in Glacier National Park at 10,052 feet, and the climbing route varies from

Class 3 to Class 4 depending on the route and the amount of snow and ice. The climbing routes are considered arduous with an approximate elevation gain of 4,800 vertical feet, high amounts of loose scree, and a significant amount of exposure on narrow ledges with steep drop offs."

While descending a snowfield on the east face on August 30, Pilipow slipped and fell an estimated 100 feet. His son also slipped but managed to self-arrest with only minor injuries. Pilipow's son was unable to find his father after the fall and decided to get help. Pilipow probably died at the time of the fall. His son descended the rest of the mountain and hiked to the Gunsight Lake backcountry campground near the base of Mount Jackson. A camper with a satellite phone was able to text for help, and the incident was reported to park dispatch at 11:08 P.M. that night. After being evacuated by helicopter, the son was treated for his injuries. The fate of the father was still unknown at this point, but preparations were made for a body recovery. The next day, August 31, two helicopters worked with park rangers to conduct a search for Pilipow. They discovered his body, and the following day a technical rescue team extricated the body.

This chapter underscores the reality that hiking and climbing in the mountains are inherently risky activities. Newcomers to mountainous terrain are well advised to travel with reputable guides or careful, experienced friends. Information on safety in the backcountry is widely available in books and online, and park service cautions are clear and prominently posted. You can avoid many mishaps by taking the time to learn about Glacier's terrain, weather, and wildlife so that you can make informed, deliberate choices, and by realizing that, ultimately, you are responsible for your own safety.

CHAPTER TEN

GRAVITY IS ABSOLUTE:
AVALANCHES
and
FALLING OBJECTS

AVALANCHES

As described earlier in this book, mountains present a number of unique hazards that have led to deaths, injuries, and close calls. The pull of gravity not only leads to people falling but also to rocks, debris, and snow coming down the mountains—sometimes at great speed and at very inopportune times. Such is often the case with snow avalanches. These can be relatively small sluffs of loose snow that can still bury a skier or a deep slab that breaks free and "propagates" around an entire basin, releasing vast amounts of snow with sufficient weight and speed to level entire forests.

Prior to the introduction of skiing for pleasure or the building of roads into the high mountain reaches, people mostly stayed out of avalanche zones during winter. There wasn't any real need to go there. However, there is a story about a Kootenai hunting party that had a close call with an avalanche. This story is described in Sally Thompson's book, *People Before the Park*, and was originally told to Claude Schaeffer, who chronicled much about the lives of the Kootenai. Sometime in the 1860s or 1870s, the hunters were on an early winter hunt along what is now McDonald Creek above Lake McDonald. Chief Paul David was among a small group who followed Avalanche Creek to Avalanche Lake and made their way to a steep slope without any trees. Paul didn't think their location was particularly safe and, while he was talking with his friend, they "heard an avalanche across on cliffs opposite. Soon . . . [an] older Indian came along. [He] moved along the edge of the snowfield to where a few trees were standing and Paul and his friend heard a noise. Looking up . . . they saw the snow start . . . downwards toward them. The older Indian ran to a tree and encircled [it] with his arms and legs. Paul and his friend started to run; the friend for the timber and Paul ran downwards on the snowfield. No sooner had Paul reached the edge of the snowfield and gained the timber, than the avalanche swept past him."

It seems likely that avalanche risks were not too common for these first occupants, but the risks became greater when people began climbing and exploring in avalanche-prone terrain for business and pleasure.

A DEATH AT BLACKFOOT GLACIER

The Glacier National Park Superintendent's Annual Report of 1913 documented an accident from the summer that led to the first death attributed to an avalanche. "On August 19, Dr. Fletcher, of Indianapolis, Ind., a tourist visiting the park and a member of the Prairie Club of Chicago, while climbing around the upper cascade of Blackfoot Glacier, was struck by a body of snow and ice, which fell from the comb at the top of the glacier, sustaining injuries from which he died within two hours. As previously reported, Dr. Fletcher was unaccompanied by a guide, having gone to this danger point of his own volition and against the advice of accompanying friends." A similar report had been sent to Hon. A. C. Miller, Assistant Secretary of the Interior, Washington, D.C., six days after the accident, suggesting that it was a fairly high-profile incident for the fledgling park, established only three years prior. (This incident occurred before the creation of the National Park Service, three years later.) All the reports were careful to absolve park and concession employees of any blame for the accident, and one report ended, "We should all try to eliminate liability to accidents as much as possible."

Dr. Calvin I. Fletcher was born in July 1859 in Indiana and served as a physician in several locations. His circle of friends and family noted his remarkable passion for travel. At his funeral service, the Rev. M. L. Haines paid high tribute to Dr. Fletcher "as probably foremost among the citizens of Indianapolis in the extensiveness of his travels." He called attention to the fact that it was not a spirit of recklessness or love of adventure that led the physician to roam the Earth but a desire to see interesting places, or as expressed by his brother, Horace H. Fletcher, "a desire to explore the picture book of the world."

The morning of August 19 found Dr. Fletcher and his wife at Gunsight Camp, a large collection of wall tents set up for the summer, which included a mess tent, with many riding and pack horses grazing in the meadows next to Gunsight Lake. J. M. Cathcart, the general manager of hotels and camps for the Great Northern Railway, was heading to Sperry Camp that day and conversed with Dr. and Mrs. Fletcher, who were also conversing with William C. Alden at their table. Dr. Fletcher and others were waiting for the main body of the Prairie Club to arrive for their horseback tour of Glacier National Park. Breakfast was served rather early, and Dr. Fletcher and several others requested permission to accompany Mr. Alden, a geologist with the U.S. Geological Survey, up to Blackfoot Glacier. Mr. Alden agreed. At the end of the day, after the accident, Mr. Alden sat down at a typewriter back at Gunsight Camp and typed a detailed account of the day to Superintendent J. L. Galen, as follows:

> Dear Sir:
> I have the honor to present herewith a statement of the circumstances attending the death of Dr. Fletcher of Indianapolis, Ind. on the Blackfoot Glacier this afternoon. I am engaged in making a study of the glaciers and glacial phenomena of Glacier National Park for the U.S. Geological Survey.
> This morning as I was starting to go up onto the Blackfoot Glacier, Dr. Fletcher, Mr. West, Mr. Tenney, Mr. and Miss Tuthill asked to be permitted to go with me and I gave them permission. On the way up I explained to them the geological phenomena and Dr. Fletcher told me of his travels and gave me to understand that he had climbed mountains

in the Alps and the Andes and elsewhere and that he was an experienced climber. While crossing the Glacier, Miss Tuthill having left us, I turned to the men and said that, while I would be glad to have them go with me if they wished to do so, I wished it understood that I assumed no responsibility for their safety, that, although I was a government employe [sic] I was not a regular guide. I told them I sometimes went into dangerous places as my professional work as a geologist required, but that I did not expect to get hurt myself, that they must go on their own responsibility if they went with me, and to this all gave definite assent.

Dr. Fletcher was particularly enthusiastic, saying it was the best day of the trip. He suggested going up to the upper glacial cascades, saying we would see a grand sight. Crossing to the rock ledges below the upper part of the Glacier we ascended over them to an elevation of about 7,600 feet above the sea (per barometer).

I had just taken a photograph looking across the Glacier to Mt. Jackson, with Dr. Fletcher standing in the foreground and had taken another and turned to put

William C. Alden snapped this photograph of Dr. Fletcher on the Blackfoot Glacier moments before an avalanche swept into him, leaving Fletcher fatally injured. W. C. ALDEN, COURTESY OF U.S. GEOLOGICAL SURVEY.

my camera in its case as Dr. Fletcher started on up ahead of us. Just then some snow came sliding down and I told the men to get close in the lee of the ledges so as to be safe if more came down. In a moment we heard Dr. Fletcher call for help. Rushing to him we found him in the snow badly hurt. Apparently his right thigh was broken and there was a great flesh wound showing through his torn trousers. We moved him up close to the ledge out of the track of snow and putting a leather string around the leg above the wound twisted it tight with a stick to shut off the flow of blood. Mr. Tenney then started down for help. We soon saw two guides, whose names I do not know, hurrying across the glacier toward us as they had seen the accident from the distance.

We immediately began moving Dr. Fletcher down. The accident occurred about 1 P.M. Dr. Fletcher was unconscious much of the time. He kept saying he was dying, spoke affectionately of his wife and called on Jesus Christ to forgive his sins. He asked for brandy. Feeling in his pocket we found his flask and gave him a little. He cried out evidently in very great pain. We made no further examination of his injuries but moved him as rapidly as possible. He soon became unconscious and we were unable to detect any pulse or respiration, though I held the mirror of my compass to his mouth. We then concluded he was dead. Other men came to help and we finally got the body to the foot of the Glacier.

There we met Mr. MacLain, who was a medical officer or nurse I understand, with the Illinois State Militia. He felt for heart action and gave a hypodermic injection of strychnine, I think, but with no response, so agreed with us that death had occurred. I think Dr. Fletcher lived about an hour after the accident.

I regret exceedingly this occurrence and of course I feel a measure of responsibility in spite of the definite under-standing with the men as stated above. I think, however, Dr. Fletcher would have gone to this place had I not been with him, as he desired to see it.

I wish to commend the work of all the men who assisted in the very difficult task of bringing the body to camp. All was done that could be done under the circumstances and no blame should attach to anyone of the party.

Respectfully,

Wm. C. Alden

Geologist, U.S. Geological Survey

While Alden and the men were struggling to get Dr. Fletcher's body off the glacier that afternoon, Cathcart, the general manager, had ridden over to Sperry Camp with some tourists, made his camp inspection, and arrived at Glacier Hotel on the west side of the park. Shortly thereafter he received a telephone message informing him of the accident, and he dispatched men and pack horses from St. Mary on the east side to go to Gunsight Camp to bring the body out. After that, he telephoned the park superintendent, Mr. Galen, and together they made arrangements for the coroner and undertaker and then rode back up to Sperry Camp, arriving about 11:30 P.M. In an August 20 letter that he wrote to the Great Northern Railway vice president, Cathcart gives a sense of how easily an accident scene can continue unraveling.

[W]e immediately called Gunsight Camp for further details and was advised the true nature of the accident. We further found that a Miss Edwards who had gone up to the glacier shortly after the accident had become badly excited and insisted on leaving at once to notify Mrs. Fletcher at the Camp. In returning she became so bewildered and confused that she mistook the Robert's Trail Camp on St. Mary River for the Gunsight Camp and soon became lost in the woods to the right of the glacier trail. It was a considerable time after the accident that her absence was noticed and immediately parties were formed to search. Everything possible was done, and from fifteen to twenty men scoured the woods most of the night. She

had, however, not been found when Mr. Galen and I arrived at the Gunsight Camp, which was at 4:15 this morning. We then made all arrangements for a systematic search to be started at 6:00 A.M. and were just commencing this search when Miss Edwards showed up at camp accompanied by two guides who had been with her during the night. She was very much exhausted but a physician in the party advised that she would be all right after a day's rest.

The body of Doctor Fletcher was moved by Lanneau down the Gunsight Trail, leaving Gunsight Camp at 2:30 A.M. We arranged for the boat at the head of the lake and for the automobile truck at St. Mary's, so that there was no delay in moving the body which arrived at Glacier Park at 11:30 this morning, where it was embalmed and will be forwarded to Indianapolis on Train Two tonight.

I accompanied Mrs. Fletcher from Gunsight Camp to Glacier Park where we arrived at 3:30 this P.M.

All members of the Prairie Club and others at Gunsight Camp speak in highest terms of the efforts of guides and employees in rescuing the body of Doctor Fletcher and in their all night search for Miss Edwards and there is not the least feeling, so far as I can tell, of placing responsibility for the accident on anyone connected with the Park.

The main body of the Prairie Club departed from Gunsight Camp at 1:00 P.M. for Sperry and will continue their trip according to itinerary.

Yours truly,
Signed, J. M. Cathcart

The high-profile snow and ice avalanche death of Dr. Fletcher stood alone for forty years despite increasing tourism and exploration of the park's glacier features.

PARK SERVICE AVALANCHE INCIDENTS

It wasn't until 1933 that another avalanche incident was reported. In a short paragraph within the superintendent's annual report, the superintendent somewhat casually and dismissively noted, "On February 21st, 1933, Ranger Ben C. Miller was caught in a snow slide, while on patrol, and was forced to spend the night and part of the day extricating himself." Given that it was a February night, during one of the coldest periods of the year, this must have been an intense experience. The superintendent goes on to write, "He was on snowshoes and had a pack on his back when a slide off Scalplock Mountain carried him down the mountain-side about 200 feet. When it stopped he was **completely buried** [emphasis added]. His principal difficulties were due to the pack he had on his back and the snowshoes on his feet, from which it took him 25 hours to set himself free. Luckily for him, his only injuries were frostbites, a few sprains, shock and utter exhaustion." Really, that's all! The superintendent seems to imply that this is well within what a ranger should expect and survive without complaint. Nonetheless, Miller had a close call with a snow avalanche.

A spotter watches for avalanches while a dozer operator shovels snow off Going-to-the-Sun Road. COURTESY OF NATIONAL PARK SERVICE.

Avalanche risks escalated once a road was built over the Continental Divide. The Going-to-the-Sun Road is, without doubt, the premier attraction of Glacier National Park. Park Superintendent Eivind Scoyen described it as "the most beautiful piece of mountain road in the world" during his speech to several thousand spectators at the road's 1933 dedication ceremony. His words still resonate today. Park surveys revealed that approximately seventy percent of the park's nearly 3 million annual visitors travel this road. More than 500,000 vehicles travel the Sun Road during Glacier's peak visitor season from June to October—about 3,500 vehicles per day.

Many people don't feel that the park is fully open until the annual clearing of snow on the road is completed. Then the floods of tourists come to drive to Logan Pass and revel in the alpine scenery. For that reason, there is always a focus on *safely* getting the road open as soon as feasible.

A snowplowing crew typically starts working its way up the Sun Road in early spring with a variety of heavy machinery. The crew often encounters snow and debris from avalanches that slide over the alpine section of the road. Crews use rotary plows, bulldozers, and excavators to remove the debris—a mix of dense snow and ice, rocks, and parts of trees.

Crews in the early years had close calls with springtime avalanches coming down while they worked. Reminiscing at a Glacier Park Alumni picnic in 2016, Roger Anderson related that in 1953, he was one of the earliest avalanche spotters; his job was to constantly scan the slopes above for any moving snow and alert the plow operators working on the road. As reported by Chris Peterson in the *Hungry Horse News*, Anderson's job could be overly exciting:

> Anderson said he got pretty good at spotting avalanche conditions. One day, he and Claude Tesmer, who was plow foreman, were up at Oberlin Bend when the sun came out. Sun was not a good thing. "On the warmer days the snow got soft and it would start to slide," Anderson said. They looked skyward. Then heard it. Avalanches. "That whole Garden Wall started to slide," he said. They thought

*they might have to spend the night up there, as the slides
blocked the way. But then a cloud went over the sun and
that was their chance, Anderson explained. They went for
it, ran down the Sun Road as fast as they could. "We got
caught between two active slides," Anderson said. On top
of that, there was a grizzly bear in a chute. He had found
a bighorn sheep carcass. He was just a few feet off the
road and not too happy to see them, Anderson said.
"He was mad, but he wasn't about to attack us," he said.
"He wanted that sheep." They were able to get by the bear
and over the slide in front of them and safely out of there.*

It was also in 1953, in May, that two crew members were killed. That year, the crews encountered an exceptionally heavy snowpack, and they were on high alert for potential avalanches. After a snowstorm ended on May 26, the crew was clearing the road of new avalanche debris and fresh snow when a massive avalanche swept down, tossing bulldozers and other machinery off the road, and overcoming four men. Buried in densely packed snow, Bill Whitford and George Beaton died. Whitford was in the cab of one machine when the avalanche hit and he was found 600 feet down the slope, thrown out of the cab and completely buried except for the tip of his boot. A bloodhound dog found Beaton the next day 1,200 feet below the road under three feet of snow. Another man, Fred Klein, was swept 300 feet below the road and partially buried. He was badly injured but alive, and rescuers dug him out. The fourth man, Jean Sullivan, probably saved his life by jumping into a trench in the snow cut by one of the snow removal machines. This prevented him from being swept over the side of the road and downslope. The downside was that he was completely buried in the trench, could hardly move, and eventually passed out from lack of oxygen. He remained buried for more than seven hours. Sullivan recalled the incident in Dave Walters' book, *Montana Campfire Tales*, saying, "I had asked Bill [Whitford], who had his head stuck out of the cab window, and George [Beaton] if they felt it was safe. George said, 'Hell yes, Jean. Let's blow it out and we'll be out of here

A mountain of slide debris dwarfs rescuers after the May 26, 1953, avalanche on Going-to-the-Sun Road. A. E. ALLEN, COURTESY OF GLACIER NATIONAL PARK ARCHIVES.

in thirty minutes.' He just got the words out of his mouth when I heard a little s-w-i-s-h. We call this kind of a quiet slide a 'sneaker.' I looked up and the snow slide was coming—no more than eighty feet above us—and I hollered." After the slide, men probed the snow with poles and discovered Sullivan; they dug him out and sent him to the hospital. Reflecting on the near-death experience more than a decade later, Sullivan's wife, May, summarized the effect that the avalanche had on her husband. According to Walters, May explained, "Before '53, there were times when Jean was just absolute hell to live with. But after he'd been buried for seven hours on Going-to-the-Sun Road he became a dear." Within a month of his ordeal, Jean returned to his job clearing the Sun Road.

In 1964, a bulldozer triggered the release of a wet slab of snow that carried the machine off the road. The driver was injured but survived. Today, avalanche experts monitor the slopes above the road, and lookouts use radios to warn plow operators of any unsafe conditions.

AVALANCHES IN THE BACKCOUNTRY

In recent years, increased interest in exploring and skiing unbroken snow in the backcountry has led to improvements in skiing and snowboarding equipment that have drawn even more people to this activity. Glacier National Park has seen its share of backcountry skiers and snowboarders checking out lines and enjoying first descents. One area that many in this adventuresome tribe use is near Elk Mountain inside the southern boundary of the park and just off U.S. Highway 2 southwest of Marias Pass. A key skill in venturing into a snowy wilderness is assessing the avalanche hazard, and it's wise to travel with competent partners. Two tales from the Elk Mountain area illustrate how different the outcomes can be when avalanches change your euphoric snow day into a matter of death or survival.

In the first incident, on March 31, 2010, a lone snowboarder, thirty-seven-year-old Brian C. Wright, likely triggered and then was caught in an avalanche. He was familiar with the terrain and, according to friends, snowboarded there frequently. Wright lived and worked in East Glacier during the winter and often rode the slopes in Glacier Park alone. He was known by the nickname "Verbal," an ironic reference to his quiet demeanor; he liked to spend time by himself. Wright worked at the Whitefish Lake Golf Club in the summer and did some work in East Glacier during the winter backcountry season. He was well-liked by co-workers and, according to his friend Jason Robertson of Whitefish, "he was quiet and kept to himself, but once you got to know him, he opened up." Robertson was a regular ski partner of Wright's and said that Wright probably snowboarded Mount Shields more than anyone in the park's history. "He was out there every single day. He maybe took a rest day once a month."

A moisture-laden Pacific storm rolled through the area beginning on March 28, leaving up to fifteen inches of new snow, a strong incentive to get out and ride a snowboard. Based on the park service investigation and press release, it appeared that Wright left his car at the Fielding Ranger Station trailhead and skied to Mount Shields. Later he completed two descents from Peak 6996, named for its elevation, along a ridge near Mount Shields. According to an April 8, 2010, *Hungry Horse News* article, at about 1 P.M. on March 31, Wright called his mother on his cell phone from the summit. Then he pushed off for his next descent and likely triggered a large slab avalanche. Investigators later found Wright's snowboard track from the point where he likely triggered it to where it was intersected by avalanche debris. From that trigger point to the top of the avalanche was 250 vertical feet—a sizable amount of the avalanched snow collapsed above him. The rushing snow swept him up and carried him more than 500 feet downslope and through some small trees. In that area, investigators found some bloodstains on the snow. They believe that he tumbled a total of 2,000 feet before he stopped. Avalanche debris was measured at twenty to thirty feet high. It appears that he lived long enough to partially descend further with his snowboard before abandoning it and continuing on foot until he died. Wright had texted his friends about 6 P.M. on Tuesday evening (March 30) saying he was on Mount Shields. When friends did not get any text messages on Wednesday, March 31, they grew concerned. On Thursday, April 1, a friend found Wright's vehicle at the Fielding Ranger Station trailhead. This friend started skiing up the mountain until he spotted the body within the slide path of the avalanche and skied out to report the fatality around 2 P.M., which initiated the body recovery and investigation. Responding personnel reported that the snowpack "whumpfed" as it collapsed under their weight, a strong indication of an unstable snowpack that one should pay heed to. Although it was believed that the victim had an avalanche transceiver, neither his transceiver nor backpack was found.

The second backcountry avalanche incident occurred on Tuesday, January 8, 2013. Justin Steck, thirty-five, and Jason Robertson, thirty-four, were steadily plodding up Elk Mountain. Steck was on skis and Robertson was on a splitboard, a two-piece snowboard that separates for ski-like use on the ascent and can then be latched together as a single snowboard for the descent. They were using ski skins that allowed them to slide forward and upward on the snow with each step but not slip back. The men forged through the snow on a climbing path called a "skin track," zigzagging back and forth until they decided on a place to start their descent. Backcountry skiers and riders often climb the same skin track for another run. Steck and Robertson had been up on Elk Mountain the previous day and enjoyed skiing parts of the lower mountain. Neither Steck nor Robertson checked the avalanche advisory the next day when they went back for more backcountry skiing adventure and fun. Unfortunately, the Flathead Avalanche Center advisory for that day read, "The general avalanche hazard will increase to CONSIDERABLE at mid and upper elevations in our region. New storm accumulations will be easily transported to form soft surface slabs on lee slopes and in chutes. The new snow should bond well with Monday's storm snow but weak interfaces on or just below recent rain crusts will be the concern."

Steck and Robertson climbed the southeast ridge of Peak 6996 (aka Little Shields) to the summit, and they descended a chute in the new snow for 2,000 feet, a wild and exhilarating ride. Deciding to go back for more, they ascended a small creek drainage to a different aspect of Elk Mountain. Robertson was about ten minutes ahead of Steck and reached the 7,835-foot summit of Elk Mountain. He then latched his snowboard together and came whizzing down to Steck, who was still climbing up the skin track. As they joined up, Steck mentioned to Robertson that he had witnessed an avalanche to his right after Robertson had gone ahead to the summit. Avalanches are, literally, slippery phenomena. They naturally occur when forces such as wind or rain trigger the release of a weak layer, or they can be directly triggered by the weight of a skier. However, a skier's weight can set in motion a collapse of the weak layer like a falling house of cards, and it can travel through the snow to release the avalanche at some distance from the skier. This is what may have caused the avalanche that Steck saw.

Steck and Robertson began their descent at this point, with Robertson going first. He rode his snowboard down about 750 feet and then pulled up on a small ridge with trees, a safe spot to watch his buddy from. Low clouds now obscured his view, but he knew Steck was skiing down. While he was waiting, he noticed avalanche debris off to his right from the avalanche that Steck had mentioned. He noticed the crown, which is where the snow slab tears away from the rest of the snowpack. If the crown is deep, the avalanche was likely large. Robertson became concerned. Just then, he looked back upslope and noticed a powder cloud blasting toward him and no sign of Steck. Fearing for his life, Robertson whipped his snowboard around and began riding down but was immediately engulfed in the powder cloud and surging snow. Fighting through the snowy maelstrom, he was able to stay upright and ride down and out of the avalanche and up onto a ridge out of the danger. Robertson had not seen Steck since he took his initial ride from up in the clouds. Desperately he scanned the terrain as the powder cloud settled and the broken, jumbled snow debris came to a stop. Almost immediately he heard shouts from the slope below. Steck had been carried by the avalanche from a point way above Robertson and then was swept past him even as Robertson himself was riding the avalanche down. Robertson struggled across the blocky and now hard snow debris and found Steck buried up to his neck with only his left arm and head out of the debris. The helmet he was wearing had shattered, likely saving his life or at the very least saving him from significant brain trauma. Steck was not wearing an avalanche transceiver and was lucky to have had his head out of the snow when the debris stopped moving. Many avalanche victims are not so lucky, and only minutes are available to dig someone out before they suffocate. A transceiver can make it far more likely that those precious minutes count for rescue.

As Robertson began digging Steck out, he noticed a bruise on his friend's forehead, and Steck reported pain in his ribs and left arm from his wild tumble through the avalanche's fury. Later, during the investigation, it was determined that Steck had been carried through a stand of small trees. Had those trees been bigger, Steck wouldn't have been so lucky. A common cause of death in avalanche incidents is that the victim collides with a sturdy tree with the force of tons of cascading snow from behind. People who have survived being in a snow avalanche report complete disorientation with no sense of up or down or of time. Steck thought he had been swept down only thirty or forty yards in the river of snow but, in fact, it was about 800 vertical feet and easily more than 300 linear yards down the slope.

Finally freeing Steck, Robertson called friends in nearby East Glacier to help with an evacuation and then called 911 to report the incident.

Despite pain and deep snow, the two men made their way downhill without the benefit of Steck's skis and equipment, which remained buried in the avalanche. At last they made it to one of the skin tracks, which made their progress a little easier, and then they were met in the fading light by a friend who brought extra skis. After dark, a rescue party arrived on snow machines, and Steck was taken the last mile and a half by snow machine to a waiting ambulance while the others skied out.

Steck had significant injuries—a broken lower left arm, six broken ribs, a head contusion, and a head laceration. The avalanche that he triggered and was engulfed in was about 150 feet wide and 2 to 3 feet deep where it started. It ran 1,400 vertical feet, gathering more snow as it barreled downslope. Steck was a lucky skier.

On January 5, 2017, Ben Parsons, thirty-six, and Joel Shehan, thirty-eight and a close friend, were on a ridge near the summit of 7,750-foot Stanton Mountain near the head of Lake McDonald. They had skied up with the intention of descending a route on a slope they had skied before. Both men were highly accomplished backcountry skiers with training in avalanche hazard assessment. Parsons was a firefighter in nearby Whitefish and an accomplished endurance athlete. After checking snow conditions, they decided that skiing down their planned route wasn't advisable. Instead, they began traversing just below the ridge looking for a safe slope to ski down. They were about 500 feet below the summit when Ben inadvertently triggered an

Ben Parsons was an expert ski mountaineer and also a mentor to many aspiring endurance athletes in northwestern Montana. BEN PARSONS, COURTESY OF RIDGE ACADEMY.

avalanche in soft snow. As reported in the *Flathead Beacon*, Shehan said, "We were 10 feet from complete safety when it slid." Shehan, skiing close behind Parsons, was not caught in the slide, but he watched as Parsons was swept down, eventually tumbling out of sight in the surging snow torrent. Using his beacon transceiver, Shehan immediately searched the entire 4,100-foot length of the slide without picking up Parsons' signal. He then began yelling Parsons' name and finally located him when Parsons managed a faint reply. The avalanche had carried Parsons about 1,000 feet in elevation and 1,700 feet in distance down the slope. Shehan found him upside down, pinned against a tree, and critically injured. At 3:15 P.M., Shehan dialed 9-1-1 on his cell phone, and a rapid response by Two Bear Air Rescue extricated Parsons from the avalanche debris shortly after 4 P.M. Although alert and conscious when the helicopter arrived, Parsons died of his injuries during the rescue.

The *Flathead Beacon* described Parsons as "a devoted family man and friend to many . . . well known throughout the community, where he was recognized for his unrivaled prowess as an elite mountain biker and ski mountaineer, as well as for his infectious smile and gregarious nature." Parsons' death was a blow to the local community, and to honor the local legend, a large crowd gathered to ski up the local ski area. A trail for "skinning up" the mountain was named after him, and there was tremendous turnout for the memorial service that included full honors from the firefighting and emergency services community. Parsons' amazing athleticism, backcountry skiing experience, and knowledge of avalanche risk made it hard for some people to believe that he would be killed in an avalanche. But nature is unpredictable and often unforgiving.

An avalanche indirectly claimed the life of a young woman in the Avalanche Lake basin, roughly in the same area that Kootenai Chief Paul David escaped a snow slide in the 1860s, as described in the first incident in this chapter. In June in Glacier Park, there is still a great deal of snow clinging to the slopes that can become unstable on warm, sunny days and give way. This is what happened on June 23, 1995. Lela Breitbart, twenty-four, from Pleasantville, New York, was enjoying an off-trail scramble with two friends above Avalanche Lake near a snowfield when an avalanche occurred upslope. Although the tumbling and sliding snow stopped before reaching Breitbart, the avalanche dislodged rocks, one of which struck Breitbart in the back of the head. She lost consciousness. One friend ran for help. Park dispatchers meanwhile were alerted by a visitor who saw the avalanche occur. Despite the timely response of rangers and the CPR that was administered by other hikers before the rangers arrived, Breitbart did not survive. Her body was removed by helicopter.

Despite its steep terrain and ample winter snowfall, Glacier sees relatively few deaths due to avalanches. This is mostly attributable to relatively low visitation during winter, particularly in avalanche-prone areas. Compared to the summer season, park access in winter is limited, and much of the backcountry terrain is remote and too dangerous for the average cross-country skier or snowshoer. Elsewhere, snowmobilers sometimes trigger or get caught in avalanches, but snow machines are prohibited within park boundaries. Because of the risks and difficulties involved, the few people who do venture into Glacier's backcountry during winter tend to be highly experienced and skilled. Finally, the monitoring and forecasting of avalanche conditions is increasingly sophisticated. Experienced winter recreationists check these forecasts daily. Proper training in avalanche awareness and the use of tools such as personal beacons, probe poles, packable shovels, and other safety gear are also helping to reduce avalanche injuries and fatalities.

FALLING OBJECTS

In addition to deaths and injuries from snow and ice falling, frequent rockfall and debris flows caused by heavy precipitation pose a danger to people. Rockfall, for instance, contributed to the falling deaths of two men, described in Chapter 7, who worked on the construction of the Going-to-the-Sun Road.

George Bristol remembered another rockfall incident poignantly, as he was one of those called to respond. It occurred in 1962, one of his first years as a Glacier Park trail crew member. He was off duty, playing baseball in Babb with some of the Blackfeet tribe kids on June 28. The call came in, and he and his Many Glacier crew of six men got in trucks and went over Logan Pass to the west side where the accident had occurred. By the time they arrived, there were all kinds of ambulances, park police, and other vehicles at the site. The crew was assigned to look for a little girl who had wandered off in the confusion. The accident itself was a staggering scene. At about 7 P.M., a huge boulder, estimated to weigh 400 pounds, had dislodged from above, fallen 500 feet, and hit a Volkswagen on the road to Logan Pass. The driver, a man from Canada, and his daughter were in the front seats, and his wife, Alice Jean Leckie, fifty-two years old, was stretched out in the back seat with her face down on the car's seat cushion because she was afraid of heights and didn't want to look out over the edge of the road to the depths below. The car was traveling thirty miles per hour, and investigators suggested that the last part of the rock's free fall just happened to be milliseconds from hitting the back of the car or not. The rock hit the back of the car and completely flattened it. Mrs. Leckie didn't make a sound as the rock crashed into the back of the car. Mr. Leckie looked back and swerved, but his daughter, Maureen, nineteen, grabbed the steering wheel and drove the crumpled car into a snowbank. When Bristol and crew arrived, the plan was to remove the rock, but he said to himself, "I can't believe there was anything left but a god-awful pancake." The dad was sitting on the stone wall in shock with his wife dead. The crew eventually found the little girl down the road and brought her up to her father, but this did not bring much solace to Mr. Leckie. Later, Bristol heard that a scientist had calculated the chances of the accident happening and announced it was a 50 million-to-one chance. But thirty-four years later it happened again.

In 1996, Tsuyoshi Kamochi, thirty, and Yoko Kamochi (variously described in reports as his wife or sister), twenty-nine, both attended school near Washington, D.C. On vacation, they had rented a car and were touring over the Sun Road on June 23, enjoying the park and probably blissfully unaware of the inherent danger of the mountains. Suddenly, at around 9:30 A.M., a large landslide blanketed the roadway with tons of rock. This rockslide began when a twenty-five-ton boulder crashed to the road from about 200 feet above. According to the local newspaper, "Although the monster boulder missed the vehicle, a shower of smaller rocks crushed the car as the couple attempted to back out of the path of the falling debris. The front of the car was destroyed, bursting into flames and then crushing the victim from the waist down. The impact flattened the wheel rims and pressed the chassis into the pavement, leaving an impression in the asphalt." Rescuers were able to free Yoko from the car in minutes and she suffered only minor injuries, but Tsuyoshi died trapped in the vehicle.

Debris flows occur when huge amounts of water, usually from an intense storm, carry rocks downhill in a slurry that piles up once it reaches a flatter surface, such as the Sun Road. On July 28, 1998, park employees were traversing the Sun Road on a stormy evening when torrential rains loosened an abundance of fractured rock on the slopes of Going-to-the-Sun Mountain above the road. As reported in the *Hungry Horse News*, three debris flows covered the road with tons of rock and soil debris. The first slide deposited an estimated forty tons of debris and stopped all westbound traffic. Just beyond, a second slide sluiced another twenty tons onto the road. The vehicles stacked up behind these blockades, unable to proceed. Then, the third slide came down behind the dozen or so vehicles that were waiting, effectively trapping them. They were now sitting ducks on the road, potential targets for any additional debris flows. One park employee described it as one of the more frightening events in his life. He was helpless to act to make himself safer and the likelihood of more debris flows sweeping down seemed quite high. Eventually, crews brought in heavy machinery to carve an escape route through the debris, but the entire road was closed for nearly twenty-four hours until the tons of mud and rock could be moved. Luckily, no people were injured and no vehicles were damaged, but the tense period when nature seemed to rule absolutely is a time remembered with dread by those who were trapped.

CHAPTER ELEVEN

MISSING,
NEVER FOUND

"Do not feel alarmed, we feel that no harm has befallen them. We have many cases of this kind every year and never any serious accidents." So wrote Chief Ranger James Brooks to Dora Whitehead, a widow and the mother of two young men who had vanished somewhere in Glacier National Park in 1924. The mysterious disappearance of the Whitehead brothers soon captured national attention.

In August 1924, Joseph Whitehead, twenty-nine, an engineer for the Universal Battery Company in Chicago, and William Whitehead, twenty-two, who attended MIT in Boston, boarded the Great Northern Railway's Oriental Limited bound for Glacier National Park. They arrived at Glacier Park Station on August 17. The two brothers had carefully planned their itinerary for a two-week wilderness experience in the park. According to Jerome S. DeSanto in "Missing in Glacier" and other sources, the young men stayed at Glacier Park Lodge the first night, then traveled by automobile to St. Mary, then by boat to the Going-to-the-Sun Chalet near the head of St. Mary Lake. On August 19, they rode horseback over Piegan Pass to Many Glacier Chalet. They stayed there for four nights while taking short day hikes to Cracker Lake, Iceberg Lake, Grinnell Glacier, and other nearby viewing points.

$1,700.00 REWARD
For
JOSEPH and WILLIAM WHITEHEAD

Brothers disappeared Sunday, August 24, 1924, on the trail between Granite Park Chalets and the Lewis Hotel in Glacier National Park, Montana.

JOSEPH H. WHITEHEAD	WILLIAM A. WHITEHEAD
Age, 29.	Age, 22.
Height, 5 ft. 11 in.	Height, 5 ft. 11½ in
Weight, 175 lbs.	Weight, 155 lbs.
Gray eyes.	Brown eyes.
Dark brown hair.	Dark brown hair.
Ruddy complexion.	Dark complexion.
Wore glasses with dark rims.	Wore glasses with dark rims.

Both wore hiking clothes: gray knickers, gray wool shirts, high tan laced hiking shoes, soft felt hats. Carried light packs. Both wore sweaters: one gray, the other tan.

Sons of Mrs. Dora B. Whitehead, ~~3040 Warren Avenue~~ *5839 Washington Blvd*, Chicago.

Notify: Charles J. Kraebel, Supt. Glacier National Park, Belton, Montana.

Despite an extensive search and $1,700 reward, the Whitehead brothers were never found. COURTESY OF GLACIER NATIONAL PARK ARCHIVES.

The Whitehead brothers wrote their mother, Dora, every day, saying they were enjoying themselves very much, and in their August 20 letter they assured her, "Don't worry, mother, we won't go into any danger." Their final letter to her was dated August 23, saying they were just leaving Many Glacier for Granite Park.

After arriving at the Granite Park Chalet, they took a short walk, then relaxed around the chalet and prepared for the much longer hike they planned for the following day. That's the last time anyone ever saw the two young men.

The Whiteheads were due back in Chicago September 1. The absence of their daily letter since August 23 alarmed Dora Whitehead, and when neither of her sons got off the train in Chicago she immediately reported them missing to park authorities.

Ranger Brooks took charge of the investigation. The young men had left a detailed itinerary with their mother and with the Universal Battery Company where Joseph worked. Rangers checked out all the places on their itinerary, including making inquiries to all the guests at Granite Park Chalet. There was no sign or clue about where the brothers were. Even so, Ranger Brooks and acting park superintendent Henry Hutchings were optimistic. They could have left the park and failed to notify their relatives.

The investigation continued, and by September 11 Hutchings was convinced that the young men had tried to hike cross-country and had become lost or had drowned in a lake or stream. He wrote to National Park Service director Stephen Mather that seven search parties were searching and all clues were being checked out. He also commented that "if the boys are lost in the park, it will only be an accident if their bodies are found. . . . It's like searching for a needle in a haystack!"

Almost immediately, the reports of the missing brothers garnered nationwide attention. Newspapers reported that President Calvin Coolidge "has interested himself in the search and had wired park officials to spare no expense." Ranger Brooks was required to wire the daily facts of the search to the National Park Service director every morning and evening.

By September 14, Ranger Brooks and other searchers concluded there was no hope of finding the brothers in the park. In a letter to Charles Kraebel, newly appointed Glacier National Park superintendent, Brooks pointed out the extra men were costing $30 to $40 a day, and the rangers from the park's east side were needed in their districts—the fire danger was high and that part of the park was unprotected. Brooks suggested that the search be abandoned. He also wrote Dora Whitehead that "[O]ur Rangers are experienced men, imbued with the spirit of going out to accomplish the task as assigned to them. When they fail it is because they have exhausted every possible means."

The next day, Mather met with Dora Whitehead in Chicago and the following day told Kraebel that he had given her his "personal assurance that you and Brooks were doing everything possible to locate her sons." In the next few days, the Bureau of Biological Survey (the forerunner of today's U.S. Fish and Wildlife Service) joined in the search. They brought in their best hunter and trapper, Chauncey "Chance" Beebe, to bring his dogs and use his outdoor skills to search for the brothers. Meanwhile, Kraebel wrote to Dora, "We have been most diligent in our search and have had a large force of experienced mountain men, rangers and old guides constantly in the field. These men have not done their work casually but with intense application. . . . The intuition of some of these men is very keen and their failure to discover any trace of the boys is a great mystery to all of us." He added, "In view of the high character of your boys . . . there seems no remotest reason for suspecting foul play. Nevertheless you may be encouraged to know that our sheriff is working on the case from this angle."

The possibility that the boys were waylaid or a victim of a hold-up was immediately regarded as a plausible theory. Dora wrote back that she was certain her boys would never have taken any chances; they had to have been the victims of a hold-up somewhere on that trail. She offered a $500 reward (today, nearly $7,000) "to anyone who gives positive and satisfactory evidence of locating her two sons." The Great Northern Railway's Louis Hill offered a $1,000 reward, and the Masonic Lodge of Chicago where Joseph was a member added another $200. The $1,700 reward brought forth several plausible theories and a few accusations of murder and robbery. The possibility of kidnapping or murder on federal property had also brought in Federal Bureau of Investigation agents to aid in the search; they investigated all the possibilities, but there was no real evidence to support any of the theories or accusations.

Dora Whitehead never gave up pursuing what happened to her sons, and she wouldn't let the government give up either. The massive search continued for months and then years, but nothing was found that would provide a clue to what really happened to the brothers. The FBI Whitehead case files remained open for thirty-seven years, until 1961, when finally the case of the Missing Whitehead Boys was officially closed and their disappearance set as a legendary Glacier National Park mystery.

The unsolved mystery of the Whitehead brothers did, however, change the focus of park ranger duties. As Curt Buchholtz wrote in *Man in Glacier*, "from that point on the job of the park's rangers forever shifted. Protecting, rescuing or finding visitors became a full-time occupation of the ranger force; at least as important as preserving the natural features of the park."

Since the disappearance of the Whitehead brothers, there have been five others who disappeared in the park and were never found. In July 1933, Dr. W. Cosby Bell hiked up Mount Brown and never returned. He was never found. The next year, on August 13, 1934, Frederick H. Lumley, a twenty-seven-year-old assistant professor from Ohio State University, left Goat Haunt Chalet at the head of Waterton Lake. He was never seen again. Canadian officials, American searchers, and FBI agents searched for him. The search was called off in October, and the park superintendent admitted "the odds are strongly against ever finding him."

On July 21 or 22, 1963, David Wilson, a twenty-one-year-old park service employee, disappeared while descending Going-to-the-Sun Mountain. He was climbing alone and had signed the register on the summit. An extensive search was organized and the FBI assisted. No clue to what happened to David Wilson was ever found.

Sometime after November 3, 2000, Patrick T. Whalen, thirty-three, had gone into the Cut Bank Creek drainage and was never seen again. Rangers found his unauthorized camp and his personal items at Atlantic Creek in May 2001. His truck was found on U.S. Highway 89 near Kiowa Junction. What happened to Whalen, or where he went, is still unknown.

Another mysterious disappearance in Glacier National Park occurred in 2003. According to Chris Peterson's article in the *Hungry Horse News*, "They've searched the trails. They've dove the lake. But there's still no sign of a Michigan man whose rig [truck] was found abandoned in Glacier National Park last month." Larry Thomas Kimball, forty, was described as tall and slender, with brown hair, brown eyes, and wearing glasses. When he was last seen by family members, his hair was mid-shoulder length and worn in a ponytail. Kimball reportedly smoked Swisher Sweets cigars and may have been wearing black steel-toed work boots. He apparently left his Michigan home sometime in April—his brother did not know why. Kimball drove across the country to Glacier National Park in a 1998 dark blue, dual-wheeled GMC truck. His truck was found in a parking area off the Inside North Fork Road across from the Rocky Point trailhead on June 16. It appeared abandoned. Based on a park entrance receipt found in the truck, Kimble had entered the park May 29.

The area where he may have disappeared was burned over after the Robert Fire crossed into the park that July. Further investigation of that area for clues to what happened to Kimball proved unsuccessful.

Five people gone missing are known or believed to have drowned in the park, though their bodies were never found. Also, two hikers fell and their bodies have not been found, although in the case of Yi-Jien Hwa, bone fragments were discovered. These incidents are covered in the chapters on drowning and hiking.

CHAPTER TWELVE

DEATH
by
EXPOSURE

Unlike the more dramatic deaths due to accidents or animal attacks, succumbing to cold seems like an uneventful way to go, but the stories are surprisingly compelling. The first recorded death after Glacier Park was established in 1910 was due to exposure. It happened during a bitter cold spell in January 1913, with temperatures ranging around 18 below zero and, according to Ranger Pearl, "the wind blowing & snowing."

On January 6, newly appointed Glacier Park superintendent James Galen traveled to the east side of the park and met with the Lower Two Medicine Station ranger, Norton Pearl. Pearl had arrived at the park in November 1912 just before James Galen took over the job of park superintendent on December 1, 1912; Galen replaced the park's first superintendent, William Logan, who had died in February 1912.

Pearl kept a detailed diary of his experiences in the park, which thankfully was later published by his granddaughter Leslie Lee in her book, *Backcountry Ranger in Glacier National Park 1910-1913: The Diaries & Photographs of Norton Pearl.* This story of the first death in Glacier National Park is excerpted from the Pearl diaries.

Superintendent Galen and Ranger Pearl planned to snowshoe to the Cut Bank Ranger Station to meet with Ranger Joe Prince where they would spend the night, and then the three men would make their way to Ranger Bill Burns' St. Mary Ranger Station. It was rough going, but Galen and Pearl made it to the Cut Bank Station. They enjoyed a good meal and a smoke with Prince. The next morning, they headed for St. Mary Station. Prince broke trail for a short distance, then Pearl took over. At the top of the hill north of the Cut Bank Station, Prince gave directions but they turned out to be wrong. Eventually the men got straightened out and headed for St. Mary Ridge. Two or three times during their trek, Galen and Pearl had to wait for Prince, which was unusual—he was usually good on the trail. Prince said he was okay except that his shoes didn't swing right on account of the toe straps on his snowshoes and he couldn't keep up. Eventually Prince fell back out of sight. Galen and Pearl went on, knowing that Prince was a seasoned backcountry ranger and would likely show up a couple of hours later. When he didn't come in that night, Galen and Pearl went out the next morning, doubled back on the trail, and found him. Pearl wrote in his diary that Prince "cashed in last night. O! The sight was hell . . . poor old man lying stark and cold on his back, his hat & mittens off, his eyes frozen open. Poor old man with gray hair, past fifty, stark and cold, with a grit that killed . . . poor Joe upon the trail cold and still. The blasts and the storms will neer bother him more and the snap of tonight he does not feel."

Ranger Joe Prince died January 8, 1913, at fifty-seven. We can only speculate, but in hindsight it appears that Prince was struggling during his trek, perhaps from heart trouble or some other illness. Uncharacteristically, he had been confused about where they were and had led them in the wrong direction to St. Mary Station. Prince had lagged behind, saying he was okay and that he was falling behind due to his shoes, but men of his times and ilk were not inclined to admit to being sick or unable to keep going and do their job. It is likely that he had been too sick to go on and had slowly succumbed to exposure, until he sat down and froze to death.

In today's world, it is unthinkable to leave a struggling person behind on the trail even if you are confident they can make it on their own.

The next deaths due to exposure to the park's unpredictable and harsh weather conditions occurred in 1925, as documented in a coroner's report and that year's annual report of the park superintendent. In August, well-known visitors to the park, Joseph and Emily Wheeler, were camping at Lake Ellen Wilson below Gunsight Pass. The couple left their car at Lake McDonald on August 10 for what was supposed to be a three-day hiking trip. Three days later, campers saw the Wheelers at the lean-to that the couple had set up as a shelter; the Wheelers told them that they planned to prolong their trip. Rain fell on the park on August 14 and 15, and then it turned cold and snowy by the evening of the 15th. Evidently now alone at Lake Ellen Wilson as the weather worsened, the Wheelers attempted to get to Sperry Chalet, which required climbing over Lincoln Pass in a snowstorm and in the dark. The snow had obliterated the trail and it could not be followed. According to the coroner's report, "They found shelter by a projecting end of a large rock and there perished. He [Mr. Wheeler] was attempting to build a fire—had a few sticks collected and some paper but everything was too wet to burn and the chill and dampness soon over-came them." A partially burned wad of paper was found that appeared to be the only attempt to light the fire. The storm produced about fourteen inches of snow, and the Wheelers were wearing clothes suitable only for summer weather. The Wheelers' absence was not reported until a week had passed because the Wheelers themselves had said they were extending their hike. Search parties were sent out, and the bodies were found August 29 by R. W. Fleming, a park ranger. They were on the south slope of Lincoln Pass, just a few miles from safety at the chalet. The coroner's report was filed August 30, two weeks after the Wheelers likely died in the storm. The cause of death was listed as "Chilled to death following exposure and exhaustion."

The next death due to exposure was in 1927 when Ole Helander, thirty-seven, died on February 7 in Lake McDonald near the Lewis Hotel. The coroner's report said that his body was found "in hole in ice," that his parents were in Sweden, and that he had with him one watch, $6.30 in cash, and keys. So how did he come to this end? Helander, a "great big husky fellow," was staying with Dave Rosier, a caretaker at the Lewis Hotel, that winter. He was a nephew of some people who ran a lumber-yard in Columbia Falls. Helander was with Rosier and a Mr. Hayworth in a boat when they hit ice and capsized, according to the report. The three men fell into the near-freezing water. Helander, being the young and strong one, took off to break trail through the snow for the older men and to get a fire started so that they could warm up, undoubtedly knowing that they didn't have much time. The older men struggled along and then came upon Helander, who had broken through ice a second time and presumably got soaked again. The coroner's report states that Helander was dying from exposure at this point, although the time of death was eventually listed as 11 P.M.

In 1977, Mrs. Gonhild "Bud" Henderson gave an oral history that provided some additional insights into this event. The men had picked up supplies in Belton, loaded them onto the boat, and were rowing them up the lake toward the Lewis Hotel but it was 20 below zero and, as they rowed, the lake began freezing over. They tried cutting the ice ahead of the boat. The wooden boat was damaged by the ice and it began to fill with water near what is now Sprague Creek Campground. Mr. Hayworth's leather shoes froze from the water in the bottom of the boat. After the boat sank and they had waded hip deep in the water to shore, they had to contend with two feet of snow. When the older men came upon Helander later, he couldn't walk and lay in the snow while they struggled on to the hotel. They couldn't find anybody to respond there for a rescue, so Rosier called Henderson, who was at the train depot in Belton, and she tried to contact rangers without success. She decided to go up on her own and try to save him. So she took off on skis and car-ried some whiskey. Skiing through the night, she said it was "awfully cold, it was just snapping, the trees would just snap, you know." Henderson got there about 2 A.M. as a Mr. Chadburn also arrived, and together they found Helander in the bright moonlight. She started to work on him by pouring whiskey into him and vigorously massaging him, moving his legs and arms to get the blood (and whiskey) to flow. Henderson demanded that a fire get started and placed her coat over Helander. In her oral history, Henderson maintained that Helander was still alive, but Mr. Chadburn was convinced he was dead. She continued working on Helander as a group of five men on snowshoes from Apgar could be seen trudging in their direction in the moonlight. They arrived about 4 A.M. and noted that a fire was going. Henderson demanded to know about the whiskey, apparently with the idea of getting more of it into Helander, but, alas, they replied that they had drunk it all on the way. Apparently, whiskey was considered not only a first option for medical treatment but an essential libation for traveling in the cold. She insisted that the new arrivals carry on with the massaging because she was utterly exhausted, but they wouldn't do it. Eventually, everyone concluded that Helander had died and they carried his body from the lakeside up to the road. The rescue party got to a cabin to warm up and have breakfast and then went back to put Helander on a sled. They pushed the sled all the way to Apgar, a distance of about seven miles.

Henderson got in trouble with her supervisor for leaving the depot as he was called in to handle an incoming train and hadn't known she had left. The tiff between them went all the way to the railroad headquarters in St. Paul, but a company executive, W. R. Smith, had heard about the entire adventure and wanted Henderson's picture and an article written up for the railroad's magazine. She kept her job.

The tale of Ranger Ness at Gable Mountain is a remarkable case of surviving substantial exposure and showing noteworthy survival grit. The 1933 superintendent's annual report briefly described the circumstances. "Park Ranger Elmer Ness was injured on November 15th when he slipped off the trail going over Gable Pass. He slid about 300 feet down the steep mountain side and unavoidably hit a large boulder at the bottom. He had gained such speed that the impact bounced him clear over the top of the rock which protruded about 4 feet above the snow. He sustained a splintered hip socket and a broken pelvis. It took him two days to reach the station after the accident. He will be in the hospital for several months, but doctors say he will recover." This account rather blithely glosses over the intense experience that Ness endured to stay alive alone in the winter for days with severe injuries.

In an oral history account given by Margaret, Elmer Ness' wife, on August 3, 1975, there is much more detail that alludes to Ness' fortitude and ingenuity in making it through his ordeal. Margaret and Elmer were stationed at the Belly River Ranger Station. They prepared for winter by bringing in all their supplies, as they were snowbound from October 10, 1933, until May 1934. As recounted by Margaret to Cynthia Mish, "Elmer set out for the Kennedy Creek Ranger Station in November and planned to continue to the Lee Creek patrol cabin to take snow course readings and count wildlife. Because he expected to get to Kennedy Creek cabin for supper, he only took a candy bar with him in his trip over Gable Pass. Hard, icy snow had glazed over on the east face of the pass, however, and Elmer slipped and fell, hitting a boulder. The packboard he wore saved his life, Margaret said, by cushioning some of the force of his fall. With a smashed hip and two pelvic fractures, Elmer cut pine trees with a jackknife to fashion crutches. It took him three nights and four days to crawl back to the station, about four or five steep miles from the Belly River Ranger

Ranger Elmer Ness, shown here in 1940, displayed remarkable composure under severe duress when he crawled five miles over the course of four days to reach safety after smashing his hip and fracturing his pelvis in a fall. JACK DODD, COURTESY OF GLACIER NATIONAL PARK ARCHIVES.

Station. During this time, Margaret didn't worry or realize anything was wrong because she knew that Elmer had planned to be gone about four days anyhow." This account underscores the exposure to cold and pain that Elmer endured.

The story goes on to say that Elmer didn't want to mention his injury to park headquarters, perhaps worried about criticism from his supervisors or because he didn't want to draw attention to his diminished physical capacity. In any case, Elmer's own report shrugs off the desperate nature of his exposure and subsequent survival. He wrote, "On the fifteenth of November while crossing Gable Pass the writer slipped on a snow bank and slid into a rock with such force that a badly sprained hip was the result. Unable to walk without support of some kind, the writer crawled to the nearest timber, a half-mile away. Two small limber pine were cut and used for crutches. With this aid the remaining three miles were made to the station by the afternoon of the seventeenth. Built a fire and camped each night."

After two weeks the pain became too great and Elmer got help. The assistant chief ranger made it in to the station to evacuate the Nesses, and Elmer spent nearly four months in the hospital. The Nesses were transferred to St. Mary, where Elmer became district ranger, and then eventually to park headquarters where he became assistant chief ranger until his retirement in 1956.

Jakson Kreiser, nineteen, was from Hudsonville, Michigan, and the summer of 2012 was his first summer working in Glacier National Park. A seasonal employee with Glacier Park, Inc. at Lake McDonald Lodge, Kreiser and his friend Ryan Whinnen were employed in the kitchen at Lake McDonald Lodge. Jakson was, by all accounts, a guy with a big personality, a warm smile, and wry humor. A tribute from his parents described Jakson's sense of self-confidence and silly day-to-day desire to have fun and enjoy life.

Ryan Whinnen and Kreiser were Hudsonville High School graduates. Ryan's mother, Cecelia Whinnen, said that the pair went to Glacier Park on June 3 and "looked forward to 'the adventure' of going to a national

Missing Person

Jakson Jeffrey-Cole Kreiser

If you have been in the Hidden Lake, Floral Park, or Avalanche Basin area and have any information regarding Jakson, please call Glacier National Park at:

406-888-7800, Option 6

Age 19
180 – 200 lbs
6' 2" Tall

Jakson was last seen at 6:00am on Saturday, July 28, 2012 leaving Lake McDonald Lodge for a day hike from Logan Pass through the Floral Park and Avalanche Basin areas, ending at Avalanche Lake.

Jakson is believed to be wearing and carrying with him:

- Plain yellow/gold Columbia cotton sweatshirt
- Long khaki pants
- Rocky brand hiking boots, size 12
- Camouflage winter gloves
- Grey/Yellow daypack with a 2 liter water bladder
- Large knife in a sheath
- Possibly a hiking pole.

Six weeks after Jakson Kreiser went missing near Hidden Lake, his remains were found submerged near a small waterfall. Cause of death was given as exposure. COURTESY OF GLACIER NATIONAL PARK.

park and being paid to work there. When they weren't working, they liked to spend a lot of time hiking and fishing." What could be more natural for a young man inspired by a beautiful and virile mountain wilderness than to meet its challenges with an adventurous traverse? On July 28, 2012, Jakson parked his car at Logan Pass and set off on his intended, and ambitious, day hike to Avalanche Lake. He had let several co-workers informally know of his plan but had not filled out a voluntary itinerary. The route he took is the one unintentionally taken by Mr. Hwa (see page 162) when he deviated from the Floral Park traverse and died. This route first descends by trail to Hidden Lake near the outlet and then involves off-trail navigation and dicey scrambling down 4,000 feet of steep country filled with rock cliffs, waterfalls, wet and slippery rocks and boulders, and dense vegetation. Jakson never showed up for work and a search operation ensued on Sunday, July 29. Ground and aerial searches were launched, with several crews staying overnight in the backcountry to make searching more efficient. The aerial searches used forward-looking infrared technology (FLIR), which uses thermal imaging cameras that detect heat sources such as a living human. The FLIR is most effective when used in early morning searches before the rocks and vegetation warm and give false heat signatures. The search also included canine teams from the U.S. Border Patrol and North Valley Search and Rescue, experts in tracking people. A park incident management team was organized. In total, about fifty people were involved in active searching and incident management.

Park personnel and local search and rescue crews searched for Kreiser for nearly two weeks without success. The assumption was that he had fallen and died on his potentially treacherous route. Eventually, according to a January 30, 2013, news article by Chris Peterson, hikers found Kreiser's body southwest of Hidden Lake on September 13, six weeks after he went missing, in a small waterfall drainage on a subalpine talus slope between two cliff bands. Flathead County Deputy Coroner Sine said Jakson was found submerged in about four inches of water. At the time he fell in, the water was likely three feet deep with meltwater from snow runoff, Sine said. As reported in the *Hungry Horse News*, the coroner concluded that "Kreiser likely slipped while trying to cross the drainage and went in the water, which was just above freezing, and he was unable to recover. Exposed to those conditions, a person instinctively gasps for air but instead sucks water into the lungs. In addition, the heart slows and the body quickly experiences hypothermia. . . . The cold water preserved Kreiser's body but also hid it from view of the search parties."

Prior to the autopsy, officials believed the cause of Kreiser's death likely was a fall since his body was recovered in treacherous country, and that he simply wound up in the pool. However, his death was later established to have been caused by exposure and not traumatic injury. Sheriff Curry said, "He could have tripped on a rock while crossing. He may have hit his head, but there was no significant vertical fall."

A final story of exposure and being lost has a happy outcome because hikers made appropriate decisions. Neal Peckens and Jason Hiser, both thirty-two and both veterinarians from Virginia, were on a fall hiking trip in the Two Medicine area. They spent their first night at the Oldman backcountry camping site on October 9, 2012. The next day, they continued up the trail to the Continental Divide, and then traversed a steep, rocky slope at 7,600 feet, below Mount Morgan and Flinsch Peak. There they encountered cold, high winds, and crusted snow up to two feet deep. As they traversed, the slope steepened. Peckens slipped from the trail and slid downslope on the snow about 100 feet. He dug in his boot heels to stop himself from sliding further and wasn't hurt, but with his slip their vulnerability was made very clear. After attempting to continue along the trail, with Peckens hiking parallel to and below Hiser, the pair lost the trail and couldn't continue. They realized that they shouldn't stay separated and that they didn't want to go back and risk another fall. A violent gust of wind sent their map sailing into the void. Taking stock of the worsening situation, the two men decided to descend the slippery slope and seek the relative cover of trees below. They set up camp and built a fire near Nyack Lakes, spending their second night out. The next day's weather

National Park Service
U.S. Department of the Interior
Glacier National Park

MISSING PERSON

Name: Jason Hiser
Age: 32 years
6 ft, 200 lbs,
Brown Hair, Green Eyes

Itinerary/Possible Routes:
Two Medicine Area
Pitamakan Pass –
Dawson Pass Loop

Possible Clothing:
Blue North Face Beanie

If you have any information or have seen Hiser please contact Glacier National Park at 406-888-7805.

wasn't any better, and after attempting to hike back up the steep slope, Peckens and Hiser decided to retreat to the valley below and wait for a break in the storm. The weather break didn't come. For the next four nights, the men camped at 6,000 feet in miserable conditions in the cold with rain pouring down. According to the NPS press release, "They rationed their food, collected fire wood and materials to create a fire and smoke, turned their cell phones on during the day, displayed their space blanket for possible reflection during the day and used it to stay warm at night, and created a SOS message with logs."

Meanwhile, the pair were reported missing on October 12 when they missed their flight home. This news led to a major search and rescue operation involving at least fifty searchers that included Glacier National Park staff, the Flathead County Sheriff's Office, Flathead County Search and Rescue, North Valley Search and Rescue, Flathead Emergency Aviation Resources, U.S. Border Patrol, and the pilots at Minuteman Aviation. The ongoing poor weather greatly hampered the search and

MISSING PERSON

Name: Neal Peckens
Age: 32 years
6 ft, 180 lbs,
Brown Hair, Blue Eyes

Itinerary/Possible Routes:
Two Medicine Area
Pitamakan Pass –
Dawson Pass Loop

Possible Clothing:
Red Hooded Rain Jacket

If you have any information or have seen Peckens please contact Glacier National Park at 406-888-7805.

Thanks to prudent decision making, Jason Hiser and Neal Peckens, both from Virginia, survived six nights in the park's backcountry in foul weather before searchers found them and airlifted them to safety. COURTESY OF GLACIER NATIONA PARK.

made it difficult for even the searchers to stay warm and safe.

Finally, on Monday, October 15, after six nights out (only one planned), Peckens and Hiser decided they would wait one more day to be found and then would attempt to hike out. Fifteen minutes later, they were found by two Glacier National Park employees who were on foot. One of the searchers saw colored flagging that led him to a tent and the missing hikers. Peckens and Hiser had been subsisting on one quarter of an energy bar each day (Hiser also sampled grasshoppers during the ordeal), huddled in a tent for days, but they were alive and uninjured. In an article from the *Flathead Beacon*, Peckens and Hiser said, "While our situation was at times tenuous, it was not insurmountable due to our faith in the dedicated and talented men and women of the National Park Service and all of the coordinating volunteer groups who were ultimately responsible for our safe return. It is to them that we owe the deepest debt of gratitude for their tireless efforts." Glacier Park chief ranger, Mark Foust, credited Peckens and Hiser for their level of preparation and prudent decisions, saying, "These hikers were prepared with appropriate equipment and they used their situational awareness skills to determine how to respond to the unexpected in the backcountry. A standard recommendation for anyone that may be lost is to "STOP" and that is exactly what they did; Stop, Think, Observe and Plan." Peckens and Hiser were airlifted from the backcountry and were with family and friends back home in Virginia the very next day.

CHAPTER THIRTEEN

LIONS *and* WOLVES *and* BEARS, OH MY

"The grizzly symbolizes the power, uncertainty and challenge of wild places."
— STEPHEN HERRERO
FACULTY OF ENVIRONMENTAL DESIGN, UNIVERSITY OF CALGARY

*"He was proud to live in a state that still has enough wildernesses
to support these magnificent animals."*
— GLENDA GIBBS
EULOGIZING HER HUSBAND CHARLES, KILLED BY A GRIZZLY.

Wild animals are unpredictable, and even non-predator species can be dangerous. As related in Chapter 1, territorial and bad-tempered non-predators such as moose and mountain goats are known to have been involved in human-wildlife conflicts. In that chapter we also told the fascinating story of goats knocking rocks off ledges onto mountain climbers below, compelling the climbers to take a different route. Fortunately, none of these encounters resulted in the serious injury or death of a human in Glacier National Park.

Four large predator species range in the park—mountain lions, wolves, and grizzly and black bears. Since establishment of the park in 1910, only grizzly bears have killed people. In the same time period, mountain lions have mauled two humans, and wolves have not caused human injuries or deaths.

MOUNTAIN LIONS

Montana had no confirmed attacks by mountain lions prior to 1989

229

A grizzly bear and her cubs survey the scene from a ledge in Glacier's backcountry.
COURTESY OF SUMIO HARADA.

(probably due to poor record keeping). But since that time, officials have recorded as many as twenty-four incidents in a single year, including the 1989 death of a five-year-old boy who was attacked while riding a tricycle near his Missoula County home.

Glacier National Park is home to an unknown number of lions (taking a census of these secretive animals isn't easy), but people do sometimes encounter the big cats. Many of these incidents occur in the "front country" —areas near main roads and facilities. Only two of these encounters involved mauling injuries.

In July 1990, nine-year-old Scott O'Hare was playing with his cousin, Chad Flanagan, on the shore of Lake McDonald near the Apgar picnic area. Scott's parents, Merry and Richard O'Hare, of Dayton, Ohio, and a group of other parents were nearby. Mountain lions are known for their stealth, and this one slipped into the area unseen and attacked Scott. The boy yelled at the first bite and then played dead. The lion continued to attack, biting him and dragging him along the shoreline. Scott's quick-thinking uncle, Michael Flanagan, who was part of the nearby parental group, ran up to the lion and kicked gravel at it. The cat, faced with a fighting foe, dropped Scott and ran away. Scott had numerous puncture wounds to his head, face, neck, and right arm. He was flown by helicopter to Kalispell Regional Hospital.

Shortly after the attack, park officials called in lion tracker Mike Clanton and his dog from Coram, Montana, to track the cat. Clanton, the dog, and park rangers found the lion within 100 yards of Lake McDonald and destroyed it.

Scott later told authorities that he had been taught to play dead if he encountered a wild animal. That's good advice if it is a grizzly, but other predators respond differently to that behavior. Lions, unlike grizzlies, will often break off an attack if the prey, human or otherwise, acts aggressively and fights back. When facing a mountain lion, playing dead is not advised.

In the second case of a lion mauling in Glacier, in August 1992, twelve-year-old Nathaniel Moore of Cornville, Arizona, was sitting on a log waiting while his father, Romano Scaturro, went into the forest to urinate, when a lion sprang on top of the boy and began clawing and biting him. The father, just a few steps away, immediately began yelling and kicking the lion, which broke off the attack. Despite being only a few seconds long, the attack inflicted numerous lacerations and puncture wounds to the boy's chest, right arm, and wrist. Moore was flown by helicopter to a hospital in Kalispell.

No maulings by a lion have been reported since the Moore incident, but encounters with lions occur almost annually. Ranger Gary Moses came out of his

The park's mountain lions are active year-round, stalking deer, bighorn sheep, and other prey.
COURTESY OF SUMIO HARADA.

house in park headquarters one morning to go to work. As he approached the shed where his patrol car was parked, a large mountain lion leaped over the hood. Gary was taken aback and then quickly found a young mountain lion under the car. The mother mountain lion and two cubs seemed unbothered as Gary yelled and motioned aggressively; they sauntered away. Backtracking, Gary and other rangers found that the cats were using a den under one of the employees' houses. Because employees' children lived in the park headquarters compound and walked daily to the school bus stop nearby, the mountain lion presence posed a threat. With the children's safety a foremost concern, the park hired a tracker with hounds who treed the cats and shot them.

Although these lions may have been habituated to being around humans, very similar behavior has been reported by trail runners in parts of the park far from buildings and developed areas. In July 2015, while hiking in the park, Trevor Rasmussen shot video of a big lion crouched on the trail in front of him. The lion slowly detoured around him while he talked and yelled at it and kept facing it—all appropriate behaviors. As of this writing, Rasmussen's remarkable video can still be viewed on YouTube.

In June 2011, two women encountered a large, dark-colored mountain lion with its ears back crouched five feet off the trail near Lake McDonald Lodge. A few days later, a large hiking party had a very similar encounter in the Upper McDonald Creek area. In both instances, the lions (possibly the same lion) showed no fear of people; park managers were concerned for public safety, but they refrained from taking action.

Big cats do odd things that are not *necessarily* dangerous, and humans simply cannot read cat behavior very well. Just ask Amy Vanderbilt, the park's public affairs officer (now retired), who was riding her bicycle on the bike path between West Glacier and Apgar Village in the park with her leashed yellow Labrador, Kootenai, only six months old but already a hefty dog, trotting along beside her. It was dusk, and up ahead Vanderbilt suddenly saw a small mountain lion approaching on the path. Fearing that her dog would see the lion and want to engage it, she hit the brakes, got off the bike, and turned around. Vanderbilt was also concerned that her dog, if it saw the lion and charged, would pull her over the handle-bars of her bike—an unwelcome action that Kootenai had done in the past. Vanderbilt remounted her bike and pedaled away in the opposite direction, but she noticed that the lion was padding along on the paved path behind her dog and closing fast. She thought the lion might become aggressive, so she followed the park's protocol for close encounters of the feline kind, which is to face the lion and act aggressively. She stopped, yelled, and threw up her hands, and the frightened lion left. An adrena-line-pumped Vanderbilt pedaled on with a mountain lion tale to tell, but one that ended well. Was the lion being predatory or just curious and responding to movement? It's hard to know.

In another incident, a research scientist working in a forested area had laid out a long measuring tape in the understory vegetation and was collecting his data. He began reeling in the tape and, as the end of the tape with a metal loop on it was approaching him through the leaves and brush, he saw a mountain lion chasing the loop as a housecat might chase a paper ball. He stopped reeling, alarmed, and the lion looked up in apparent utter shock to see a human standing there holding the reel. The lion took off.

In the following incident, it was Leo Marnell who took off. Marnell told us his story about how he was riding his bicycle on the same path as Vanderbilt, albeit years earlier, and was blissfully listening to music on headphones on a bright, sunny summer evening. Suddenly, an elk calf came frantically fleeing out of the woods with a lion in hot pursuit. The lion pulled down the calf just a few yards ahead of Marnell who slammed on his brakes. With music still pumping through his headphones, he witnessed the cow elk mother rush up to the lion and her thrashing calf to intervene. The lion screamed, the elk bleated, and Marnell left the area quickly as the caterwauling continued. Despite how close he was, Marnell didn't think that the lion or the elk noticed him, but it was certainly one fray he didn't want to get involved in because predators can be very aggressive in defending their catch.

WOLVES

Once nearly extinct in the United States, the northern gray wolf began its recovery in the 1980s when a pack of wild wolves crossed the border from Canada into Glacier National Park. Protected by the 1973 Endangered Species Act, these first wild wolves to return to the United

Wolf encounters are fairly rare in Glacier, though lucky visitors sometimes find tracks, hear howling, or even catch a glimpse of these wary animals.
COURTESY OF GLACIER NATIONAL PARK ARCHIVES.

States were known as the Magic Pack. Currently there are nine or ten wolf packs; in the park, some no doubt, are descendants of the Magic Pack.

Wolves are an apex predator, at the top of the food chain, and no other creature, except humans, preys upon them. They are known for their intelligence and strict pack hierarchy. Their return to the park and the Crown of the Continent ecosystem provides balance by controlling populations of plant-eating animals such as elk and deer, which prevents overgrazing and maintains healthy, vibrant plant life that provides food and habitat for all wildlife.

Despite their fierce reputation in folklore, wolves rarely attack people. Rarely is the key word here. When a wolf encounters a human, generally the wolf runs away, but wolves have killed humans. As recently as 2010, wolves killed a person in Alaska and one in Saskatchewan. Since 1910, there have been no recorded human fatalities caused by wolves in Glacier. Interestingly, there is an incident—captured on film—of wolves harassing a grizzly with cubs.

If you see a wolf or wolves, keep your distance and treat them with caution. Avoid areas of wolf activity such as fresh kills and denning areas. In the event of an encounter, calmly and slowly leave the area if you can. If the wolf approaches, stand tall and make noise. Yelling will usually drive off a wolf and so will bear pepper spray.

GLACIER IS BEAR COUNTRY

According to Glacier National Park supervisory wildlife biologist Dr. John Waller, there are more bears in the park now than in the 1960s. Before passage of the National Environmental Policy Act and the Endangered Species Act in the 1970s, predators were "controlled" outside the park boundaries. Ranchers, hunters, and sportsmen killed wolves, bears, lions, and other predator species, which impacted the number migrating into the park. Currently, there are about 600 black bears and 250 to 300 grizzlies in the park. A more precise estimate has not been made since 2004.

Black bears are expert tree climbers and instinctively know they can escape most threats when they are in a forested environment. This makes them typically less aggressive than grizzlies. In contrast, grizzlies evolved in the treeless expanses of the mountains and plains where there was no convenient natural escape from threats. Their instinct is to neutralize a threat, which explains

Bears roam throughout Glacier, including on trails and at campsites. DAVID RESTIVO, COURTESY OF NATIONAL PARK SERVICE.

their aggressive-defensive reaction if surprised or threatened.

An average of 20,000 people visit the park every day during June, July, and August. Generally, bears tolerate humans in their domain. But sometimes they don't! Death or injuries occur when a person invades the bear's individual space or comes upon the bear suddenly, which the bear perceives as a threat. In the century since Glacier became a national park, ten people have died due to a grizzly attack, one death was suspected but unconfirmed, and about 136 people have been injured (some were mauled, but most were bites). Given the bears' considerable physical advantages over humans, this suggests that even when bears react with force, most are not murderous, and a hike in bear country is statistically safer than a walk in any big city. As Dr. Waller says, "According to the CDC [Centers for Disease Control], statistically there is less chance of being mauled by a bear than being hit by a falling vending machine."

In the introduction to this book, we tell the story of Johan and Jenna Otter's attack by a grizzly and how they survived it. The following pages are about others who have survived grizzly attacks and those who did not.

LEGENDS OF THE MEDICINE GRIZZLY

In Blackfeet legends, as related by Walter McClintock in The Old North Trail: Life, Legends, and Religion of the Blackfeet Indians, *the "medicine" of the grizzly is "most powerful" and can be harmful or helpful. McClintock passed on the Blackfeet story of Calf Robe, the Piegan (Piikani) warrior who had been wounded in a raid far to the south against the Snake (Shoshone). Calf Robe was saved and cured by a grizzly bear. The bear carried him northward along the Backbone (mountain range) to the Piegan camp on the Marias River. Calf Robe invited the bear to live with them, but the bear refused and said it was time for him to find a den in the mountains. The bear asked a favor in return for saving Calf Robe. He asked Calf Robe to never kill a bear in winter. And so it is, from that day to this,* that the Piegans will never kill a hibernating bear.

In the Blackfeet story of the Medicine Grizzly of Cut Bank Canyon, Mad Wolf led a war party across the Rocky Mountains to battle the Flathead Indians. Victorious in their battle with the Flatheads, they returned through Cut Bank Pass and were attacked by a war party of Kootenai (Ktunaxa) who were returning from an expedition into Blackfeet country. Again they defeated their enemy, then continued on until they came to the camp of Running Wolf, Black Bear, Ear Rings, Stock-stchi, Ahpases, and other Blackfeet chiefs on Cut Bank Creek. In those days, the Blackfeet traveled so far in a year that their lodge poles were worn too short. Every spring they went into the mountains to cut new poles and to dig camas roots. As McClintock recounts the story:

> It happened that in the evening, the chiefs were assembled in Stock-stchi's lodge, listening to Mad Wolf's story of his war expedition against the Flatheads. It was a warm moonlight night and the women were sitting outside singing and talking together. Stock-stchi called to his wife to go to the stream for water. But she was afraid, saying, "The woods are dark down there and the water deep." But her husband made her go. She soon returned, badly frightened, and said, "I was dipping my bucket when a man came from the forest. He jumped across the stream and ran up the trail. He carried a rifle and wore a war bonnet." Just then another woman came into the lodge saying, "We saw a stranger go to the big fir tree yonder. He hung his war bonnet there and then stole over to the lodge. He looked in and went away. He was an enemy. We saw him plainly in the bright moonlight."
>
> Mad Wolf and the other chiefs hurriedly seized their rifles and ran down to the stream just in time

to see a small party of Gros Ventres emerging from the forest. The Blackfeet opened fire and killed all except their leader. He stood his ground until his ammunition gave out, when he took refuge in the underbrush.

Our people clipped the branches off all around him with their bullets, but could not hit him. Finally they made a charge, but the Gros Ventre chief fought savagely with his knife, roaring all the time like a grizzly bear at bay and calling to the Blackfeet, "Come on, I am not afraid. My name is A-koch-kit-ope and my medicine is powerful." When day broke, our people were uneasy, thinking the Gros Ventre chief might have supernatural power. They told him he was free to go, but they would scalp the others. A-koch-kit-ope replied, "No, they are my brothers and I will not leave them."

When our people finally killed him, they discovered that the grizzly bear was his medicine. He had a grizzly bear claw tied in his front hair. The Blackfeet were so afraid that some of his power might escape, that they built a fire and burned A-koch-kit-ope's body. If a spark or coal flew out, they carefully threw it back into the fire, to prevent the possible escape of any of his power.

When the fire had burned out, the Blackfeet hurriedly moved camp. But in spite of their pre-cautions, A-koch-kit-ope transformed himself into an enormous grizzly bear and followed them. He came upon the Blackfeet when they were pitching camp, killing some, while the rest escaped by flight. The people were afraid to shoot, because they recognized the bear as A-koch-kit-ope. He appeared beside the fir tree, where the year before the Gros Ventre medicine man had hung his war bonnet. The grizzly boldly went through

*camp eating all the food he found and tearing to
pieces hides and parfleches. Whenever our people
camp near the fir tree in the canyon they see the
medicine grizzly. He comes only at night and
disappears before daybreak. The Blackfeet know
his medicine is strong and are afraid to shoot at
him. When we made peace with the Gros Ventre,
we told them about the grizzly and they said that
he was A-koch-kit-ope, their great medicine man.
They declared he could not have been killed, if all of
his followers had not been slain first. A-koch-kit-ope
had predicted to them that he would be killed, if he
should ever be left alone in battle with no one to
make a "medicine smoke." As this happened many
years ago, A-koch-kit-ope, the medicine grizzly, must
now be very old.*

THE OTOKOMI GRIZZLY BEAR ATTACK

"Suddenly, I was overwhelmed by a sense of intense anxiety. I felt with
certainty, that we were going to be attacked by a grizzly bear," wrote
Smitty Parratt while recalling the fateful day when he was ten years old
and his life abruptly changed. Nearly fifty years later, Smitty helped
his older brother, Mark, after their brother Monty died, write of their
childhood adventures in Glacier National Park in Mark Parratt's book
Fate Is A Mountain. The following account of the Otokomi grizzly bear
is excerpted from that book with the permission of Sun Point Press in
Whitefish, Montana.

Lloyd Parratt, the boys' father, was a seasonal ranger naturalist in the
park. Every summer from 1945 to 1963, the Parratts left their home in
southern California to live and work in the park.

On July 18, 1960, young Smitty Parratt begged to go along on a
fishing trip to Otokomi Lake with friends and co-workers of the Parratts,
ranger naturalist Alan Nelson and Ed Mazzer. The three fishermen did

A grizzly bear and her cubs hurry across an open slope in the park. ANDREW ENGLEHORN, COURTESY OF NATIONAL PARK SERVICE.

not have much luck that day. They fished until late afternoon and their creels were still empty when they decided to head home. Along the trail, they were joined by Swedish tourists, teacher Brita Noring and companion Gote Nyhlen. About a mile below the lake, the trail narrows. The group of five walked single file, Mazzer in the lead and Smitty in the rear, carefully making their way down the steep path, through a meadow and then into dense forest. Mazzer, who was slightly ahead of the group, rounded a bend in the trail and caught sight of a sow and cubs moving up the trail toward him. He raced back to warn the group, yelling, "Grizzly, run for your lives!" The enraged mother grizzly was quickly gaining on him, but Mazzer climbed to safety in a nearby fir. The Swedish tourists, Noring and Nyhlen, quickly reached trees and began to climb.

Smitty later wrote, "My parents had drummed into my head never to run from a grizzly. So there I stood as my four companions ran for the trees. I quickly glanced down the trail at the gigantic grizzly bear churning straight toward me. The sound of the rasping, deep, guttural grunt that accompanied each stride sent waves of panic through my body. Then, when perhaps half the original distance was consumed, I, too, fled. I ran like the wind, dodging bushes and leaping over downed trees."

Alan Nelson had not yet made it up a tree, and he and Smitty headed for a grove of evergreens on the far side of the trail. As they neared the trees, the grizzly pounced on Smitty, knocking him to the ground. Then the bear picked up the boy, tossed him about, chewed and clawed flesh from the back of his head, and raked his face with her massive claws.

Nelson, now standing behind a tree, shouted at the bear to distract her. The furious bear spun around and charged him. As Nelson struggled to climb the tree, dead branches broke off in his hands, dropping him down toward the bear. The enraged bear reared up, grabbed Nelson by his buttocks, and pulled him down. He screamed as he slammed into the forest floor, face first. The bear hovered over him, using her claws and snout trying to turn him over. Nelson knew his best chance to survive was to remain face down and play dead. He spread his arms and legs to gain leverage and grasped vegetation. The bear bit the back of his thighs again and again. Then suddenly she stopped biting him and turned toward sounds coming from the opposite side of the trail. Brita Noring stood at the base of the pine tree that Gote Nyhlen had climbed for refuge. The bear charged in Noring's direction, reared up on its hind legs, and stood face-to-face with her. Noring froze and wisely remained motionless for a long while. Finally, the bear dropped to all fours and started to move away.

Nyhlen, still clinging to a branch in the pine, reached down to Brita. She grasped his hand and struggled up the tree. Seconds before she could reach a safe distance, the bear lunged toward her, crushed her ankle in its mouth, and dragged her from the tree. The bear tore at her side again and again, laying her flesh bare, then she grabbed Brita's leg and dragged her into the underbrush and bit her arm.

The still-enraged grizzly finally left Noring and went to the injured Smitty and Nelson, who were still lying on the ground, conscious, but motionless. The bear hovered over them for a while, watching for signs of life.

Smitty later recalled that after the bear left him, "time drifted aimlessly. Although I was aware of my surroundings, the events that followed seemed to play out in a detached fashion. I felt no pain and my fear vanished. As the minutes dragged on I began to explore the extent of my injuries, first discovering the opening in my side. With each breath, air made a hissing sound as it escaped from my punctured lung. I felt about me and found a leaf that worked fairly well to block the air leak. The bone from my right upper arm protruded from the flesh an inch or so. It alarmed me to feel its jagged edge. Next, came the stark realization that I couldn't see. Both of my eyes had been pulled from their sockets.

Moments later I found that if I lifted one eye from where it rested on my cheek, a tiny fraction of my surroundings came into view. Realizing the gravity of my injuries, I felt a deep sense of loneliness and wanted, more than anything, to be near another human being."

A few yards away, Nelson, still lying on the ground with his arms covering his head, was listening for the bear. He waited for a while, then, satisfied that the bear had moved away, he looked over his shoulder to check his injuries. Seeing the blood bath around his legs, he decided not to try to stand for fear he would bleed to death. Then, from across the meadow Nelson heard Smitty's soft cries. He called out to the young boy. "Hearing Nelson's calls, I rose out of my timeless drifting long enough to take a course of action," wrote Smitty. "Using the tiny square of my vision that remained and guided by Alan's calls I rose. Cradling my broken arm, I slowly made my way to where he lay, at the foot of a tree. As I approached him, I recall his shocked expression. He blurted out, "Oh, my God." At his direction I nestled close to him. He covered me with his jacket and peace came at last with the knowledge that I would not be alone when I died."

Mazzer and Nyhlen watched from the trees, and after about thirty minutes the sow and her cubs wandered away. When they were convinced that the bears had left the area, Mazzer and Nyhlen climbed down. They found Nelson and Smitty, but a quick search of the area showed no trace of Brita Noring. Both men realized they needed to get help and fast if the lives of Nelson and Smitty were to be saved, but they wondered where Noring was and if she was alive. They decided that Mazzer would hike out first and then Nyhlen would follow. They spaced their departures so that if the bear attacked again, at least one of them might survive and be able to get help.

Luckily both of them arrived at the Rising Sun Campground within minutes of each other. It was 6 P.M., nearly two hours since the attack. They jumped into Mazzer's car and sped to the St. Mary Ranger Station, to the home of District Ranger James Godboldt. Godboldt listened as Mazzer gave a hasty account of the attack. He shook his head in disbelief and said, "I'll get my team together and meet you at the fire cache." (The fire cache houses a map room, radio room, and fire and rescue tools.) Before he left, he asked his wife Barbara to let the Parratts know that their youngest son had been attacked by a grizzly.

A bear attack of such prolonged fierceness as the one just described to him was rare in the park. Godboldt, a seasoned ranger, sensed the danger this night held for the victims and those about to rescue them. When he reached the fire cache's radio room, he mobilized the St. Mary search and rescue crew and broadcast an urgent need for backup rescue, medical personnel, and armed marksmen to all stations in the park.

Meanwhile, Lloyd and Grace Parratt were having a quiet dinner with friends and beginning to feel a little uneasy about Smitty's late return from his fishing trip. A knock came at the front door, and when Lloyd opened it he saw the wide-eyed alarm on Barbara Godboldt's face. Barbara asked him to step outside for a moment, and she told him of the bear attack and as much as she knew about Smitty's condition. From inside the house, Grace could tell by her husband's anguished expression that her young son was hurt or dead. Lloyd turned to her and held her close as he told her what happened. Then he grabbed his jacket and rucksack and went to the fire cache to help rescue his son.

The news of the bear attack spread quickly throughout the park community. A makeshift command post was set up at Rising Sun Campground. Dr. Lewis Reese, resident physician at Many Glacier, was notified, and he and his wife, a registered nurse, assembled emergency medical equipment and hurried to Rising Sun. At 6:45 P.M. the first search and rescue team left the Otokomi trailhead, hurrying up the trail to reach the attack site and set up rescue operations. By 7 P.M. a second, larger rescue crew, including Lloyd Parratt, was hiking up the mountain, equipped with additional wheeled stretchers and medical supplies. At the Otokomi trailhead, crew members set up camp stoves on picnic tables as volunteers brought food and blankets to help with the rescue effort and await news of the injured.

Mark Parratt had just finished a day of testing equipment at the Many

Glacier fire cache and was making his way to the crew bunkhouse nearby when Ranger Larry Dale came toward him. Dale's voice was hoarse with urgency. "Mark, there's been a grizzly bear attack near Otokomi Lake," he said. "They've put out an urgent call for our search and rescue team. There were several people injured and they need our help to get them out of there."

Dale quickly assembled Team Three—his Many Glacier crew. Mark Parratt was among the group who grabbed gear and jogged to the waiting trucks; they arrived at the base camp at 7:30 P.M. It was then that Larry Dale took Mark Parratt aside and quietly told him, "Mark, you know a number of the injured personally. One is your brother, Smitty. I didn't want to tell you until we got here. If you choose not to go with us, I'll certainly understand. Your dad headed up with Team Two not long ago."

"Larry, I have no choice. That's my little brother up there," Mark answered. Team Three moved along the steep trail at a brisk pace, each man keeping a wary eye on the shadows. The group's safety lay in the pair of rifle-bearers who were in the lead.

Team One arrived at the attack site at 8 P.M.; they approached cautiously. "Over here," Alan Nelson called out. A jittery lead rifleman instinctively swung his weapon toward the sound. Nelson quickly added, "Don't shoot, Smitty and I are over here."

A group of men searched the meadow and the periphery. Much to their relief there was no sign of the grizzly sow and her cubs. They heard anguished calls from deep within the forest and searched for Brita Noring. They were walking among scattered trees when suddenly the ground near them shuddered and a bloodied hand emerged from the forest floor. Fearing another bear attack, Brita Noring had covered herself with a thick carpet of earth and pine needles. She was hurt but alive and grateful to be found.

While rangers applied compression bandages to the deep, bone-baring gashes and shredded flesh to stem blood loss of the attack victims, other team members readied the stretchers mounted on bicycle wheels to take the victims down the trail. One ranger gasped, "Unbelievable," then muttered, "These people need skilled trauma surgeons and they need them now!" Smitty's injuries were life-threatening and he would be carried out first.

Team Two from St. Mary arrived at 8:30 P.M. Lloyd Parratt scanned the scene, looking for Smitty. He slowly approached his son who was already heavily swathed in bandages. Ranger Al Kytonen blocked his way and seized him by the shoulders, saying, "Lloyd, I tell you as a father and your friend do not look at Smitty. He isn't good."

Moments later Team Three with Mark Parratt arrived. Lloyd stepped forward, embraced Mark, and wept as Smitty was being strapped to the first stretcher. "Mark, the bear got his face. He's really bad." Then Lloyd walked over to his son's side and spoke to him. At the sound of his father's voice, Smitty responded, "Dad, please hold my hand. Don't leave me." Lloyd Parratt took his son's hand and spoke gently to him throughout the five-mile-long rocky trek to base camp. Every fifteen minutes an alternate crew stepped in to carry the stretcher. They reached base camp at 10:45 P.M. Dr. Lewis Reese was awaiting their arrival and quickly assessed Smitty's injuries. Smitty was moved onto another stretcher and placed into the back of a park service vehicle. A ranger huddled near Smitty holding the IV saline drip for the long trip to the hospital.

The nearest hospital was in Cardston, in Alberta, Canada, about forty-two miles north. The park service alerted Cardston Municipal Hospital, and the staff immediately brought in additional trauma physicians from medical centers farther north. Customs agents at the U.S.–Canadian border had been notified of the situation, and the gates at the Piegan Port of Entry, which normally close at 10 P.M., swung open for the approaching ambulance carrying Smitty. Meanwhile, a Royal Canadian Mounted Policeman departed from Lethbridge, Alberta, carrying two pints of blood. The lone police sergeant was driving in excess of 100 miles per hour to bring the life-giving blood to the hospital for Smitty.

A short time after Smitty had arrived at the hospital, ambulances carrying Alan Nelson and Brita Noring arrived. Three and sometimes four trauma surgeons labored nine hours over the three injured victims of the grizzly attack. One of the surgeons was a Canadian flight surgeon during

World War II. He said that not since the war had he seen a face wound as severe as Smitty's.

It was 5 A.M. when the head surgeon appeared in the doorway of the waiting room. "I am always honest about a patient's prognosis," he told Lloyd and Grace Parratt. "Smitty is not good." He went on to explain the difficulty in getting him stabilized then said, "We feel it is doubtful that your son will survive the next twenty-four hours. If he does, he will be blind for the rest of his life. I wish I could give you more encouraging news. We've done our best. Now it's up to the Man Upstairs." Hours later, the Parratts listened as they got another update on Smitty's condition from the head nurse. "The left eye was torn from its socket and severed from the optic nerve. It was removed along with bone fragments from the eye socket. The right eye, which had also been torn from its socket, was surgically replaced in its moorings. We have every reason to believe he is blind at this time and we see little hope for significant change. There were severe compound fractures of the entire facial area. His scalp suffered serious lacerations and we basically had to suture it together around his skull. He has five broken ribs. As a result, his right lung was punctured and has collapsed. We've managed to repair the puncture. Smitty also has a compound fracture of his right upper arm. His condition is extremely grave. I am so very sorry. We are doing all that we can at this time to keep him stable."

A number of park service employees from St. Mary drove to Cardston the next morning to donate record quantities of blood. Over thirty-two pints were required for the three victims in the first week alone.

Alan Nelson and Brita Noring were listed as stable and in fair condition. Nelson had extensive damage to the backs of both thighs. Noring had severe muscle damage to her lower right leg and deep lacerations to her buttocks. Following several weeks in the hospital, Nelson and Noring were well enough to be transferred to hospitals near their respective homes: Nelson was hospitalized in his hometown of Bismarck, North Dakota, and Noring was flown from Calgary to her home in Stockholm, Sweden.

As time passed, Smitty began to amaze everyone. It was a miracle that he survived at all, and slowly he began to improve. Smitty surprised the doctors when his one remaining eye with its badly bruised and abraded optic nerve actually functioned and he could see. Eventually, Smitty was strong enough to be airlifted to a hospital close to the Parratts' home in Upland, California. They landed at Los Angeles International Airport where he and his family were met by attendants from the Children's Hospital of Los Angeles. Smitty spent many weeks enduring further surgical procedures in that renowned hospital. Finally Smitty was released from the hospital and continued his recovery at home. He had to return to the hospital many times over extended periods for plastic surgery.

Smitty had one good eye and a strong will. His brother Mark wrote, "With his obvious disfigurement, all of his steely determination was required to brave the constant stares and questions whenever he ventured out."

A home teacher provided daily school lessons for Smitty during the first year he was home. The next year he returned to school and his regular classes. Smitty began to excel in his studies and lettered in cross-country running on the high school varsity squad despite having only one lung. He earned two college degrees and a number of academic honors and became a career employee with the National Park Service. Today, Smitty and his wife Shawn are avid hikers. They have hiked the entire Pacific Crest Trail and many trails in distant lands.

In *Fate Is A Mountain*, Smitty reflected on the day of the Otokomi grizzly attack some forty-seven years in the past: "Yes, this day forever changed my life. However, if you were to ask me, 'If you could do it over again would you avoid the bear encounter?' To this, I would say 'No.' The experience, however horrifying and painful, led me to where I am now . . . to find my soul mate, Shawn. It led me to see life from a far different perspective and to discern textures of life I may not have noticed otherwise. I guess the worst day of my life paved the way for the best days of my life to come. . . ." (More of the Parratts' exciting adventures in Glacier National Park are recounted in *Fate Is A Mountain*, available

IMPORTANT SAFETY INFORMATION INSIDE

Glacier is bear country—all of it— so every visitor is well advised to read the National Park Service safety information regarding bears. COURTESY OF GLACIER NATIONAL PARK ARCHIVES.

online and at bookstores in northwestern Montana.)

NIGHT OF THE GRIZZLIES

On August 13, 1967, two grizzly bears attacked two different groups of backcountry campers separated by ten miles of mountainous terrain. At the Granite Park campground near Granite Park Chalet, nineteen-year-old Julie Helgeson was killed and partially consumed by a grizzly, and her companion Roy Ducat was mauled. Ten miles away at the Trout Lake campsite, another nineteen-year-old, Michele Koons, who worked summers at the Lake McDonald Lodge gift shop, was mauled in her sleeping bag. Her arm was ripped off and she was dragged up a hill. She died before rescue crews could take her out of the mountains.

Julie Helgeson and Michele Koons were the first people killed by grizzlies since Glacier became a park in 1910. The fact the deaths occurred in a single night drew national attention. Speculation in newspapers and among park employees and visitors on what caused the bears to attack and kill the women ranged from "the bears were drunk on overripe huckleberries" to "the victims had not followed established backcountry procedures and invited disaster." Critics of the National Park Service claimed that shoddy backcountry management allowed employees at Granite Park to invite bears to come near the chalet for the viewing enjoyment of guests by dumping garbage; this was against park policy, but was not aggressively enforced at the time. Bears had been feeding on garbage in Glacier since the late 1800s and had never killed a human in the history of the park. No one believed they ever would. Jack Olsen, author of the 1969 book *Night of the Grizzlies,* in his quest to find out why the attacks occurred after six decades of relatively peaceful coexistence, concluded that it was inevitable. He wrote, "By 1967, man with his hated smell and his bumbling manner was pushing harder and harder on the grizzly." Almost 1 million visitors had come to the park that summer, and a "goodly number of them were taking to the beautiful trails that led straight into the domain of the grizzly and camping out in areas the bears considered their own."

It had been a hot summer, and the bears' favorite food—the berry crop—was lean. Olsen argued that the bears were hungry, crowded, and angry, and it was no wonder someone was killed. The park launched an aggressive program to reduce bear-human confrontations. They strictly enforced the rule about not dumping garbage, closed trails where bears were feeding, and expanded public awareness programs on how to avoid contact with bears while camping and hiking.

THE PAISLEY UMBRELLA

The following story is from an interview with Lanny Luding, who built and operated the Belton Chalet taproom in West Glacier.

> This goes back to 1967 and the "Night of the Grizzly" and the Belton Chalet when I used to have the Belton tap-room. During the late 70s and early 80s it was the main watering hole for everybody that worked in and around the park. Since the night of the grizzlies there was a lot of discussion about grizzly confrontations and what could be done to deter them. This was before bear spray (pepper spray). Someone brought up that postmen were using

spring-loaded umbrellas when they delivered mail to a place where there was a bad dog in the yard. The postmen used these spring-loaded umbrellas to deter dog attacks with considerable success, so the talk in the bar was "that was a great idea and would it work on a bear?" In those days, we had a lot more rain in the summer than we get now and didn't have Gore-Tex, so any of those . . . plastic slickers you wore, you got wetter from sweating than you would from the rain.

So I started carrying one of these little spring-loaded fold-up umbrellas in my backpack—when it rained you popped it up and when it quit, you put it away. You're nice and dry, not sweaty. It worked well and a lot of us carried them in place of those awful plastic slickers, and I figured if we ran into a bear on the trail, maybe it would prevent an attack.

But then we come to the paisley umbrella. Okay. You know who Arnie Schwarzenegger is? This particular umbrella used to belong to Arnie. There's a guy named Douglas Peacock, who as part of his PTSD [post-traumatic stress disorder] self-help program spent a lot of time in Glacier, doing cinematography on the grizzly bear. That was his thing! He worked a lot of the lookouts, and he spent a lot of his spare, free time out photographing the bears. He and Arnie did a Sports Illustrated TV special on the grizzly bear. Anyway, the upshot is that Arnie gave the umbrella to Douglas Peacock, who gave it to his wife. Well I had a bartender at the Belton by the name of Big Dave Reynolds. Peacock's wife gave the spring-loaded paisley umbrella to Dave. So Dave started taking it when he went hiking. It was too big to put in his backpack so he carried it like a walking stick and he found out that when it's raining it works really well.

Everybody used to go hiking somewhere in the park in the summer. One day we had a bunch of people come in, old friends and people from back East, and people already here [seasonal employees] and whatever, and they wanted

to go hiking up to Granite Park and so they got it on.
I think they had about fourteen people. They were going
to hike up to Granite Park for lunch and back down. They
got up the Loop Trail before the first switchback and before
the little creek crossing, they got up in that area where you
go from rock layer to rock layer and there's a little clearing,
and they ran into a momma grizzly with a cub and she put
the run on them. She ran a bunch of them up some trees,
and then she came back after the rest—they were sprawled
along the trail and Dave was with us and some other
people and one of these gals he was with—little gal named
Margie and some of the other people. The guys up the
trees watched all the action. Margie got to a tree, hugged
it, and froze. Dave tried to push her up but couldn't get her
to budge. Big Dave is six-feet-four and he is standing there,
the bear is coming, and he's got this umbrella and says,
"Well, I guess we get to try it." So he says, "All I did is
I popped that darn thing in front of me and Margie and
I hid down behind it waiting to see what happened."
He said, "I just hid there and didn't move." It was a big
umbrella and the guys watching from the trees said the
only thing they could see was umbrella. The bear ran up
there, sniffed the umbrella, snorted, and then rounded
up her kid and took off.

That was the story of the paisley umbrella from Arnold
Schwarzenegger on the Loop Trail.

Postscript: Lanny hiked the mountains in Glacier for forty-seven years and never confronted a bear, he said, "because I didn't surprise them. I always made noise."

1970S AND 1980S

Despite the management changes that park officials made as a result of the "Night of the Grizzlies," there were four deaths in the 1970s and 1980s. Mary Patricia Mahoney, twenty-one, of Highwood, Illinois, was a student at the University of Montana in Missoula. On September 23,

1976, she was camping with friends at the Many Glacier Campground when a grizzly entered their tent, just 200 feet from the Many Glacier Ranger Station. In the predawn dark, the bear ripped through the side of the tent where Mahoney and two other women were sleeping. As the bear clawed at her, Mahoney screamed and the bear backed away only to return, collapsing the tent and dragging Mahoney away. The two other women in the tent were unharmed. Rangers later shot and killed two grizzlies that were guarding Mahoney's body.

In 1980, there were three grizzly-caused deaths. On July 24, Jane Ammerman of Stillwater, Minnesota, and Kim Eberly, of North Lawrence, Ohio, both twenty-year-old park concession employees, were camped on a sandbar on Divide Creek near St. Mary, one-half mile from a commercial campground outside the park. At about 4 A.M. a grizzly attacked the sleeping pair. According to reports from United Press International, "The bear ripped the campers' tent to pieces, destroyed their belongings and mauled their bodies." Then on September 27 or 28 of that same year, thirty-three-year-old Lawrence Gordon of Dallas, Texas, was killed at the remote Elizabeth Lake campground. His mauled and partially consumed body was not discovered until several days later. Interestingly, a week earlier at nearby Glenn's Lake, a bear had treed three hikers and torn into their backpacks. A bear had also ransacked a local patrol cabin.

GABBING WITH GRIZZLIES

On August 1, 1976, Ranger Clyde M. Fauley was returning from a hike to Harrison Creek to see what remained at the old Dan Doody homestead. He was on his way back and stopped at the snowshoe cabin on the trail. Nearby, a big grizzly bear had pulled down a bush and was eating the berries. Fauley hid in the cabin for a while, then decided he couldn't stay there all night, so he sneaked out of the cabin and had no trouble with the bear that was busily eating berries. A little later, Fauley encountered three grizzlies, and when it was all over he filled out a case incident report. Sometime later, he retold the story in the following interview.

I was about a mile and a half out of West Glacier. I came around the bend and three grizzlies, an adult and two sub-adults which were almost as big as the sow, exploded out of the brush, which anybody knows that's encountered a grizzly bear, that's just what they do—they just explode up on the trail from nowhere. I was about sixty or seventy feet away when they did this. Then they raised up and that made me feel good, because it has been my experience that when they raise up and sense you, then they figure you're alright and then they take off. But these guys didn't do that. She came down on all fours and charged. The two sub-adults were by her side and did just exactly what she did. And here they come! They stopped again at about thirty feet and they all raised up; fortunately those sub-adults did everything she did. If one of them little buggers were to come on to me I'm sure I would have had it. But, boy they were well disciplined. They did everything she did. They raised up again. I kind of hate telling this part of the story, but I started talking with them calmly. I wasn't calm by any means, but I talked like I did with my dog, and started telling them, "We're on your side, guys. The management plan looks into your interest." Just rattling on, somebody would have thought I was completely nuts. But it kind of worked; it kind of surprised them that I was standing there talking to them. They just looked at me, and I kind of backed up. I came around this corner, and kind of just slowly backed up and kept talking to them. And pretty soon I was out of sight. Apparently they decided I wasn't a threat, and apparently they weren't hungry. I don't think they were looking for anything to eat in this particular case.

Then I was trying to decide what to do. I had seen canoers on the river, so I thought maybe I'd better look for another boatman coming down the river and hitch a ride although the river was quite a ways down. But while I was thinking about it, and the more I thought about it, "Well, they're probably gone by now." I probably spent ten or fifteen minutes back there thinking so I said to myself,

"I'm going to sneak around the corner again and see what's happening." So I peeked around the corner and they had gone up on this hill in the meantime. And they were eating. They had kind of forgot all about me. I came around the corner and they probably caught my scent. They're pretty alert to what's going on around them. Here they raised up again. I thought 'Oh, oh, they're going to charge down that hill.' They just raised up, the two sub-adults doing the same as the sow. As I went by and looking back it looked like they were waving. So I waved back and away I went into West Glacier. I had already called it in, because I had the radio. But it brings out a point I had a gun with me. I had a .38 in my packsack and I often wondered if I had that gun [out] I might have started shooting and then I would really have had it with them that close, and three of them.

Over the years, Fauley had a number of grizzly encounters and survived them all.

FOR WANT OF A PICTURE

"He wanted to get closer for a picture," said Charles' wife Glenda. "He really wanted a good grizzly bear photo."

It was Saturday, April 25, 1987. Libby, Montana, school bus driver, wildlife photographer, and all around good guy Charles "Chuck" Gibbs and his wife Glenda, a first-grade schoolteacher, were spending several days hiking in the Fielding area in the southern section of Glacier National Park just southwest of Marias Pass. On Friday, they photographed goats at Goat Lick and hiked Autumn Creek Trail at Marias Pass. On Saturday, they took a day hike to Ole Creek and were returning to the trailhead at Fielding when they spotted bears high on the southwest face of Elk Mountain. Charles wanted to hike up the mountain and get photos of the bears. The hike up Elk Mountain is short but strenuous. The trail climbs 3,020 vertical feet in two and a half miles. Glenda was recovering from a recent surgery and decided not to go. Glenda and Charles agreed to meet later at the trailhead. They split up less than a mile from their pickup camper parked at the boundary.

An hour went by, then another. Glenda was accustomed to Charles being gone for long periods in search of a good photo. She waited a worrisome two more hours for Charles to return, then drove to the Walton Subdistrict Ranger Station and reported him missing.

Ranger Charlie Logan hiked into the area and fired three rifle shots. He did not get a response. By then it was late and getting too dark to continue the search. At first light the next morning, Logan and twenty-five other searchers from Glacier Park, North Valley Search and Rescue, and the Flathead County Sheriff's Office resumed the search. They found Charles partway up Elk Mountain. The film in his camera helped determine what happened.

Charles was an avowed friend of grizzlies and wanted to get a great photograph. He had taken about forty photographs, several showing the bears looking at him. He moved closer. The last photo was from about fifty yards—the mother grizzly was moving toward him. She had three cubs to protect. She charged.

According to assistant park superintendent Alan O'Neill, the evidence at the scene showed that Charles tried to climb a thirty-foot tree. He was about eighteen feet up the tree when the bear pulled him down. The ground was torn up at the base of the tree. It appeared that the six-foot, 170-pound Charles had tried to fend off the bear while facing it. There were no wounds on his back or body, but there were numerous bites and scratches on his arms, legs, and head. He did not try to slowly retreat, lie flat, or roll up in a ball to show the bear that he wasn't a threat. Neither did he fire the .45 semi-automatic pistol (illegal in the park at the time) that he carried in a shoulder holster.

The attack was not immediately fatal. Somehow Charles managed to get himself about fifty yards from where he was attacked. There was no predation and he was not dragged. Charles bled to death.

His friends told reporters that Charles really loved the bears and said, "He believed he was for the bear, so the bear would not hurt him."

"Charles Gibbs will be remembered as an avid outdoorsman and wildlife photographer," said Glenda. "He shared this enthusiasm of life and nature with many adults and children." Glenda asked park officials to not destroy the grizzly that killed her husband. "He had a great love and respect for grizzly bears and accepted any risk involved when in their territory. His wish was that no harm would come to the bear."

GRIZZLY COURT OF APPEAL

Assembling a board of inquiry consisting of wildlife biologists, bear experts, and park officials is standard procedure following deaths by bear. No ranger wants to destroy a bear that is doing what is instinctive to their own survival, in their own territory. Rangers responding to an incident routinely interview witnesses, inspect and photograph the scene and any physical evidence, and write up detailed reports. They present their findings to the board, along with their educated guess of what happened.

There is no management action taken against bears that are protecting their young, protecting their space or their food, or made to feel threatened by the human. Bears that are irreversibly aggressive toward humans or that see humans as food are incurable and dangerous. Depending on the circumstances, these bears usually have to be destroyed.

A three-person board met to review the facts. Charles knew the danger, but he kept getting closer to the bears, ultimately leading to a defensive attack. "It appears to be a classic example of protection of the young," said O'Neill.

The bear attack on Elk Mountain was not the first in that area. In July 1983, Richard Kirchhoffer, sixty-three and a minister at the Holy Nativity Church in Whitefish and St. Matthew's in Columbia Falls, was hiking down the mountain when a grizzly with two cubs charged him and his companion Bill Beacham. Kirchhoffer tried to climb a tree, but the bear pulled him down. Kirchhoffer assumed the fetal position, prayed, and listened to the bear breathe above him. Soon the bear wandered away. Kirchhoffer had puncture wounds on his right thigh, right bicep, and left knee. The two men managed to walk to the Walton Ranger Station for help; Kirchhoffer was taken to a hospital in Kalispell where he recovered after undergoing surgery for his wounds.

Three months after Charles Gibbs was killed on Elk Mountain, park concession employee Gary Goeden, twenty-nine, from Madison, Wisconsin, was found dead at Natahki Lake near Many Glacier. According to the *Hungry Horse News*, Goeden was last seen on July 23, 1987, walking east on Many Glacier Road. He carried a daypack, lunch, and a light jacket. Fellow workers said Goeden was an experienced hiker and had hiked more than 200 miles in the park that summer. He told friends he was planning to hike in the Apikuni area. That night he did not return to the Swiftcurrent Motor Inn where he worked. The next day he was reported missing. An extensive search was begun, but helicopters, numerous ground searchers, and Flathead County search dogs and their handlers were unable to find any trace of Goeden. For the next three days, rangers conducted grid searches of the twenty-five-square-mile area around Apikuni Cirque. By August 5, there was still no sign of Goeden, so they moved the search area to Siyeh Pass.

On September 1, an off-duty park dispatcher found and reported what he believed to be a shoe of Goeden's in the Natahki Lake area. Many Glacier subdistrict ranger Randy Coffman and three other rangers hiked into the area. They found Goeden's remains about a half mile east-northeast of Natahki Lake. The body was off the trail in a dense stand of stunted alpine fir. Goeden's wallet and pack were nearby. Less than twenty feet away was a fifteen-foot tree with freshly broken branches, and, according to Coffman, "broken a certain direction that would indicate that someone had tried to climb it." The base of the tree was scuffed up, indicating that a bear was there, and it either pulled Goeden down or Goeden may have climbed down and tried to make a run for it. Based on the evidence—a blood-stained visor with bear teeth marks and a ripped sweater—it appeared that Goeden first encountered the bear more than sixty-five feet from where he was killed.

In Ranger Coffman's interview with the *Hungry Horse News*, he made the point that Goeden was in a seldom-hiked area, alone and off the trail. There were bear droppings, diggings, and other sign indicating that the area had been frequented by bears. "We want to get the message out that staying on the trail, you're less likely to have an encounter," Coffman said. He added that a bear bell was found nearby, but it was neither large nor loud enough to give proper warning.

Goeden's remains were sent to his family in Madison, Wisconsin.

THE OCCASIONAL OUTLAW

"Ninety-nine percent of the bears spend their time staying away from us and are doing quite fine," said Chris Servheen, grizzly bear recovery coordinator for the U.S. Fish and Wildlife Service. There is, however, that one percent! In bear populations just as in human populations, there are a few rogues. In ranger speak, they are classified as "food conditioned." These are bears that seek unnatural bear foods such as people food (garbage, backpack snacks, etc.) or, worse, see people as food. They are aggressive toward humans. These bears are considered incurable and for human safety they are destroyed.

BLOND AND DANGEROUS

Recounting his experience of the morning of October 3, 1992, Buck Wilde says, "I was spooked out of my mind, but I had every reason to believe I was alone in that situation and that this guy's life was on the line." In addition to ranger reports and newspaper accounts, Wilde's personal story about a bear attack on John Petranyi was chronicled in Scott McMillion's book *Mark of the Grizzly* (Falcon Publishing, 1998). It is retold here because, as Scott McMillion put it, this was "the incredibly rare situation."

Wilde, forty-three, from Julian, Pennsylvania, had given up his career as an electrical engineer three years earlier to become a wildlife photographer. He spent most of his time in Yellowstone National Park, Alaska, and Florida. In 1992, he was exploring Glacier National Park. Wilde hiked into the Granite Park area on October 2 and spent the night at Granite Park Chalet campground. A seasoned camper in bear country, he carefully hoisted his food high into the air on the food pole and slept some distance away. The next morning, he went for a short walk, then returned to the campground to make his breakfast. While he was enjoying his cereal and tea he saw a grizzly cub, heard a "woof" that he guessed was from its mother, and watched as the cub ran off toward the Loop Trail. Anxious to get a picture, he hurriedly cleaned up his food, hoisted food stuff and gear up the pole, grabbed his camera, and headed down the Loop Trail. It was around 11:30 A.M.

Earlier that same morning, John Petranyi had begun his day hike on the Loop Trail from the Going-to-the Sun Road to Granite Park Chalet. Petranyi was forty years old, single, and a custodial service coordinator for the city of Madison, Wisconsin. He spent his free time hiking, camping, and photographing scenery in Alaska, the Arctic Circle, and the Canadian Rockies. Petranyi was nearing the spur trail to Granite Park campground when he ran into trouble.

Just hours later, Buck Wilde walked along the Loop Trail, visually scanning the scenery for a photograph opportunity. About 150 feet from the campground spur, he saw a blue hat lying on the trail. A camera and tripod and a red backpack were lying nearby. Curious, Wilde walked back up the trail. He saw blood spots on the ground that he had not noticed earlier. About three feet into the brush Wilde saw a pool of blood. Further on he saw blood smears on the ground, a drag-path, grizzly tracks, and more blood. He knew somebody was badly hurt and, if not already dead, would die if he didn't help. Wilde was alone. He knew the danger. He had a can of bear pepper spray, and he made a lot of noise as he followed the blood trail into the brush. He found coins, a wristwatch, and a boot, and then he found Petranyi. The man had been bitten and clawed, and the flesh from one arm and one buttock had been eaten. Wilde was not sure whether the man was dead or dying. He could not find a pulse, but the man's body was warm. Wilde ran the few hundred feet back to the red backpack to get a coat to cover the man to keep him warm. When he returned, the man was gone—the bear had come back and taken him away. Wilde followed the trail for a few steps and then saw that the trail led into a patch of thick timber. "That's when I knew I had really been more foolish than I thought I was being," recalled Wilde. "I had the pepper spray in my hand the whole time with the safety off. I was scared shitless. That was the point when I made the decision that I was in over my head and had to get out. It was time to think about myself and other people who I knew were alive."

It was late in the season; no one other than Wilde had stayed in the Granite Park campground the night before, but it was a weekend. Wilde was sure other hikers would be coming along the Loop Trail soon and could be in danger. It was now noon or a little after. He backtracked to the trail, went a quarter mile up-trail from the attack site, and put a note in the middle of the trail, anchoring it with a rock. The note read, "A man has been attacked by a bear. Turn around and go back to the highway. Shout and make noise every hundred feet or so. Don't run, but move fast. Send help." Wilde left his pepper spray with the note and then walked back up the trail to the chalet. He met some hikers who had just arrived. He sent them back to Logan Pass with a note for park rangers.

The note for the rangers read, "Help. Discovered signs of bear mauling about a quarter to a half a mile downhill from chalet backcountry campsite. Followed another quarter-mile and found body. He was in bad shape but alive. Went back to get coat to cover him and body was gone. Met these people at chalet. I plan to stay here for two reasons. 1. To turn people back toward Logan Pass visitor center; 2. To take National Park Service personnel to site I last saw victim." It was signed "seriously Buck Wilde."

Wilde left another note at a second trail intersection and then returned to the chalet, climbed to the second-story deck, and scanned the area with binoculars, looking for bears and watching for hikers.

Numerous people began notifying park officials of the bear attack. Park rangers Charlie Logan and Curt Frain were flown in by helicopter and with help from Wilde located the body. Wilde had initially found Petranyi 175 feet from the trail. The bear had moved him another 500 feet and shoved dirt on the body, a clear sign that the bear was claiming the body and was nearby to protect it.

It was getting dark. There was a clear and present danger. Logan decided to "quickly document and mark the scene and exit the area." Frain flagged and documented while Logan stood guard with a shotgun.

The three men then backtracked, photographing and documenting evidence as they went. They walked back to Petranyi's backpack to check for food and identification. They wanted to know if food in the pack had lured the bear. Frain was searching the backpack when he heard "heavy, rapid pounding of feet on the trail section below us, followed by repeated woofing sounds." Logan reported that "I could not see what was running up the trail at us but guessed it was a bear so began yelling 'back bear.' Within a moment a grizzly appeared at the bend in the trail below us and stopped. I caught a glimpse of a smaller bear just behind but did not take my eyes off the larger bear, now squarely in the sights of my shotgun."

Logan would later report that the adult bear had a distinctive blond collar around her neck that flowed onto her chest.

The bear charged to within fifty feet of the men. She bounced back and forth on her front paws, a sign she was agitated, then she looked back at her cub and woofed.

According to Wilde's account, Logan aimed his shotgun and calmly said, "Safety off, one in the chamber. Bead down. Start yelling."

"Stop bear, stop bear," they all yelled, and the bears turned away and took off.

The charge "looked like a pretty deliberate deal on the bear's part," Logan said. "But there were three of us there and we were yelling at her. I think she sized us up and decided we were too much."

Wilde's assessment of the situation was that Logan showed commendable judgment to not shoot those bears right then. "The bears were close and coming fast. But he gave them more than a fair chance and they did enough to avoid getting shot."

Logan said he didn't shoot for two reasons. The bear stopped when they started yelling at it, and he had no idea if these bears were the ones that killed Petranyi. "I certainly didn't want to kill the wrong bear, especially one with cubs."

The men quit for the night, went to a nearby backcountry ranger station, filled out reports, and tried to figure out what had happened to Petranyi. "In all my other cases, the bear attacks, neutralizes the threat, and leaves," said Logan. In this case a grizzly bear had killed and eaten a man, an extremely rare occurrence.

The next morning, they called in a ground crew of armed rangers and pilot Jim Kruger of Kruger Helicopter to pick up the body. The bears had moved it another seventy-five feet and were close by, guarding it. Kruger used the helicopter to haze the bears away so they could recover the body. It was not an easy task. The bears refused to leave their kill. Kruger would get them going one way and they would come around another. Eventually he was able to keep them away long enough for the rangers to load the body.

On Monday, Chief Ranger Steve Frye, Logan, and other rangers met to discuss what to do about the bears. They conferred with various bear experts, then decided the adult bear's behavior was predatory. She would likely continue to view humans as lunch and the cubs would learn from their mother. All three bears—the sow with the blond markings and her two cubs—would have to be destroyed.

The necropsy (an animal autopsy) revealed that the adult bear was about fifteen years old, generally in good health. She had recently injured her left front foot, had deep cavities in her molars, and a front tooth was rotted away. Biologist Keith Aune speculated that the sore foot and the constantly painful toothache made the grizzly more cantankerous. Others noted that it was getting close to the bear's time to hibernate as well. She may have been hungry and unwilling to leave an easy meal.

CHOCOLATE LEGS

Six years after John Petranyi was killed by a bear, a twenty-six-year-old newly hired Red Bus jammer named Craig Dahl set out alone, hiking up the steep, winding Two Medicine Scenic Point Trail above Two Medicine Valley. He never returned.

A trail crew worker found Dahl's body in a patch of vegetation downslope from the trail near Appistoki Falls. Physical evidence at the scene indicated Dahl came upon a grizzly sow and two cubs. He turned, ran downhill for several hundred yards, and was chased, caught, killed, and partially consumed.

Scientists isolated human DNA in the bear droppings taken from the scene, removing any doubt that bears, not other scavengers, had fed on the body. Just as with John Petranyi six years earlier, this was a rare incident—a mystery. Why had these bears become man-killers?

On a hunch, based on events from a year earlier, park rangers suspected that the adult bear was a grizzly nicknamed Chocolate Legs.

In 1998, Chocolate Legs was sixteen years old. In bear years, she was middle-aged. She started getting in trouble around 1983 as a cub. At eighteen months old, she had lost her wariness of people and was causing "bear jams" as tourists stopped their cars to watch and photograph her.

Bears such as Chocolate Legs that have adapted to foraging near humans along roads and at campgrounds are considered "habituated." In the 1980s, biologists considered habituated bears a potential risk for grizzly-human conflict and relocated them to the backcountry. Chocolate Legs was captured in the summer of 1983, ear tagged and radio collared, and then flown twenty miles across the Continental Divide to the remote headwaters of Pinchot Creek near Mount Stimson. During the next few years, she repeatedly crossed the Continental Divide, traveling through the peaks of the Lewis Range. In 1986, she removed her radio collar at her den near the headwaters of Pinchot Creek and could no longer be electronically tracked. Based on sightings, Chocolate Legs occupied a range that included Two Medicine for the next eleven years. She was believed to have been involved in an incident in 1995 in which a bear raided food from the packs of a pair of hikers.

By 1997, Chocolate Legs and her cubs were so thoroughly habituated that they had become "pushy" around people. In May, the three bears strolled through Red Eagle Campground on the Blackfeet Reservation. It was there that Daniel Carney, wildlife biologist for the Blackfeet Tribe, captured Chocolate Legs and her son. He put a new ear tag and collar on Chocolate Legs and collected hair samples. Then he turned the bears loose while exploding "cracker shells" to scare them and hopefully restore their wariness of people.

Shortly afterward, Carrie Hunt of the Wind River Institute in Heber City, Utah, and Tim Manley, a bear management specialist with the Montana Department of Fish, Wildlife and Parks, used trained dogs, loud noises, and rubber bullets to drive the bear family from the Two Medicine Campground.

Neither effort to restore the bear's wariness of people worked. Chocolate Legs and her cubs continued to show no fear of people. In July, when rangers were searching the area around Mount Sinopah for a missing hiker (twenty-five-year-old Matthew Truszkowski, of Michigan), they reported the "strange and erratic behavior" of the female bear as she came onto the trail, sniffing the air and looking around, as if searching for Truszkowski. In September, the bears again charged at hikers, backing away just a few feet from them.

While investigating Craig Dahl's death in 1998, experts matched the bear DNA from hair samples gathered at the site of Dahl's death with that collected a year earlier from Chocolate Legs. It was clear that Chocolate Legs and her cubs had no fear of humans because they were habituated. The bears also saw humans as food providers and as food; bear experts refer to this as "food conditioned." Habituated bears are not always problem bears. Bears that are food conditioned always are. There was no other choice than to destroy Chocolate Legs and her cubs.

As of this writing, Craig Dahl was the last person killed by grizzlies in the park. However, in 2016 a man was killed by a grizzly while mountain biking in West Glacier just outside park boundaries.

	Black Bear	**Grizzly Bear**
Shoulder:	No hump	Hump
Ears:	Taller	Short and rounded
Face:	Straight profile	Dished profile
Front Claws:	Dark ~ 1.5" long	Light ~ 2-4" long

In the field, a few key characteristics can help to distinguish black bears from grizzlies.
COURTESY OF NATIONAL PARK SERVICE.

Black bears can also become food conditioned and dangerous. In July 2014, a black bear came toward a family that was eating at a picnic table at the Two Medicine picnic area. The family yelled and clapped their hands. This bear was not only food conditioned, he was also habituated to humans. The bear charged the table and the family ran to their vehicle. While the bear was eating their food, a park ranger arrived. He hazed the bear with rubber bullets and bean bags until the bear finally left. This same bear was seen digging in a fire pit in the area and scavenging for food along the shore of Two Medicine Lake. The trails and picnic area were closed until rangers could euthanize the bear.

"ALL HELL BROKE LOOSE"

Jim Schroeder, sixty-four, from Reedsburg, Wisconsin, was an experienced outdoorsman. Over the years, Schroeder had made dozens of visits to Glacier and had hiked probably thousands of miles in the park. In September 2015, he told his local news media, Wake Up Wisconsin, of his encounter with a grizzly and two cubs in Glacier National Park that year.

Schroeder was off-trail near Mount Henkel in the Many Glacier area when he spotted a grizzly and two cubs foraging for food several hundred yards away. He waited an hour to ensure his route down the mountain would not intersect with the bears. He was hiking below a shelf of cliffs on his way down the mountain when, as he recollected, "all of a sudden, all hell broke loose." Schroeder said he heard "this tremendous roaring sound and three bears came flying down off the cliff above me."

The sow landed right next to him, "so I was looking straight into her face while she had me by the leg, shaking me." Fortunately, when Schroeder first saw the bears he had taken the safety off the bear spray canister he carried in a holster in the front of his backpack. "I just grabbed the pepper spray out and let her have it smack dab in the face. She dropped me instantly and ran off." Schroeder hiked back to his vehicle and drove to a hospital emergency room where he was treated and released.

In recounting his experience later, Schroeder said, "Being clutched in the bear's jaws sparked not panic, but resolve. It was just, keep your head, and do what you have to do." Schroeder also reported to rangers that the attacking sow was startled by his proximity. She didn't attack from a distance. Her behavior was defensive. Schroeder "did everything right" and still had an unnerving encounter, but this is part of the risk of enjoying an untamed landscape.

VACATIONING WITH BEARS

Since the first fatal grizzly attacks in 1967, park officials have worked to understand bear behavior and to proactively manage the park in a way that bears and humans can coexist. They have accomplished much toward that goal. In the last several years, the number of people who visit the park has increased exponentially and bear populations have also increased, but bear-caused human deaths have remained at less than one per year since 1981.

The three most effective ways to avoid a bear attack are to carry bear spray and be ready to use it, make noise, and hike with a group. Ninety percent of attacks have been on solo hikers or pairs. Except for a few bluff charges, bears rarely attack a group of four or more people, although it has been known to happen.

BEAR FACTS AND FOLKLORE

- *Bears and dogs share a common ancestor from 38 million years ago.*
- *Native Americans referred to the grizzly as "Real Bear." The Blackfeet believed that a form of human spirit existed within the Real Bears.*
- *In the long ago, Real Bears had killed many of the Blackfeet people and were dangerous foes. In those days, to kill a grizzly was considered as brave a deed as killing an enemy.*
- *Grizzlies are intelligent, dignified, and individualistic, and they like to be left alone. They generally try hard to avoid people.*
- *Grizzlies are extremely curious and will almost always investigate anything out of the ordinary—a sudden noise, an unexpected movement. Their instinct is to neutralize a perceived threat.*
- *They have a keen sense of smell but only average eyesight. They associate a new odor with danger until they investigate.*
- *You can't outrun a grizzly. Don't try! They are fast and tireless. They can run fifty yards in three seconds, up to forty miles per hour.*
- *Bears don't like surprises. They'll usually move out of the way if they know that you are approaching. Make noise—call out, sing, and clap frequently as you walk along. Avoid yelling "bear" (unless you actually see one) so that other hikers don't react to a nonexistent danger.*
- *Bears don't like to be bothered when they are eating. Be aware of bear habitat and where they are feeding so you can avoid hiking in those areas.*
- *Actually, bears don't like to be bothered at all. They have their own personal space requirements that vary depending on their mood and if they have cubs.*

- You are less likely to encounter or surprise a bear if you stay on the trails.
- Bears are incredibly athletic and an angry bear can do amazing things; a grizzly can break the back of an 800-pound elk.
- Bears sometimes interpret direct eye contact as threatening. Daniel Boone, Jeremiah Johnson, and Hugh Glass would all strongly advise you to never appear to be threatening a bear.
- Bears are attracted to odors. Keep a clean camp and store all food properly. See Bear Aware safety brochures for park rules.
- CARRY BEAR SPRAY. Have it easily and quickly accessible. Know how to use it. Bear spray has been proven to be one of the most important tools in bear management and in deterring an attack. It's usually effective in an encounter and it "allows the bear to learn" as opposed to using firearms and killing them.
- Memorize the park's guidelines on bear behavior and safety before hiking or camping in Glacier. It may save your life and the life of a bear.

CHAPTER FOURTEEN

FLYING

the

BIG SKY

Flying the Big Sky over the mountains of Glacier National Park in a light airplane or in a search and rescue aircraft is no "piece of cake." More often than not there are conditions not experienced in the lowlands—conditions that challenge a pilot's flying abilities and the aircraft's performance capabilities. There are wind waves that create strong up- and downdrafts and other turbulence, sudden storms, microbursts, mountain-top cloud caps that obstruct line of sight, and density altitude effects on the airplane that can reduce its lift and rate and angle of climb when it is needed most. In the hundred-plus years that the park has been keeping records, there have been seven deaths in four airplane crashes. Given the likely high number of flyovers, and add to that the inherent risks in the numerous search and rescue flights over the years, this low number of aircraft accidents is a testimonial to the skill of those who fly.

Throughout this book we have chronicled the search and rescue of those who survived everything from being lost, falling off a mountain, and being attacked by grizzlies to near drowning, freezing, or suffering a heart attack. Later in this chapter, we add stories of people who died or survived an airplane crash. As these reports attest, most of the survivors owe their lives to the skill and dedication of the ground and aerial search and rescue crews. One prime example is included in the Introduction, where we recounted the 2005 story of Johan and Jenna Otter, who, after being attacked by a grizzly, were rescued by ground and aerial rescue crews.

In that aerial rescue, Ranger Gary Moses was dropped in by helicopter earlier and administered intravenous fluids to Johan and put a cervical collar around his neck. At that time, Moses reassessed Johan's condition and determined that his injuries were life-threatening. The initial plan to carry Johan on a litter to the trail and then to the helicopter landing zone would be too traumatic and take too long. Moses recommended to the incident commander that a rescue helicopter be sent to airlift Johan off the ledge. The incident commander agreed and ALERT was called. (When ALERT was established in 1975, the Kalispell Regional Medical Center offered one of the first hospital-based air ambulances to serve a rural area. It still is one of the few hospitals in the country that owns and maintains its aircraft and employs the pilots and crews rather than contracting these services).

Ken Justus was the pilot on that aerial rescue. At the time of this rescue, Justus had been flying for ALERT for two years. He had short-haul training, but until that August day in 2005 he had never been called to fly a short-haul

Established in 1975, ALERT continues to provide rescue services in Glacier National Park and northwest Montana. COURTESY OF KEN JUSTUS.

rescue. When he got the call to rescue the Otters, Justus was at the Blackfeet Hospital in Browning picking up a cardiac patient to transport to Kalispell. When the call came, he flew to the Kalispell Regional Medical Center, unloaded his Browning patient, then picked up the necessary short-haul gear and flight nurse Travis Willcut and paramedic Jerry Anderson. They flew to the park to "scout out the situation." Johan Otter was on a ledge on a cliff. Justus had to make sure there was enough space for the Bell 407 helicopter's rotors to clear the rock face. With 150 feet of line below it, the helicopter could rise far enough away from the cliff to give his rotors room to spin. He then flew to the landing pad at Keyhole near Many Glacier Lodge (the landing zone is cut out of the trees and from the air looks like a keyhole). Anderson put on a backpack of medical gear and, with a Bauman bag and flying litter strapped at his waist, he harnessed himself beneath the helicopter. Justus lifted off with Anderson and the rescue equipment dangling below. When they were over the ledge on the mountain, Justus eased Anderson into position. Then, keeping a watchful eye on the treacherous sheer rock of the mountain, he lowered Anderson onto the ledge.

Anderson unhooked himself from the cable and conferred with Moses. It took Moses and Anderson about twenty minutes to prepare Johan Otter for the flight. Johan was bundled in the Bauman bag and strapped to the air litter, and then he and the litter were strapped to Anderson at chest level. Justus slowly and gently flew the dangling rescuer and patient to the Keyhole helipad at Many Glacier where a ground ambulance was waiting. If Justus flew too fast (over forty knots) Anderson and Johan would spin or swing beneath the helicopter and risk tangling the lines, and it would be hard for them to breathe or for Anderson to see.

As soon as Johan was in the ambulance, Justus returned to Grinnell Mountain for Johan's daughter, Jenna. When he returned to Keyhole with Jenna, the on-site medics determined that Johan was the more critical of the two and needed to be immediately transported to Kalispell Regional Medical Center. Justus reconfigured the helicopter from short-haul to patient transport and away they went.

It was a busy day—and all survived! Jenna and Johan were in the hospital getting medical care. The ground crew made their way back to their respective headquarters. The aircrew—Ken Justus, Travis Willcut, and Jerry Anderson—was back at the hangar unloading gear. All of the rescue crews—ground and aerial—surely had that good, warm feeling that comes with knowing they had done their job well and saved lives.

SHORT-HAUL RESCUES AND RESCUE HOIST OPERATIONS

Short-haul is a rescue technique first used by the military, further developed by the Swiss Air Rescue Agency (REGA) in the 1960s, and adopted by the National Parks of Canada in 1970 and the U.S. National Park Service in 1986. The short-haul is used when the rescue is in locations that are in extremely difficult terrain and time consuming to get to by foot. The duration of the flight is as short as possible—the intent is to get the injured person to a landing zone where they can then be loaded into the helicopter for the flight to the hospital or transferred to an air or ground ambulance for increased medical care and quickly taken to a hospital.

Hanging below a helicopter, a park service ranger cradles an injured climber during a short-haul rescue. COURTESY OF NATIONAL PARK SERVICE.

A short-haul involves lowering and raising a rescuer and the injured person via a fixed line under a helicopter. The rescuer is clipped onto a cable attached to the helicopter. The helicopter pilot lowers the rescuer wherever he needs to go to bring out the injured person—often on vertical cliffs or in narrow canyons or moving water. Flying into these locations is extremely risky for the helicopter pilot and crew and especially the rescuer (usually a paramedic) who is hanging on a cable below the helicopter. If the helicopter gets in trouble (entanglement or emergency) during the approach to the location or during the extraction of the patient, the pilot may have to "dump the load"—meaning dump the rescuer or the rescuer and patient. It's a dangerous job, but it has saved many lives.

The short-haul is a proven rescue protocol, and rescuers still use it as needed. In recent years, however, due to the obvious dangers associated with flying with people suspended from a helicopter, experts have developed and improved rescue hoist operations. Depending on the situation and the availability of hoist-equipped aircraft, military and public agencies, including national parks, consider rescue hoist operations the preferred protocol. In hoist operations, the rescuer and injured are immediately reeled up and onto a side platform or into the cabin of the helicopter for the flight. Rescue hoist operations provide less exposure and risk to rescuers and the injured and are often faster flights.

Throughout the years, whenever a short-haul rescue was necessary in Glacier National Park, Parks Canada or a U.S. Air Force unit from Malmstrom AFB in Great Falls were called in, depending on the location of the incident and the availability of air rescue responders. The ALERT helicopter of the Kalispell Regional Medical Center is single-engine. U.S. Department of the Interior regulations require twin-engine aircraft for short-haul extractions except in a life-threatening emergency when no twin-engine aircraft is readily available. Such was the case with the Johan Otter rescue. Currently, the park calls in Two Bear Air Rescue's twin-engine Bell 429 helicopter and crew, which are equipped and trained for both short-haul and rescue hoist operations. Two Bear Air Rescue was established in Whitefish in 2011 and began flying rescues in Montana and Idaho in January 2012.

DARING YOUNG MEN
IN THEIR FLYING MACHINES

Park officials keep records of deaths in the park, but because not all plane incidents result in a death there isn't a complete record of aircraft incidents within the park. One incident that did get documented was of particular interest. It involved two historic icons of the park—Harvey Dimon "Dimey" Apgar, grandson of Milo Apgar, one of the first settlers in the area, and artist Ace Powell's younger brother Bobby Powell. At one time, the Apgars owned most of what is now Apgar Village and much of the area around it. In 1944, they still owned quite a bit of land but occasionally sold off parcels.

Rae Marie Fauley grew up in Apgar. She was the daughter of park road foreman Ray Price and was married to Ranger Clyde Montana Fauley, the district manager for the east side of the park who later became the park's wilderness specialist. In an interview with historian Jennifer Bottomly-O'looney, Rae recalled that twenty-eight-year-old Dimey knew how to fly, and in March 1944 he rented an airplane to take Bobby Powell on an aerial tour of Apgar. The two young men were having a grand time. They buzzed low over Powell's house, which was on McDonald Creek upstream from where Eddie's Cafe and Mercantile is now. Apparently the

In 1944, Dimey Apgar and Bobby Powell were sightseeing in a rental airplane when the engine stalled, leading to this unusual landing site in Jean Sullivan's yard in Apgar Village. R. A. NELSON, COURTESY OF GLACIER NATIONAL PARK ARCHIVES.

engine stalled, the wheels caught on a power line, and the plane crashed in Jean Sullivan's yard. (Jean Sullivan was one of the snowplow operators who cleared the Going-to-the-Sun Road every spring. In 1953, Jean was caught in an avalanche and survived being lost in the snow for over seven hours. (See story on page 199.)

Dimey Apgar was badly smashed up and Bobby was injured but not as badly as his friend. They were both patched up at the hospital. In good neighborly fashion, Rae Marie's dad, Ray Price, helped Dimey out with the groceries while he recuperated, and when Dimey was well enough he helped her dad build their house.

AIRPLANE DOWN WITH TWO ABOARD

On Saturday, November 1, 1975, Donald Donovan, forty-five, and Kathryn See, thirty-one, were on their way from Coeur d'Alene, Idaho, to Shelby, Montana. They refueled their single-engine Beechcraft in Kalispell and headed for Shelby via the most direct route—over Glacier National Park and the Continental Divide. Donovan had thousands of hours of flying time as a former military pilot and was experienced in mountain flying. He was known to be a disciplined pilot, but on this occasion he did not file a flight plan.

When the plane did not reach Shelby, authorities contacted the Montana Aeronautics Division. Search coordinator Gerald C. Burrows speculated, based on Donovan's flight path, that Donovan would fly over the Continental Divide via Marias Pass, which is less than a mile high and close to where residents reported seeing or hearing a plane. Unfortunately there was heavy turbulence in the area, which made searching from the air risky. Burrows limited the air search until conditions improved the following Monday. Searchers were not receiving any signals from the Beechcraft's emergency-locator beacon, which meant either something as simple as beacon failure or a catastrophic crash. In either case, it would make the search in this snow-covered mountainous terrain difficult if not impossible. The Civil Air Patrol flew the possible flight paths, watching for the plane or for flares that Donovan might have

Flinsch Peak (9,225 feet) is named for Austrian Rudolf Ernst Ferdinand Flinsch, who came to these mountains in 1892 to hunt mountain goats. Flinsch's guide was a Piegan scout, William Jackson, for whom Mount Jackson and Jackson Glacier are named.
COURTESY OF U.S. GEOLOGICAL SURVEY.

placed in the snow. They found no aircraft debris or flares, indicating that they were either nowhere near where the plane went down or there were no survivors.

Even though changing weather patterns hampered visibility, the search for the lost plane continued for another eight days. Idaho pilots searched the Priest River area following up on a call from a hunter who said he heard an airplane and had seen a "bright flash" about the time the plane was believed to have gone down. After several days of bad weather and with no sightings of any kind, the Idaho pilots decided to stop searching. By the end of the week there was still no clue about where the plane went down. The search planes and crews were at risk—ice was forming on the search planes, and severe turbulence over the park continued. The search was too dangerous to continue and was called off.

The following July, the wreckage of the plane and the bodies of Donald Donovan and Kathryn See were found on Flinsch Peak above Dawson Pass on the Continental Divide.

AIRPLANE DOWN WITH FOUR ABOARD

On September 5, 1985, a single-engine Piper Cherokee with four onboard was flying low, 150 to 200 feet over the Going-to-the-Sun Road. The pilot and passengers were a Canadian family on their way to Kalispell, Montana. The pilot, James "Jim" Conway was twenty-nine and an experienced pilot with more than 5,000 hours of flight time. He worked for an aviation company in Edmonton. His wife, Shirley, thirty-one, was a nurse. On board with James and Shirley were James' father, Leo Conway, fifty-eight, and James' mother, Judith Conway.

It was a cold, rainy day and Ranger Jerry Ryder said, "We figured he [Conway] was flying low for the weather conditions. He was flying just off the deck near the road and when the road made the hard turn at Siyeh Bend, he may not have been prepared to make the turn. He possibly tried to make a turn up the valley, but we don't know what brought him down." The plane flew up the drainage and crashed into the trees. One wing sheared off and the other wing tore back as the plane augured in. James and his mother, Judith, both on the left side of the plane, were killed in the crash. Passengers Shirley and Leo, on the right side of the plane, survived.

Shirley, who had a shoulder injury, managed to pull Leo from the wreckage, then she hiked the half mile or so to the Going-to-the Sun Road for help. She caught a ride to St. Mary and reported the accident.

Rescue crews reached the site around 2 P.M. They stabilized Leo, who had a badly broken leg, a compression spinal fracture, and hypothermia. They carried him out on a litter over the steepest part of the terrain, then wheeled the litter for a short stretch on the trail to the Sun Road. Rescue crews transferred Leo to a Babb ambulance that took him to St. Mary to a waiting Mercy helicopter, which flew him to Great Falls. Shirley was driven to Great Falls for treatment.

CANADIAN INVASION

On Wednesday, February 12, 1992, two Canadian military personnel parachuted onto Logan Pass. "We were surprised," said Chief Ranger Bob Andrew. He had not yet been advised that a rescue attempt was underway.

The U.S. Air Force Recovery and Rescue Service at Scott Air Force Base in Belleville, Illinois, had alerted Canadian and U.S. authorities about an overdue airplane from Lacombe, Alberta. Mike Strand of Strand Aviation in Kalispell was searching the area and picked up signals from the downed Grumman aircraft's emergency locator transmitter as he flew over the area southeast of Logan Pass. He notified authorities, and personnel from the 440 Squadron, Canadian Armed Forces in Edmonton dropped two jumpers nearby to search for survivors. According to Ranger Andrew and the *Hungry Horse News*, the parachutists ". . . were extremely well-equipped and extremely efficient. They traveled lightly and everything they needed was in the plane circling overhead." The parachutists verified the fatalities and were picked up by the ALERT helicopter and taken to Glacier International Airport where the squadron airplane was waiting to take them back to Canada.

Willard and Marion Smith of Lacombe, Alberta, were flying from Lacombe to Glacier Park International Airport in a 1976 single-engine Grumman Tiger. They were traveling to Kalispell to purchase new navigation and communication equipment. They crashed about 300 to 400 yards south of the Logan Pass Visitor Center. According to Pete Mangum, air safety investigator for the National Safety Transportation Board, "The airplane's engine was operating normally . . . the plane was heading east when it hit the snow at a high rate of speed and at a steep angle." He believed the pilot had become disoriented. The pilot, Willard Smith, had 700 hours of flight experience but was not qualified to fly by instruments, which is necessary in bad weather. At the time of the crash, the mountain peaks were obscured by clouds and a snow squall was forecast. Both Willard and Marion were killed in the crash.

The weather cleared later that afternoon. Park rangers Charlie Logan and Gary Moses were taken to the site by Kruger Helicopter. They removed the bodies and turned off the airplane's emergency locator transmitter. On Friday afternoon, a Bell helicopter from River City Helicopter in Coeur d'Alene, Idaho, removed all the wreckage from Logan Pass.

AIRPLANE DOWN NEAR KENNEDY LAKE

On Saturday, April 16, 2000, Dale Laird, forty-two, was flying his Maule M-5-210C from Polson, Montana, to Lethbridge, Alberta. He had filed a visual flight plan with the FAA indicating he was flying over the park using visual navigation references. When his plane was overdue at Lethbridge, he was reported missing. FAA radar records indicated that his plane had disappeared from radar in the Many Glacier area. An immediate search for the plane began. Planes from the Montana Civil Air Patrol, a helicopter from Malmstrom Air Force Base in Great Falls, and Canadian pilots joined in the search. Three days later, Ray Sanders of the Montana Aeronautics Division reported that a helicopter pilot and crew found the wrecked plane two miles northwest of Many Glacier near Kennedy Lake, north of 8,770-foot Mount Henkel. The pilot, Dale Laird, was dead.

In the four airplane accidents within the park involving deaths, all occurred during turbulent weather typical of mountainous terrain. Search and rescue was delayed in two of the accidents for the same reason. As we said in the beginning of this chapter (in WW II pilot jargon), flying over the mountains of Glacier National Park is no "piece of cake."

CHAPTER FIFTEEN

LASTLY

Although this book is a compendium of deaths and survivals in the mountainous landscape of Glacier National Park, it is not just about dying or surviving. It's about balancing the pleasures of exploring incredible wildernesses with the risks of unbounded adventures. It is also about the courage, skill, and dedication of those who take care of the park and take care of the people. To them, it's not just a job. It's a special kind of living.

A recent example of the bond between the people who live and work in and around the park occurred in June 2016. This incident occurred outside the park but within shouting distance of the park boundary. On June 29, 2016, mountain biker Brad Treat, thirty-eight, was cycling at a fast pace on a forested trail south of the park not far from Halfmoon Lake. He collided with a grizzly bear at such speed as to flip over the animal, and he was immediately attacked and killed by the startled bear.

Brad Treat was a respected and revered law enforcement officer for the U.S. Forest Service, and he was accorded the highest honors in a moving public ceremony attended by thousands. The response to Brad's unfortunate death by the community and the multiple agencies that have jurisdiction in and around Glacier National Park underscores how close-knit people become when they face the common challenges of living, surviving, and, sometimes, dying in a mountain landscape. Politics, personalities, and pride fall by the wayside when someone is in trouble and a search and rescue needs to be launched. This is especially true for the professionally trained search and rescue personnel, both volunteer and agency based, who are ready at all hours of the day and night to respond to an emergency, whether in Glacier Park, Flathead National Forest, or elsewhere in northwest Montana. In every incident described in this book, in addition to the search and rescue people who were called from warm beds in the middle of the night to endure harsh weather

Brad Treat's fifteen-year career as a USDA Forest Service law enforcement officer was tragically cut short by an off-duty encounter with a bear.
COURTESY OF SOMER JOY TREAT.

or other challenges while trying to save a life, their families also had to make sudden adjustments as their lives were disrupted. And when a mission ends with a death in or near the park, it impacts the community of people who work and live there—especially when they lose one of their own. Brad is the perfect example. The thousands who attended his service are a tribute to Brad, and a community gathering of that size also speaks volumes about the people who reside in the landscape of which Glacier is part.

Another perspective that emerges from chronicling the death and survival stories in Glacier National Park is the somewhat conflicted role that the park service plays in trying to ensure the safety of visitors while accommodating people's tendency (and right) to have adventures that come with risk. A park superintendent report from 1925 indicates that this was already an issue that managers wrestled with early in the park's history:

> *While this severe toll of life can in no way be ascribed
> to any fault of the Park Administration, we are nevertheless
> greatly concerned over it and anxious to find a means of
> preventing a reoccurrence of such needless loss of life.
> The question arrises [sic] as to how far the Government may
> go in paternalism, by restricting the privilege of hikers to
> travel thru the Park without the attendance of a paid guide.
> Glacier Park has already been given the stigma of being a
> rich man's Park and if such a restriction is established one
> can well believe that the title will be deserved. Means of
> registering the hikers and checking them from place to
> place was devised during the past winter, as a result of
> the disappearance of the Whitehead Boys last year, but it
> was found that in practice this registration would require
> more than double our present force of rangers. An effective
> check on individual hikers has yet to be found.*

Fast-forward to today: Glacier Park has a voluntary hiker registration program intended for climbers or those planning arduous, off-trail trips, in which people fill out their itinerary and other information and leave a form in their cars. Many trails have voluntary trailhead registers for people to sign in if they are more spontaneous about starting a hike. However, only the backcountry overnight use permit system is a mandatory and fairly precise way for officials to know where people are and whether they are overdue. The park strongly encourages visitors to use common sense and let someone know of their plans, especially when solo hiking. Closures of trails do occur, such as after a grizzly bear incident (e.g., a close encounter with a hiker). But, in general, the park does not stop visitors from exploring the mountains.

What role should the parks play in keeping visitors safe? Earlier in this book, we referenced Joseph Sax's book *Mountains without Handrails* and the early and philosophical debates of maintaining a wilderness experience versus responsibility for visitor safety. In a 2013 article by Karl Puckett of the *Great Falls Tribune*, park officials and backcountry experts talked about the tools available for managing risk and the most common things that get people into trouble. The article listed visitors being too casual or underestimating the real risk, hiking alone, failure to prepare well (even for a short hike), poor decision-making, and, finally, not having the necessary expertise, equipment, or fitness for the activities they choose to do. Sara Newman of the National Park Service's Office of Risk Management described the training for park personnel that is intended to reduce risk for park visitors. This includes actions already described in this book, such as issuing warnings via signs and other means, disseminating educational materials, providing interpretive programs where safety can be discussed, and making contacts by rangers and other park personnel who can provide advice. Newman described how the park can reduce accidents by encouraging visitors to be better prepared and make better decisions, but ultimately visitors must take responsibility for their own actions. She went on to say, "That's sort of the beauty and the reward of enjoying nature is having that freedom to enjoy the wilderness and not have a Disney World experience where all risk is managed. It's not risk free to come to a park like it really is in Disney World."

People will undoubtedly continue to die in Glacier, but new technologies and capabilities will likely continue to lower the fatality rate. Perhaps not the overall death rate, as annual visitation at Glacier approaches 3 million, but probably on a per capita basis. An increase in visitors creates more opportunities for getting into trouble, but for people who do, the prospects of rescue and earlier medical care will shift some incidents from being fatal to incidents with happier outcomes. A case in point is the availability of high-tech helicopter rescues. Thanks to the concern and commitment of Whitefish philanthropist Mike Goguen, Two Bear Air Rescue was established in 2011. Crews began air rescues in January 2012, serving areas throughout Montana and Idaho. Two Bear is equipped for both hoist rescues and short-hauls, and is readily available a few miles from the park. Prior to 2012, the air rescue team just across the international border in Glacier's sister park, Waterton Lakes National Park, was called upon a number of times for short-haul rescues. One such event occurred in July 2007 when Denis Twohig, sixty-eight, one of the founders of the Glacier Mountaineering Society, and his partner were climbing the "Gendarme" on Little Chief Mountain in the St. Mary Valley. At about 5:30 P.M., Denis fell while leading a technical section and was injured. His climbing partner lowered Denis and secured him on a ledge after providing what first aid he could. This was before the days when cell phones worked in backcountry situations (coverage is still spotty), and before satellite phones were feasible for most people to own. Denis' partner had to rappel and otherwise descend the fairly technical climbing route and go for help. He made contact with rangers around 11 P.M., and they began planning the rescue during the night. The location of the ledge that Denis was marooned on presented daunting challenges—a helicopter could not land a rescue party anywhere near the ledge. Thus, Glacier rangers would have had a very technical climb just to get to Denis and would then face the prospect of lowering him in a litter by rope for thousands of feet. The Canadian rescue crew was called in and, after they did a reconnaissance flight, they performed a short-haul rescue relatively quickly. Denis was then transferred to the ALERT air ambulance and flown to medical care. Not only was the rescue not as prolonged, which would have left Denis exposed for a longer time and decreased his resilience to his injuries, it also meant that fewer rescuers were put into a dangerous situation performing a prolonged and tricky rescue. The cooperation between Parks Canada and Glacier National Park on this rescue was hailed as another example of true partnership stemming from the Waterton-Glacier International Peace Park designation.

When benefactor Mike Goguen's high-capacity advanced rescue helicopter operation, Two Bear Air Rescue, became operational in 2012, it revolutionized search and rescue by greatly speeding up rescues as well as reducing risks to responding rescuers. Faster rescues add a huge safety margin to successful outcomes since injured parties in backcountry situations are often extremely vulnerable to changing and inclement weather.

Jack Beard's story is a testimony to Goguen's contribution to safety. On June 27, 2015, Beard, sixty, and his climbing partner, David Steele, were climbing and establishing a new route on the Lithoid Cusp, a complicated and technical climb in Glacier National Park. An experienced climber, Beard nonetheless fell on the final section of a snowfield. In the *Flathead Beacon*, Beard's 600-foot fall is described as follows: "He slid to the bottom of the snow chute and slammed into a scree bench before falling another 200 feet over the rock ledge and down a waterfall. He landed on a rock outcropping and sustained a concussion, fractures to eight ribs, his spine and his right arm. The fall occurred around 11:30 A.M." Just beyond the rock outcropping was a 3,000-foot drop to the valley far below, from which a fall would have been fatal. Steele had to spend an hour negotiating the steep terrain they had just climbed to get to Beard. For much of the descent, Steele assumed that Beard was dead. He was relieved to find his friend alive but disoriented. Beard was extremely lucky to be alive but was severely injured; Steele rapidly secured him to the ledge but worried that Beard, in his injured and disoriented state, would roll over and fall into the abyss. After leaving him some provisions and a sleeping bag, Steele went for help.

This left Beard alone and exposed on the mountain pondering his own fate and worrying over the safety of the rescuers who would have to climb up to his location. "We were in a really bad location for rescue," Beard later explained to *NBC News*. "But I was aware of Two Bear Air, which was a great comfort to me because I knew they were capable of possibly rescuing me without inserting rescuers on the ground." After waiting for hours, Beard finally heard the rotor chop of the incoming Two Bear Air helicopter. Once the chopper was overhead, it took less than ten minutes for rescuers to hoist Beard aboard and transfer him to an ambulance at Many Glacier.

For decades, search and rescue teams in Glacier have relied on helicopters for air support, but according to Flathead County undersheriff Jordan White, who in 2011 initiated the Flathead County program to raise money for search and rescue equipment, Two Bear Air is unique. The

Two Bear Air's Bell 429 helicopter is specially equipped for a range of rescue scenarios. COURTESY OF TWO BEAR AIR.

company's Bell 429 is equipped with infrared cameras, a moveable searchlight, and a 3-D mapping system, all of which aid in finding a person in the remote backcountry, even after the sun goes down. But searching is just half of the mission. The twin-engine Bell 429 also has a hoist to lower rescuers and retrieve victims without landing—a critical ability in many mountain rescues where rugged, often vertical terrain precludes setting the helicopter down. But perhaps the most important aspect of Two Bear Air's operation is the people. Undersheriff White told *NBC News*, "When it comes down to what we really do, it's not about the helicopter and it's not about the camera and hoist. It's about a team of people working together with other teams of people making public service and public safety more readily accessible, even in the most remote places." That team includes Flathead County sheriff deputies who volunteer as crew for Two Bear Air.

"I just feel like I owe them a lot," Beard told *NBC News*. "I put myself in that position, and I'm really sorry that somebody had to rescue me. But the training, and the professionalism, the skill, and the equipment they have just made it pretty unbelievable."

Jim Bob Pierce, the Two Bear Air pilot the day of Beard's rescue, described the rescue as "textbook," but also noted that Beard was incredibly lucky to be alive. "My goodness, he fell a long way. He's one of the luckiest guys I've seen," Pierce said. "He landed on the only possible place on the wall that could have stopped him. If he'd gone any further, we wouldn't have been on a rescue mission."

In addition to today's high-tech capabilities from the air, ground search and rescue capacity is greater now than in the past. After all, bad weather conditions can still ground even the most advanced aircraft.

Nowadays, even ground search crews can carry thermal imaging equipment, have lightweight global positioning systems (GPS) to navigate in complex terrain, employ superior communication technologies, and carry lightweight gear for technical extractions, first aid, and advanced patient care. Computer algorithms and geographic information systems (GIS) aid search planners in efficiently deploying their personnel to maximize success. Changes in strategy necessitated by updated information can be easily communicated to field personnel. Lost people can sometimes be located by signals from their cell phones even if they can't communicate with them for whatever reason. DNA testing can conclusively identify a victim from tiny bone fragments or pieces of clothing. Despite these advances, as this book chronicles, people still sometimes disappear or their remains are not found until years later.

Lost or injured visitors can help themselves by remaining calm and using common sense but also by using tools such as cell phones. Cell phone reception has increased in recent years in backcountry locations and is the fastest way to get an urgent message out to the park and county search and rescue by calling 9-1-1. Although there are still many "dead" zones, an uninjured person in a hiking party can improve the chances of getting a signal by climbing (safely) higher in the terrain. Some park staff and visitors now use satellite-based phones and locator devices that do not experience "dead" zones.

Some groups of hikers carry inexpensive two-way radios to stay in touch with others in their group. These can be used to relay information to others for many miles if in line of sight. Other options include LED flashlights and headlamps that have a strobe option, which can operate for many hours, or all night, while preserving much of the battery charge. Some even flash the universal Morse code distress signal, SOS—three short flashes, three long flashes, and three short flashes. Another way visitors can help themselves is simply by being prepared with clothing, food, shelter, and first-aid supplies to allow rescuers time to get to them before their condition worsens due to exposure.

Of course, the sense that help can be called up reliably can lull people into a sense of false security. Even a relatively speedy rescue is often hours away once authorities are alerted by a cell phone call or a hiker from the injured party's group getting out to report in person. It can take a while to mobilize a rescue team, especially during the busy summer months when resources may be spread thin. People need to take full responsibility for their safety without the assumption of a timely response if they get in trouble.

Park visitors have plenty of resources and opportunities to increase margins of safety for their adventures. The first is when visitors go through the entrance gate—rangers give them a tri-fold brochure with pertinent information on the park. In addition to a map, interesting information on park features, and the details of where to camp and what services are available, there are many basic safety messages. These include instructions about not approaching wildlife, specific information about bears, cautions about being around water, and letting people know your itinerary if you venture out on trails, particularly if you go alone. People are exposed to more safety information via signage at trailheads and displays along roads and at visitor centers. But people are in vacation mode and probably give only a cursory glance at all of these passive avenues of creating appropriate safety awareness. A more active approach is employed when people get a permit to access Glacier's backcountry. When they pick up the permit, they view a mandatory training video that describes backcountry ethics, leave-no-trace camping techniques, recommended food storage, and how to filter water from lakes and streams. There also is considerable discussion about bear awareness and other backcountry hazards.

Although visitors now have less chance of becoming a death statistic in Glacier National Park thanks to the ample safety awareness information available, and indeed the persistence of park management in keeping the safety message front and center, there are new developments that may somewhat reverse that trend. One is the rise in extreme sports such as BASE jumping (described earlier), use of "squirrel" suits (used to glide in flying-squirrel style before a parachute is deployed), ice climbing, freestyle skiing, and long-distance trail running. Although these sports are generally practiced by experienced athletes who try to minimize the likelihood of an accident, the consequences of a mishap are very high. Catching a ski edge on a descent down an icy couloir will result in severe injury and possible death. People who engage in extreme sports are aware of the risks they deliberately take, and they work hard to reduce them. But such activities are still risky.

Another development is the speed with which information on other people's activities and exploits can be transmitted by social media. Whole networks of park lovers, climbers, and backcountry users can find out about new places to go, new hiking or climbing routes to traverse, and new experiences to enjoy from friends and bloggers, all in very short order. While convenient, such networking also tempts—or pressures—some people to attempt mountain activities beyond their experience and abilities.

Although this book has chronicled the deaths and survivals in a mountain landscape and an iconic national park, it is not our intent to discourage anyone from visiting and experiencing one of the best national parks in the world. Indeed our intent is just the opposite. Please visit Glacier National Park! Its scenery, wildlife, and wilderness are truly exceptional. Although it can be hazardous too, we hope our cautionary tales help people to better avoid the risks and enjoy the pleasures.

Hikers enjoy the vista atop Cut Bank Pass. JACOB W. FRANK, COURTESY OF NATIONAL PARK SERVICE.

1910 to Present

Year	Date	Name	Age	Location	Cause
1913	1-8	Joe Prince, ranger	57	between Cut Bank and St. Mary ranger stations	exposure, froze to death while snowshoeing
	8-19	Dr. Calvin Fletcher, visitor	54	Blackfoot Glacier	hit by falling ice, avalanche
	8-21	Frank Ellis, visitor	63	George Snyder's saloon just inside GNP west entrance	gunshot (on 8-18)
1914	9-16	George McKinnon, contract employee	32	Two Medicine	bridge collapsed
1915	7-21	George White, visitor	57	Many Glacier	intoxication
1916	6-25	Jane Davis, visitor	39	Two Medicine River	drowned
1919	9-1	J. D. Kettlesand, visitor	?	St. Mary Lake	heart attack
1922	7-27	Dr. Frank Wynn, visitor	63	Mt. Siyeh	fell, likely due to stroke
	9-8	Charles Barker, bus driver	23	Divide Hill	tour bus accident just outside park boundary
	10-12	Daniel C. Doverspike, resident	70	Doverspike homestead, North Fork Valley	heart attack
1923	7-1	Samantha Jones, visitor	18	Lake McDonald	drowned, never found
	7-1	Fred W. Huber, Jr, visitor	19	Lake McDonald	drowned, never found
1924	6-29	Ester Peterson, concession employee	20	Mt. Altyn	fell while hiking
	7-4	Donald T. Fly, concession employee	?	St. Mary Lake	drowned
	8-24	Joseph Whitehead, visitor	29	between Granite Park and Lake McDonald	lost, never found, presumed dead
	8-24	William A. Whitehead, visitor	22	between Granite Park and Lake McDonald	lost, never found, presumed dead
1925	4-28	Charles F. Robinson, visitor	23	North Fork Flathead River	drowned trying to cross river
	6-21	Jack F. Davis, NPS employee	36	Lake McDonald	drowned, vehicle accident
	7-13	Ben J. Cushing, visitor	41	6 miles from Sperry Chalet	fell while hiking
	7-15	Lena Longini, visitor	20	St. Mary Falls	drowned trying to save brother Henry
	7-15	Henry Longini, visitor	11	St. Mary Falls	drowned
	8-14 or 15	Joseph D. Wheeler, visitor	42	Lake Ellen Wilson area	exposure, caught in a storm
	8-14 or 15	Emily Wheeler, visitor	36	Lake Ellen Wilson area	exposure, caught in a storm
1926	2-7	William Byron McAfee, NPS employee	35	Kishenehn Ranger Station	suicide, gunshot
	6-24	Charles Rudberg, contract employee	?	Going-to-the-Sun Rd., 10 miles east of Lewis Hotel	fell from ledge
1927	2-7	Ole Helander, resident	37	Lake McDonald	exposure after falling into lake
1931	6-27	Stanley Clark, NPS employee	35	St. Mary Lake	drowned
	8-26	Carl Rosenquist, contract employee	26	Going-to-the-Sun Rd.	hit by falling rock
1932	7-14	Gust Swanson, contract employee	48	Going-to-the-Sun Rd., 1.5 miles east of Logan Pass	hit by falling rock
1933	7-8	Frank E. Whalen, NPS employee	42	park headquarters, West Glacier	cerebral embolism

Year	Date	Name	Age	Location	Cause
	7-?	Dr. W. Cosby Bell, visitor	?	Mt. Brown	Unknown, never found, presumed dead
	7-19	William Richeson, CCC employee	20s	near CCC Camp #15, Apgar area	hit by falling tree
	11-26	John Joe Pearce, NPS employee	31	14 miles north of East Glacier Park station	fell into a rock crusher
1934	7-7	Harry Clifford Carlson, CCC employee	43	North Fork Rd.	fell from truck, broken neck
	7-20	Rt. Reverend W. F. Faber, visitor	74	Two Medicine	exposure, found 7-23
	7-23	Michael Greppo, CCC employee	18?	Sherburne Lake	drowned
	7-23	Amato Montemarano, CCC employee	18?	Sherburne Lake	drowned
	7-23	Gilbert Cooper, CCC employee	19	Sherburne Lake	drowned
	8-13	Dr. F. H. Lumley, visitor	27	Goat Haunt	unknown, never found, presumed dead
	8-20	Fred. M. Johnson, NPS employee	24	Middle Fork Flathead River	drowned
	9-6	William Haines, CCC employee	17	Hidden Lake Fire 17 miles east of West Glacier	skull crushed by falling tree
1935	1-15	Frank Kelly, resident	80	Lake McDonald, Kelly's Camp	pneumonia
	1-16	Emeline Kelly, resident	58	Lake McDonald, Kelly's Camp	pneumonia
	3-21	Dudley Hayden, Jr, NPS ranger's son	2	Lubec Lake	drowned
	7-7	Geraldine Bogar, visitor	15	North Fork Road between Apgar and Fish Creek	vehicle accident
	7-19	Charles White, CCC employee	52	CCC camp 2 miles north of Polebridge	heart attack in tent after breakfast
	7-26	Robert McCormack, CCC employee	18	2 miles from CCC Camp Sherburne	dump truck rollover
	8-12	Kenneth R. Friend, CCC employee	21	CCC Camp Sherburne	died after brief illness
1936	7-26	Herbert Gray, visitor	15	Garden Wall	fell from cliff, found 8-12
	8-2	Dr. Frank Oastler, visitor	65	Many Glacier	heart attack
	12-1	John Albert Lonson, CCC employee	50	CCC Camp #1, Apgar	heart attack, died in sleep
1937	8-24	Lloyd Campbell, NPS employee	34	Going-to-the-Sun Rd. above tunnel and Loop	skull fracture (from crane he was operating)
1938	6-20	Gilbert Shephard, concession employee	19	Grinnell Point	climbing accident
1939	1-6	Andrew J. Aldrich, CCC employee	20	Apgar Flats	hit by chopped, falling tree
1940	7-15	Arrah Owens, visitor	69	Josephine Lake	natural causes (on boat)
	8-12	Newton A. Kippen, visitor	67	Many Glacier	heart attack
1941	2-17	Antone Shiller, CCC employee	45	CCC Camp #15, Apgar area	alcoholism complicated by lemon extract
	6-2	Alice Olson, visitor	49	Avalanche Creek	drowned, fell into gorge
	7-18	John Webster Sherwood, resident	72	at his home on Lake McDonald	cerebral blood clot
	12-27	Cal Irvin Sibley, resident	23	Apgar	home fire, suffocation
1942	7-5	Eunice Fehlbert, visitor	40	Kintla Lake	drowned
1946	8-2	Susan Colleen Apgar, resident	4	Apgar area	pile of lumber fell on her
1949	10-12	Major Fred Lee, visitor	48	McDonald Creek	drowned rescuing daughter
1950	7-12	Robert Stokes, visitor	18	Mt. Wilbur	climbing accident
	7-27	Frank A. Denney, visitor	60	St. Mary Lake	drowned

Year	Date	Name	Age	Location	Cause
	9-13	James B. Pinney, visitor	35	Kintla Lake	drowned, never found
	9-13	John C. Provine, visitor	33	Kintla Lake	drowned, never found
	9-13	Aubrey Clyde Olinger, visitor	37	Kintla Lake	drowned
1951	7-10	J. Louis Thomas, visitor	60	Two Medicine Lake	drowned
	7-29	Charles Norris, visitor	19	Going-to-the-Sun Rd. at St. Mary Bridge	his motorcycle ran into a horse
	8-5	Bernida M. Byrd, visitor	8m	Going-to-the-Sun Rd. 1/2 mile west of Sprague Ck. Campground	tree fell on car she was in
	8-30	Samuel I. Stokes, contract employee	64	Going-to-the-Sun Rd. 1 mile east of Loop	fell from road
	11-25	Jesse A. Bemis, resident	68	Bemis/Covey homestead, North Fork Valley	heart attack
1952	7-29	Robert Dion, visitor	17	Little Chief Mtn.	fell while climbing
	8-3	Frank B. Stewart, visitor	74	St. Mary River	drowned
	8-22	Asa August Powell, resident	65	Apgar	heart attack
1953	5-26	George H. Beaton, NPS employee	45	Going-to-the-Sun Rd.	avalanche
	5-26	William A. Whitford, NPS employee	45	Going-to-the-Sun Rd.	avalanche
	8-6	Peter Alan Kasen, visitor	18	Mt. Helen	fell while climbing
1954	6-30	Pat Kays, concession employee	18	Sherburne Lake	thrown or fell from horse, drowned
	8-8	James Larson, concession employee	18	Swiftcurrent Lake	drowned
1955	2-15	Albert L. Showen, NPS employee	65	at home, park headquarters, West Glacier	heart attack
	2-28	John Lewis Washburn, resident	49	Apgar, 150 ft. from home	heart attack after shoveling snow off neighbor's roof
	7-21	June B. Johnson, concession employee	20	Mt. Altyn	climbing accident
	8-21	John S. Jam, NPS employee	26	Many Glacier	vehicle accident
1956	4-21	George McMullin, NPS employee	51	park headquarters, West Glacier	heart attack
	7-15	Ken Matheson, visitor	44	Going-to-the-Sun Rd.	fell 250 ft. from roadside
	7-21	William L. Meuser, visitor	70	Swiftcurrent Campground	natural causes, died in car
	7-27	L. E. Miller, visitor	62	Swiftcurrent Pass	heart attack
1958	7-10	Victor Ernest Seargent, visitor	60	West Entrance	heart attack
	8-16	Jean Jensen, concession employee	23	Lake McDonald Lodge	natural, exact cause unkown
1959	5-31	Leo Bowman, visitor	50	Many Glacier	motorcycle accident
	6-21	John Carmack	64	park headquarters, West Glacier	coronary
	7-23	James D. Grist, NPS employee, resident	52	US Hwy 2	vehicle accident
1960	7-11	George Engle Keller, visitor	49	Lake McDonald Lodge	unknown
	7-25	Michael Stone, visitor	13	Upper McDonald Creek	drowned
	7-28	Frederick R. Steinmetz, concession employee	19	Redgap Pass	slipped on wet rock at stream and fell
	8-28	Lillian Mayall, visitor	52	McDonald Falls	fell from roadside ledge
1961	6-21	James Moylan, concession employee	17	Mt. Henkel	climbing accident

Year	Date	Name	Age	Location	Cause
	7-29	Boyd H. Evans, visitor	73	Going-to-the-Sun Rd., below West Side Tunnel	heart attack
	7-29	Gordon E. Scott, visitor	43	St. Mary Campground	natural causes, probably heart attack
1962	6-28	Alice Jean Leckie, visitor	52	Going-to-the-Sun Rd., 1.5 miles west of Logan Pass	hit by falling rock
	6-28	Alberta Dickman, visitor	42	Upper McDonald Creek	drowned in rescue attempt
	9-2	Ronald W. Larson, visitor	23	near Sprague Creek Campground	vehicle accident
	9-7	Harry Culp, visitor	1	Many Glacier Hotel	natural (in sleep)
	9-25 or ?	Frank McPhillips, visitor	70	Two Medicine Lake	drowning, vehicle in lake, found 8-23-63
1963	6-18	Jerome T. Delaney, visitor	19	Mt. Pollack	fell descending
	6-27	Gregory W. A. Trenor, visitor	6	Upper McDonald Creek	drowned
	6-28	Thomas Dumay, rescue person	21	Upper Lake McDonald	drowned in search for Trenor
	7-21 or 22	David Paul Wilson, NPS employee	21	Going-to-the-Sun Mtn.	climbing solo, never found, presumed dead
1964	7-17	Paul Gerrish, NPS employee's child	5	park headquarters, West Glacier	hit by truck while riding bicycle
	7-19	Clara R. Fulton, visitor	64	Lake Josephine	natural causes (on boat)
	7-25	Kenneth Gelston, concession employee	22	St. Mary Falls	fell while hiking, never found, presumed dead
1965	5-10	Paul E. Jones, visitor	46	Avalanche Campground	suicide (.22 pistol)
	7-20	Christine C. Pettee, visitor	8m	Lake McDonald Lodge	respiratory failure
	7-25	Henry M. Noldan, visitor	65	Lake McDonald	heart attack after swimming
	8-4	Laurie Van Mun, visitor	6	Running Eagle Falls	fell while hiking
	8-12	Cornelius K. B. Smith, visitor	78	Two Medicine	heart attack
	8-19	Audrey Ley, visitor	56	Many Glacier	heart attack
1966	6-14	Everett Flammond, visitor	20	Many Glacier Rd.	vehicle accident
	6-14	James Kittson, visitor	16	Many Glacier Rd.	vehicle accident
	7-29	Rev. Joseph H. DeVaney, visitor	52	Mt. Oberlin	fell while hiking
	8-13	Rev. Paul F. Schreiber, visitor	37	Going-to-the-Sun Rd., Logan Creek area	fell from road
1967	3-7	Hans Jungster, resident	49	at home, Apgar	heart attack
	7-3	Douglas Tettlebach, visitor	20	Mt. Custer	fell while descending
	8-13	Julie M. Helgeson, concession employee	19	Granite Park backcountry campground	grizzly bear
	8-13	Michele L. Koons, concession employee	19	Trout Lake backcountry campground	grizzly bear
	12-28	Keith Moors, contract employee	33	Nyack Flats, inside park	hit by falling tree
1968	5-26	Larry R. Jones, visitor	29	Apgar picnic area	suicide (.22 pistol)
	6-22	Diane Neale, concession employee	19	Many Glacier Rd.	vehicle accident
1969	7-24	Paul Gettys, visitor	17	Altyn Peak	fell while climbing
	8-23	Rodney R. Long, visitor	50	Fish Creek Campground	heart attack
	12-30	Jerry Kanzler, visitor	18	Mt. Cleveland	avalanche, body recovered 7-3-70
	12-30	Clare Pogreba, visitor	22	Mt. Cleveland	avalanche, body recovered 7-3-70
	12-30	Mark Levitan, visitor	20	Mt. Cleveland	avalanche, body recovered 7-3-70

Year	Date	Name	Age	Location	Cause
	12-30	Ray Martin, visitor	22	Mt. Cleveland	avalanche, body recovered 6-29-70
	12-30	James Anderson, visitor	18	Mt. Cleveland	avalanche, body recovered 6-29-70
1970	5-19	Melvin M. Mellett, NPS employee	63	Eddie's Cafe, Apgar	heart attack
	6-30	Robert Personett, visitor	23	North Fork Flathead River	drowned in boating accident
	7-5	Neil T. Fisher, visitor	9	Lower McDonald Creek, Apgar	drowned
	7-22	Christine B. Straley, visitor	56	Many Glacier Hotel	coronary
	12-11	Roscoe M. Perry, visitor	72	Goat Lick area, US Hwy 2	vehicle accident
1971	2-6	Lowell Mattson, visitor	41	North Fork Flathead River	drowned, snowmobile went in river
	7-4	Maynard E. Kitzman, visitor	55	Many Glacier Road	vehicle accident
	7-5	Francis Pokorney, visitor	59	Many Glacier Hotel	heart attack
	7-30	Sally Boughner, visitor	22	Upper McDonald Creek	drowned, raft capsized
	8-15	Ronald Matthews, visitor	32	Sperry Glacier	fell in crevasse while skiing
1972	7-5	Perihan North, wife of NPS employee	46	St. Mary Lake	drowned
	8-24	Nathan Grove, visitor	64	Grinnell Glacier Trail	heart attack
1973	8-6	Adrian Harry Sanders, visitor	62	St. Mary Campground	heart attack
	8-21	Karl J. Staner, visitor	72	McDonald Falls area	fell from cliffs
	8-23	Michael Dunn, visitor	22	Upper Two Medicine Lake	fell into lake, drowned
1974	7-6	Roy Crissman, visitor	18	west of Goat Lick, US Hwy 2	his motorcycle hit oncoming car
	7-15	Michael Neyer, visitor	22	Rising Wolf Mtn.	slid on snowfield and off cliff while descending
	8-18	John P. Hunting, concession employee	20	near Stoney Indian Pass	fell at start of climb to Mt. Cleveland
1975	7-4	Greg A. Finley, concession employee	19	Mt. Brown	fell while descending
	11-1	Donald Donovan, visitor	45	Flinsch Peak	airplane crash
	11-1	Kathryn M. See, visitor	31	Flinsch Peak	airplane crash
1976	6-18	James Krell, visitor	42	Lake McDonald	never found, presumed drowned
	7-3	Sam Raider, visitor	27	Mt. Clements	fell while descending
	7-15	David Boos, concession employee	17	Mt. Siyeh	fell while climbing
	8-1	Don William Ash, visitor	29	Haystack Creek below Going-to-the-Sun Rd.	head injury from fall into creek
	9-23	Mary P. Mahoney, visitor	21	Many Glacier Campground	grizzly bear
1977	6-23	David Noel Barry, concession employee	20	Wilbur Creek	drowned trying to save another swimmer
	6-23	Randy Hill, concession employee	22	Wilbur Creek	drowned trying to save another swimmer
1978	7-28	Margaret W. Squibb, concession employee	20	Rising Wolf Mtn.	fell while descending
	7-31	Nancy Brown, visitor	24	Grinnell Point	fell while hiking
1979	6-13	Doug D'Arcy, visitor	17	St. Mary Lake	drowned, inflatable kayak capsized
	6-13	Troy Berger, visitor	17	St. Mary Lake	drowned, inflatable kayak capsized
	8-31	Coleen G. Griggs, concession employee	20	St. Mary	motorcycle accident
1980	7-24	Jane Ammerman, concession employee	19	Divide Creek, St. Mary area	grizzly bear
	7-24	Kim Eberly, concession employee	19	Divide Creek, St. Mary area	grizzly bear

Year	Date	Name	Age	Location	Cause
	7-27	James Coke, visitor	53	Swiftcurrent Pass	heart attack while hiking
	9-27 or 28	Lawrence Gordon, visitor	33	Elizabeth Lake	grizzly bear
1981	6-16	David H. Ellis, visitor	69	Many Glacier	heart attack
	7-12	Carla McLean, visitor	26	Two Medicine	vehicle accident
	7-22	Kevin P. Dolack, visitor	7	Upper McDonald Creek	drowned
	7-27	Don Danielowski, visitor	41	Upper McDonald Creek	drowned
	7-27	Betty Danielowski, visitor	40	Upper McDonald Creek	drowned
	8-22	Charles Bareham, visitor	30	off Hidden Lake Trail	fell while taking shortcut
	8-29	Harry J. Donaghy, concession employee	23	Mt. Stimson	fell while climbing
1982	6-15	Devali Oakes, visitor	13	Avalanche Creek	fell into creek, drowned
	8-6	Lisa Handford, visitor	20	Haystack Creek, Going-to-the-Sun Rd.	fell into creek above road, then through culvert off cliff
	8-24	Walter E. Lieser, visitor	84	Many Glacier Hotel	heart attack
1983	5-28	Teddy Hatley, visitor	20	Kintla Lake	presumed drowned, never found
	7-14	Frederick H. Pongrace, visitor	31	Crystal Point, Going-to-the-Sun Rd.	stabbed, pushed off road
	7-21	Paul Sullivan, visitor	48	Village Inn, Apgar	heart attack
	10-12	Steven Fernekes, visitor	27	Swiftcurrent Glacier	fell into bergschrund while descending
1984	7-21	Robert W. Herron, visitor	34	US Hwy 2, east of Walton Ranger Station	vehicle accident
	8-30	Mary E. Trolley, visitor	72	Bowman Lake Campground	heart attack
1985	5-4	Robert S. Walton, visitor	39	St. Mary entrance station	motorcycle accident
	6-10	Thor Tangvald, concession employee	19	below Ptarmigan Falls	fell while descending cliff
	9-5	Gerald Frahn, visitor	68	Apgar Campground	heart attack
	9-5	Jim Conway, visitor	29	Going-to-the-Sun Rd. near Siyeh Bend	airplane crash
	9-5	Judith Conway, visitor	55	Going-to-the-Sun Rd. near Siyeh Bend	airplane crash
1986	4-26 or 27	Peter Soderlund, visitor	24	Going-to-the-Sun Rd. near Packers Roost	suicide by asphyxiation
	5-31	Charles Bauer, visitor	27	Mt. Reynolds	fell while climbing
	7-5	James McCauley, visitor	80	on bus near Avalanche Campground	unknown
	8-2	Ross Alden Reed, visitor	43	Going-to-the-Sun Rd. below Weeping Wall	drove off road
	8-8	Geraldine Jacobsen, visitor	64	Upper Lake McDonald Road	thrown from concessionaire horse
	8-31	Yvonne V. Waslovich, visitor	34	Going-to-the-Sun Rd. just east of Logan Pass	fell while taking or posing for photo
1987	4-25	Charles Gibbs, visitor	40	Elk Mtn., Walton area	grizzly bear
	5-13	Sue Grace Williams, visitor	92	Trail of the Cedars	natural causes
	6-4	Bradley J. Cox, visitor	32	Going-to-the-Sun Rd. near Triple Arches	motorcycle accident
	7-7	John A. Hamilton, visitor	57	Rising Sun Motor Inn	heart attack
	7-23 or 24	Gary Goeden, concession employee	29	Apikuni Cirque area	grizzly bear, remains recovered 9-1
	8-31	Robert Clarence Hall, visitor	34	Many Glacier Rd.	motorcycle accident
1988	7-21	Harry Isch, visitor	69	near Hidden Lake	heart attack
1990	4-2	Barbara Schustrom, visitor	50	head of Lake McDonald	drowned

Year	Date	Name	Age	Location	Cause
	6-24	Thomas E. Skeen, visitor	81	Apgar Village	heart attack
	7-15	Dale Grapatin, visitor	45	Chief Mtn.	fell while climbing
	8-8	Norman J. Wiebe, visitor	29	Going-to-the-Sun Rd. near Triple Arches	motorcycle accident
	9-6 or 7	Brian McCartie, concession employee	21	between Bishop's Cap and Mt. Gould	fell while traversing cliff
1991	8-3	Edgar M. Fetter, visitor	52	Going-to-the-Sun Rd. east of East Side Tunnel	drove off road
	8-14	Gordon Ochenrider, visitor	46	southern slope of Mt. Siyeh	fell while descending
	8-17	Sandra Leckie, visitor	46	Going-to-the-Sun Rd. near Logan Creek	heart attack
1992	2-12	Willard A. Smith, visitor	57	near Logan Pass	airplane crash
	2-12	Marion V. Smith, visitor	54	near Logan Pass	airplane crash
	5-19	Merwin Hodges, visitor	79	Two Medicine	heart attack while hiking
	7-12	George Efraimson, visitor	63	Kelly's Camp	heart attack
	7-19	Josh Skibsrud, visitor	20	Mt. Gould	fell while climbing
	10-3	John Petranyi, visitor	40	trail to Granite Park	grizzly bear
1993	6-18	Suzanne E. Wood, visitor	53	Many Glacier Campground	heart attack
	6-20	Sophia Dexoirt, visitor	79	Goat Lick Overlook, US Hwy 2	vehicle accident
	7-24	Francine A. Nixon, visitor	47	Upper McDonald Creek	fell into creek and hit head
1995	6-21	Lela Breitbart, visitor	24	above trail on southeast side of Avalanche Lake	hit in head by falling rock from avalanche upslope
1996	1-13	Taggart Schubert, NPS seasonal employee	25?	Mt. Jackson	fell while descending
	6-14	Margaret Swanson, visitor	78	Going-to-the-Sun Rd. near Sprague Ck. Campground	unknown, vehicle accident
	6-23	Tsuyoshi Kamochi, visitor	30	Going-to-the-Sun Rd., Rimrock area	rockslide fell on vehicle
	7-28	Toma Jercinovic, visitor	22	above Avalanche Lake	fell while bushwhacking from Sperry Chalet
1997	7-3	Mark Robison, NPS seasonal employee	24	Rainbow Peak	fell while climbing
	7-3	Chris Foster, NPS seasonal employee	23	Rainbow Peak	fell while climbing
	7-7	Matt Truszkowski, concession employee	25	Mt. Sinopah area	missing, unknown, presumed dead
	9-1	Roger Dokken, visitor	62	Mt. Cleveland	fell while descending
1998	5-17	Craig Dahl, concession employee	26	Appistoki Falls	grizzly bear
	7-5	Connie J. Lindsey, visitor	47	north side of Ptarmigan Tunnel	fell, dragged by horse off cliff
	7-15	Brian Donald-Nelson, visitor	27	Redgap Pass	bent for a drink of water, slipped, and fell 150 ft.
	8-4	William Simpson, visitor	47	Rising Sun	heart attack
1999	7-20	Craig Ryan, visitor	56	Mt. Clements	fell while descending
	8-13	Harold Addison, visitor	74	Going-to-the-Sun Rd. just east of East Side Tunnel	stepped over retaining wall, fell
2000	4-16	Dale Laird, visitor	42	Kennedy Lake/Mt. Henkel	airplane crash
	7-24	Henry Mayer, visitor	59	Going-to-the-Sun Rd. 2 miles west of Road Camp Overlook	heart attack on bicycle tour
	8-9	Christopher B. Wolk, concession employee	26	Swiftcurrent Creek	while swimming below waterfall, hit in head by a dislodged rock

Year	Date	Name	Age	Location	Cause
	11-3 or ?	Patrick T. Whalen, visitor	33	Cut Bank Creek drainage	missing, presumed dead; personal items found 5-21-01
2001	6-12	James M. Parks, visitor	83	Lake McDonald Lodge	complications from pneumonia
	6-14	Don Fogg Harris, visitor	85	Crystal Point turnout, Going-to-the-Sun Rd.	exited vehicle and fell to road below
	8-5	David Olseth, visitor	30	Going-to-the-Sun Rd. at Triple Arches	bicycle accident, fell off road
	8-13	Wojciech Krajewski, visitor	22	Mt. Jackson	fell while descending
2002	6-28	Manita Felicidad Diaz Nery, visitor	59	Avalanche Gorge	slipped into creek above gorge, drowned
	7-23	Thomas Hart, visitor	17	Hudson Bay Creek near Red Eagle Lake	drowned, slipped and fell over waterfall
	8-5	Matthew Colin Wiesike, visitor	20	Reynolds Mtn. above Hidden Lake	fell while hiking
	8-5	Manville J. Smith, visitor	61	near Sperry Chalet and Comeau Pass	heart attack
2003	5-29 or ?	Larry Kimball, visitor	40	Fish Creek, Rocky Point area	missing, presumed dead
	8-15	Richard Peckham, visitor	73	near Siyeh Pass	collapsed while hiking
2004	7-8	Mark Horter, visitor	49	Two Medicine, 3 miles up Scenic Point Trail	heart attack
	7-19	J. Gordon Edwards, visitor	84	base of Divide Mtn. just outside park boundary	natural causes, collapsed at start of climb
	7-27	Howard Cohn, visitor	46	Grinnell Glacier	fell into crevasse, died of exposure and injuries
	9-3	Angel Star Makes Cold Weather, visitor	19	Going-to-the-Sun Rd., Granite Creek area	vehicle accident
2005	7-20	David Johnston, visitor	64	Upper Grinnell Lake	heart attack while hiking
	11-21	Dennis Brooks, visitor	40	Upper McDonald Creek	fell into creek, drowned
2008	6-19	Ronald Grecco, visitor	66	Iceberg Lake Trail	heart attack while hiking
	8-?	Yi-Jien Hwa, visitor	27	above Avalanche Lake	likely fall while hiking
	10-10	Bruce Colburn, visitor	54	near head of Kintla Lake	suicide, gunshot
2009	7-14	James R. Greene, concession employee	22	Swiftcurrent Lake	drowned, canoe capsized
	8-22	William Labunetz, visitor	67	Ahearn Pass	fell while descending
	9-9	George S. Zlatnik, visitor	51	Going-to-the-Sun Rd. west of Wild Goose Island Overlook	motorcycle accident
2010	3-31	Brian C. Wright, visitor	37	Mt. Shields	avalanche, body recovered 4-1-10
	6-18	Elizabeth G. McNamara, visitor	62	Virginia Falls	fell off bridge, drowned, recovered 6-19-10
	7-29	Clinton Croff, visitor	30	Two Medicine Rd.	apparent suicide
	8-12	Charles Trisdale, visitor	81	Going-to-the-Sun Rd. Logan Pass parking lot	heart attack in car
	9-21	Michael Sloan, visitor	30	Lake McDonald at Upper McDonald Creek	drowned while wade fishing, recovered 9-24
2011	2-22	Ladell Friesen, visitor	34	mile marker 182, US Hwy 2	semi-truck slid into his car
	7-18	Nicholas Ryan, visitor	30	Grinnell Glacier Trail	fell, slid down snowfield
	7-23	Richard Fish, visitor	70	Going-to-the-Sun Rd. near Logan Creek	motorcycle accident
	8-23	David Fergason, visitor	69	Gunsight Pass Trail	heart attack
	8-28	Jacob Rigby, NPS seasonal employee	27	Peak '8888' between Park and Ole Creeks	fell while climbing
2012	7-28	Jakson Kreiser, concession employee	19	above head of Hidden Lake	probable fall while hiking
	8-20	Blair Merrill, visitor	69	Rising Sun Restaurant	unknown, collapsed

Year	Date	Name	Age	Location	Cause
	9-25	David Hughes, visitor	67	North Fork Flathead River, 1st bend downstream from Camas Creek Bridge	drowned while wade fishing
	11-6	Martin Crundall, visitor	49	Bowman Lake parking lot	suicide, generator running in vehicle
2013	3-13	Amy Marie Reddig, visitor	28	Lake McDonald Lodge area	drowned
	6-26	Charles Huseman, visitor	64	Highline Trail, Rimrock area	slid down snow, fell onto Going-to-the-Sun Rd.
	7-7	Cody Johnson, visitor	25	cliff next to the Loop Trail	pushed by wife off cliff
	7-9	Cesar Flores, concession employee	21	Apikuni Ridge	fell while climbing to cliff's edge
	7-25	Matthew Needham, concession employee	21	Grinnell Point	fell while climbing
2014	7-12	Abigail Sylvester, visitor	33	Upper McDonald Creek	drowned, slipped into creek while taking photo
	7-28	Robert Rock, visitor	67	St. Mary Falls Trail	heart attack
	7-29	David Middleworth, visitor	76	Ptarmigan Trail	heart attack
	9-13	Beau Weiher, visitor	22	Mt. Siyeh, north face	fell while BASE jumping
	9-18	Brandon Avalos, visitor	18	Going-to-the-Sun Rd.	unwitnessed fall at night from Big Drift area
2015	3-24	Robert Douglas Haetinger, visitor	40-49	Going-to-the-Sun Rd. near foot of Lake McDonald	suicide, gunshot
	5-9	Porter Gifford, concession employee	60-69	Lake McDonald Lodge	heart attack
2016	5-4	Clint Cory Not Afraid, visitor	26	Running Eagle Falls	jumped from waterfall into shallow pool
	7-22	Erik Belgrade, visitor	49	Two Medicine Camp Store	natural causes
	8-30	Dann R. Pilipow, visitor	56	Mt. Jackson	fell while descending east face
2017	1-5	Benjamin Parsons, visitor	36	Stanton Mtn., 500 yards below summit	avalanche while skiing

DEATHS IN GLACIER
NATIONAL PARK BY CAUSE

1910-2017

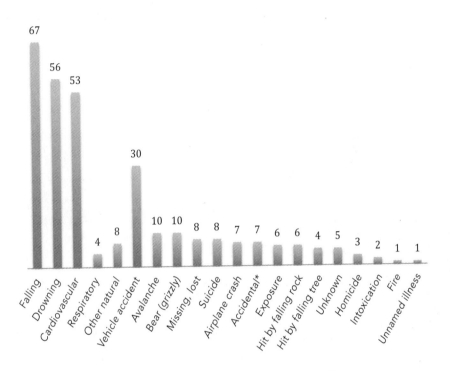

Cause of death as recorded in park incident reports and coroners' reports.
*Deaths not covered by other "accident" categories.

Buchholtz, Curt. *Man in Glacier.* Glacier Natural History Association, West Glacier, MT, 1976.

Cederborg, Julie. "Survival Story: Surviving a Grizzly Attack in Glacier National Park," *Backpacker Magazine.* Boulder, CO. 2008.

Clark, Ella E. *Indian Legends from the Northern Rockies.* University of Oklahoma Press, Norman, OK. 1966.

Columbian Newspaper. "Shoots Partner after Quarrel at Snyder's Saloon." Columbia Falls, MT. 1913.

Curwen, Thomas. "A hike into horror and an act of courage in Glacier National Park." *Los Angeles Times,* Los Angeles, CA. 2007.

Daily Inter Lake. Various editions, Kalispell, MT.

DeSanto, Jerome S. "Missing in Glacier! The Disappearance of the Whitehead Brothers in 1924." *Montana, the Magazine of Western History,* Helena, MT. Summer 1989.

Edwards, J. Gordon. *A Climber's Guide to Glacier National Park.* Mountain Press Publishing Company, Missoula, MT, 1995.

Fisher, Frances. *Glacier National Park, Going-to-the-Sun Corridor Management Plan—Existing Conditions of the Transportation System.* John A. Volpe National Transportation Systems Center, Cambridge, MA. 2014.

Fladmark, Bruce. *Evaluation of Older St. Mary Buildings in Glacier National Park.* Glacier National Park. 1991.

Flathead Beacon. Various editions, Kalispell, MT.

Flathead County and Glacier County coroner's reports. Various, Kalispell and Cut Bank, MT.

Fraley, John. *Wild River Pioneers: Adventures in the Middle Fork of the Flathead, Great Bear Wilderness and Glacier National Park.* Big Mountain Publishing, Whitefish, MT. 2008.

Glacier National Park Archives. Various oral histories, West Glacier, MT.

Glacier National Park Press Releases. Various releases, West Glacier, MT.

Going-to-the-Sun, Journal of the Glacier Mountaineering Society. Various editions, Kalispell, MT.

Great Falls Tribune. Various editions, Great Falls, MT.

Green, Charles. *Montana Memories. Vol. I and Vol. IV.* Coram, MT. 1972.

Guthrie, C. W. (editor). *The First Ranger.* Redwing Publishing, Huson, MT. 1995.

Hanna, Warren L. *Montana's Many-Splendored Glacierland: All You've Ever Wanted to Know about Glacier Park.* Superior Publishing, Seattle WA. 1976.

Hanners, Richard. Various newspaper articles about Johnson murder. *Hungry Horse News,* Columbia Falls, MT. 2013.

Herrero, Dr. Stephen. *Bear Attacks: Their Causes and Avoidance.* Lyons Press, 2002.

_____. "Aspects of Evolution and Adaptation in American Black Bears (*Ursus americanus Pallas*) and Brown and Grizzly Bears (*U. arctos Linné*) of North America." *Bears: Their Biology and Management, Vol.* 2, International Association for Bear Research and Management, 1972.

Hubbard, W. P., Seale Harris. *Notorious Grizzly Bears.* The Swallow Press, Chicago, IL. 1960.

Hufstetler, Mark, Kathryn L. McKay, Janet Cornish. *Going-to-the-Sun Road, Glacier National Park, Montana: Cultural Landscape Report.* Renewable Technologies, Inc., Butte, MT. 2002.

Hungry Horse News. Various editions. Columbia Falls, MT. 1946-2016

The Inside Trail. Glacier Park Foundation, Minneapolis, MN.

Lee, Leslie. *Backcountry Ranger in Glacier National Park 1910-1913.* Elk Rapids, MI. 1994.

Luding, Lanny. *The Paisley Umbrella.* Unpublished manuscript. 2016.

Madsen, Robert. *The White Death.* Knopf Doubleday Publishing, New York, NY. 2002.

McMillion, Scott. *Mark of the Grizzly.* Falcon Publishing, Inc., Helena, MT. 1998.

Miller, Alice. Various newspaper articles about Johnson murder. *Missoulian.* Missoula, MT. 2014.

Missoulian. Various editions, Missoula, MT.

Montana Death Index website: deathindexes.com/montana/.

Moravek, Vince. *It Happened in Glacier National Park.* Globe Pequot Press, Guilford, CT. 2005.

Moynahan, J. M. "Western Realist: Asa Lynn Powell (1912-1978)." *The Pacific Northwest Forum Volume III, Number IV,* Eastern Washington University, Cheney, WA. 1978.

The New York Times. Various editions, New York, NY.

Parratt, Mark W. *Fate Is A Mountain.* Sun Point Press, Whitefish, MT. 2009.

Reeves, Dr. Brian. *Mistakis: The Archeology of Waterton-Glacier International Peace Park.* Technical Report Between Montana State University and the National Park Service. Bozeman, MT. 2003.

Reeves, Dr. Brian, Dr. Sandra Peacock. *"Our Mountains are Our Pillows": An Ethnographic Overview of Glacier National Park.* Final Report. Glacier National Park. 2001.

Rockwell, David. *Glacier: A Natural History Guide.* FalconGuides, Falcon Press, Helena, MT, 2007.

Sax, Joseph. *Mountains without Handrails: Reflections on the National Parks.* University of Michigan Press, Ann Arbor, MI, 1980.

Shultz, James Willard. *Blackfeet Tales of Glacier National Park.* Houghton Mifflin Company, Boston and New York. 1916.

State of the Wilderness and Backcountry. Report, Glacier National Park Archives, West Glacier, MT. 2014.

Superintendent's Annual Reports. Various reports, Glacier National Park Archives, West Glacier, MT.

Thompson, Sally. *People Before the Park: The Kootenai and Blackfeet Before Glacier National Park.* Montana Historical Society Press, Helena, MT. 2015.

Vaught, L. O. Manuscripts and various letters. Glacier National Park Archives, West Glacier, MT.

Walters, David. *Montana Campfire Tales.* Rowman and Littlefield Publishing, Lanham, MD. 1997.

Waterman, Ed. "Going-Off-the-Sun." *A View Inside Glacier National Park.* Glacier Association, West Glacier, MT. 2009.

C. W. (Carol) Guthrie's love affair with Glacier began when she and her dad drove the Going-to-the-Sun Road when she was nine years old. For the past twenty-five years, following a career working for the Air Force, she has explored the park and its history and authored five books about the park.

Dan and Ann Fagre have been backpacking, climbing, skiing, and exploring mountains and national parks since the early 1970s. Over these decades, they've been wilderness rangers, fire lookouts, firefighters, and outdoor trip leaders in various western landscapes. For the past twenty-six years, they've made their home in West Glacier, Montana, and Glacier National Park, where they've worked, played, and raised their daughters who are following in their footsteps.